Emotional Literacy
at the Heart of the School Ethos

A Lucky Duck Book

Emotional Literacy
at the Heart of the School Ethos

Steve Killick

P·C·P
Paul Chapman
Publishing

Paul Chapman Publishing
A SAGE Publications Company
1 Oliver's Yard
55 City Road
London EC1Y 1SP

BF
721
.K479
2006

SAGE Publications Inc.
2455 Teller Road
Thousand Oaks, California 91320

SAGE Publications India Pvt Ltd
B-42, Panchsheel Enclave
Post Box 4109
New Delhi 110 017

www.luckyduck.co.uk

Commissioning Editor: Barbara Maines
Editorial Team: Sarah Lynch, Mel Maines, Wendy Ogden
Designer: Jess Wright

A catalogue record for this book is available from the British Library
Library of Congress Control Number 2005932397

ISBN 10 1-4129-1155-9
ISBN 13 978-1-4129-1155-9 (pbk)

Printed on paper from sustainable resources
Printed in Great Britain by The Cromwell Press Ltd, Trowbridge, Wiltshire

Contents

To my Mother and Father,
and Sarah, Seamus and Ciara

Acknowledgements

Firstly, Headlands School must be thanked for commissioning HELP (the Headlands Emotional Literacy Programme) that created the springboard for this book. I would like to thank all the staff of the school who contributed towards the development of the project, particularly Dave Haswell and Mike Church, for their energy, enthusiasm and vision.

There are many friends and colleagues who have inspired me and helped clarify or correct my thinking and there were also angels who held me when I fell. Particularly, I would like to thank Prof Neil Frude, Stuart Lindeman, Liz Platt, Lucie Robinson and Sue O'Shea. Thanks too to Barbara, George, Jess, Wendy and Sarah at Lucky Duck for their help and support throughout. Thanks to Sarah for endless proofreading and toleration of absences whilst writing this book.

Foreword

I have had an association with the author for a number of years now. We worked together at Headlands School, a residential special school for children and young people with challenging behaviour. Steve Killick was our Clinical Psychologist and although I had come across the concept of emotional literacy before, conversations with Steve inspired me to find out more.

In January 2002 I invited Peter Sharp, of Mouchel (formerly Chief of Educational Psychology Service Southampton City Council and author of *Nurturing Emotional Literacy* (2001)) along to Headlands. Peter delivered a whole-school training day for us and this experience cemented my belief that we should become an emotionally literate organisation.

Achieving this goal was not an easy task. Following the training day, some colleagues told me they liked the idea but still didn't understand how to 'make the kids more emotionally intelligent'.

I could understand why some people felt this way as Peter had focused his training on the staff and the organisation, and not on children and young people's learning. However, it was an indication of the challenge that lay ahead. We needed to bring staff on board with the concept of an emotionally literate school otherwise we would make little impact on children and young people.

My challenge was to help my staff improve their knowledge and the level of skills that they needed in order to make a difference. Regular whole-school training events and the establishment of Headlands Emotional Literacy Interest Group made an impact and we established a new Psychology Service that could provide support for staff.

Steve continued to provide consultancy to the School and we commissioned him to produce *The Headlands Emotional Literacy Programme* (HELP). The HELP handbook outlined the key features of emotional literacy and also described a number of practical activities and lesson plans teachers could use.

Training events are more likely to be a success if they are followed up by an implementation programme that includes supervision and refreshers. It was useful to have HELP as a manual to refer to and to draw practical ideas from. In this book the author has developed the toolkit idea and I believe he has produced a handbook that will sit on teacher's desks rather than their bookshelves.

Steve describes how our emotional life is at the core of human nature and experience. He shows that our rational and intellectual abilities can only function to their full potential when we are able to utilise and manage emotions rather than be consumed by them, or to act on them without reflection.

This book describes how emotional intelligence and its application in education, emotional literacy, provide a basis for understanding the emotional life of children and for helping them to develop skills in understanding their own complex emotional life and those of others.

The students at Headlands School have very challenging behaviour and helping them develop their emotional literacy is one of the keys to unlocking their potential. The author shows that this is equally true whether you teach in mainstream primary, secondary or special schools.

The emotionally literate school can be achieved.

I advocate a whole-school approach to this; emotional literacy should not be bolted on to the curriculum but must underlie and inform all our actions and interactions throughout the day.

The concept of emotional literacy described in this book is becoming more widely known and in schools in England it is currently the subject of a government backed initiative. This is welcome indeed and it is pleasing to see that more resources are becoming available to assist in establishing emotionally literate cultures in schools.

This book draws upon teachers' real life experiences in the classroom and beyond. I believe it will prove to be an informative and useful tool for teachers in a variety of settings.

Dave Haswell, NCH Schools Manager and Headteacher,
Headlands School, NCH Cymru from 2000-2005.

Introduction

The concepts of emotional intelligence (EI) and emotional literacy (EL) have started a revolution in many schools. Teachers see the importance of valuing the emotional lives of children and young people and the implications of this for the ethos and organisational climate of schools. These ideas have given a theoretical, practical and evidence base for considering not only how children think about learning but for considering how they feel about themselves. The concepts reveal a connection between how children manage their emotions and relationships with their academic learning. Emotional literacy has been practised in schools for longer than there has been a name for it. What is new is how the theoretical ideas of emotional intelligence can give a structure and framework for developing this work and that developing these skills is important for all children, not just those experiencing difficulties.

However, in a climate of almost continual change in schools, of competing targets and pressures to achieve, it can be difficult to become familiar with the theory and to see what difference it can make to children and teachers. The last few years have seen significant advances in what is known about how the brain works. This has implications for helping children (and adults) learn. Some of the most significant findings are that our emotional functioning affects both learning and behaviour. This has led to a phenomenal interest in the concepts of emotional intelligence in the areas of physical and mental health, work settings and schools. There have been many publications worldwide exploring the importance of emotional literacy in schools. This resource aims to:

- explain the ideas that form the foundation of emotional intelligence

- explain how they might apply in the school setting

- give a number of practical communication skills that teachers can use to help to develop emotional literacy and encourage cooperation in the classroom.

These skills can make a practical impact to how children and adults communicate and learn together.

The message is simple. Teachers can make a significant difference to children by how they communicate and relate to them. However, to reach its full potential, emotional literacy needs to be placed at the heart of the school ethos and many schools are now implementing the ideas at an organisational level. Organisational change is often difficult to achieve, especially when there is uncertainty about the implications for schools. It is by teachers working together and with others who share an interest in this area that change occurs. We best help children develop emotional literacy by developing it in ourselves.

> You must be the change you want to see in this world.
>
> **Mahatma Gandhi**

Individual development leads to organisational development. Teachers can place emotional literacy on the agenda for schools by knowing what emotional intelligence and literacy are all about and bringing these ideas into their everyday work. The classroom is a complex environment and teachers work with great skill in managing the needs of children and young people. In the many everyday interactions that take place in every school between teacher and child, as well as between staff and between the school and parents, the ideas contained in the philosophy of emotional literacy are already carried out in many ways. However, there are so many ways that considering emotional functioning can unlock the potential of children in learning, not only academically, but also in problem-solving and relating to others, that developing and extending this expertise is now being seen by many as a priority.

In the UK the green paper Every Child Matters (8 September 2003) has placed the emphasis on ensuring children will have the support they need to be healthy, safe, happy and confident enough to contribute to their communities. The Department of Education and Skills launched the Social, Emotional and Behavioural Skills Strategy (SEBS) (September 2005) that has led to the development of curriculum material to address this area in primary school. In secondary schools, initiatives such as Behaviour Improvement Programmes (November 2005) and the Five Year Strategy for Children and Learners (July 2004) address how students in secondary schools can become more involved and take greater responsibility for their learning. The practice of emotional literacy in schools will contribute to reaching the goals of these developments.

The National Healthy Schools Programme places emphasis on the development of emotional health and well-being. There is also a curriculum resource available for primary schools as part of Primary National Strategy to develop 'Social and Emotional Aspects of Learning (SEAL) that is available from the DfES (2005).

Using this resource

The format of this resource recognises that teachers and educators are busy people who need information and techniques delivered in straightforward and manageable units.

This resource is in two parts: this book (which consists of two sections) and a CD-ROM. The sections are:

1. Creating the Climate for Emotional Literacy

This is an introduction to the central concepts of emotional intelligence and emotional literacy and how these concepts can be applied in schools.

2. Communicating Emotional Literacy

This focuses on communication skills that facilitate emotional learning and cooperation in the classroom.

The CD-ROM contains a PowerPoint slide presentation and the exercises in the book with accompanying activity sheets that can be used in whole or in parts by teachers to help with professional development in this area.

The reader might use this resource in two ways:

*   as a workbook to promote understanding and develop skills in emotional intelligence
*   as a source of ideas for training and discussing emotional literacy with staff.

Throughout the book there are exercises that may be used to help reflect on the content. You can do many of these exercises alone as you work through the book, though some can only be done in groups with the aim of encouraging discussion, debate and assimilation of learning around the subject. Teachers and trainers may use these exercises to help run emotional literacy training sessions for staff. These can range from short 'twilight' or after school training sessions through to longer, more intensive courses as part of a structured in-service or external training programme.

Using the pack as a workbook

Although readers will have their own learning styles and will want to read the book in the way that suits them best, some suggestions are given to use this book most effectively. Before beginning to read, quickly skim through the content by flicking through the chapters noticing anything that catches your eye. Consider any questions you have or ideas about what particular chapters may say. When you start to read, work through the chapters sequentially pausing after each chapter to do some of the exercises within each one. Many of the exercises aimed at groups will, of course, be less easy to complete alone. However, there may be value in imagining vividly what might happen if you were doing this with a group of people you know.

Using the pack in learning and training

You do not need to have specialised knowledge about emotional literacy to lead a session, although it is important that you feel comfortable with the material and in facilitating a discussion with a group of learners. We are all experts in our own emotional lives so it is important for the facilitator not to take an 'expert' position. Rather, it may be better to explore what a group's 'baseline' level of knowledge is and to develop that based on familiarity with the content of this resource or other sources of information. Integrated into the chapters are slides that can be used to talk about some of the information presented in the chapter. There are also exercises presented throughout the text. The aim of these is to facilitate discussion around some of the points made. The presenter need not feel she should work through everything systematically in the order presented, rather to select and, if necessary, adapt the material to particular audiences.

Part One

Creating the Climate for Emotional Literacy

Chapter One

Emotional Intelligence and Emotional Literacy

'Fish swim, birds fly, and people feel,' was a statement of Haim Ginott (1965), a teacher, therapist and writer. Ginott was a pioneer in the area of effective communication between children and adults. He wrote in the 1960s and 70s about how adults, both parents and teachers, could attend to the emotional lives of children and help those children develop confidence and self-esteem. This attention to feelings also aids children's ability to listen, to cooperate with others and develop personal values. This focus helps make young people more able to solve problems in their lives and to be able, 'to learn, to grow, to change'. His work foresaw the development of emotional intelligence and his contribution to this area has been recognised by Daniel Goleman (1995) and John Gottman (1998).

That 'people feel' is central to the concept of emotional intelligence; our emotional life is the heart of human experience. Our moods and feelings influence how we think and what we do, and are at the core of our feelings of wellbeing. How children mature emotionally and the skills they have in managing those feelings will influence their abilities to fulfil their potential in school and in life; to be able to learn, solve problems, and, fundamentally, how they feel about themselves. The child's journey from being newborn to becoming a healthy adult, able to work and to love and to grow from life's many challenges, is a perilous one.

Problems related to emotional health

The concepts of emotional intelligence and emotional literacy can help schools help children in many ways. Developing problem-solving, thinking and social skills can increase confidence, motivation and academic performance and decrease behaviour problems. These skills are of tremendous importance, especially given the increasing prevalence of problems in our society related to our emotional health. At a time of increasing affluence and raising standards in health, education and the workplace, mental health problems such as depression and anxiety are increasing at a alarming rate. More people are suffering and the onset of such problems is happening at younger and younger ages. A recent study in the UK found a 70% increase in such problems in secondary schools over the last 25 years (Collishaw et al., 2004). It has been estimated that as many as 20% of children will experience some form of mental or emotional health problem before they reach adulthood, creating a higher demand than child and adolescent mental health services are able to meet. These findings suggest that it is likely that in every school, possibly in every class, there will be children with unmet emotional or mental health needs. Children with special educational needs may be particularly vulnerable. Teachers have a lot to deal with in helping children learn.

Emotionally literate children will have greater resilience to emotional problems. Schools have an important role to play in this development of emotional competence alongside that of parents and the child's wider social network (Mental Health Foundation, 1999). The reasons for the increase in mental health problems, for children as well as adults, remain unclear. However, despite such problems being likely to affect one in three of us at some point in our lives, they are still surrounded with stigma and shame.

Emotional problems also underlie behavioural problems that are seen in the classroom. The child who feels angry, frightened of failure or humiliation or not confident in herself may avoid or disrupt the learning situation, affecting her own development and perhaps the learning of others. At home, more children are experiencing family difficulties and breakdown which, for some, will contribute to difficulties in learning effectively. Not uncommonly, a child can spend up to four hours a day watching TV or in front of a computer screen. This is passively receiving information rather than learning, playing or interacting with others – the basic building blocks of emotional development. Most young people have had to face experiences where they have felt frightened, angry or unhappy. Many have experienced failure, rejection and abuse of a severity that will affect their self-belief and capacity to learn. For a significant few, this may lead to avoiding or being suspended from school. Early emotional experiences lay the foundation of neural development and emotional neglect and abuse can affect the brain's capacity to learn. Some can become unable to engage in relationships where they might experience success, learn to see themselves differently or to trust others. Their experiences or lack of support from home may influence their capacity to learn both academically and emotionally. However, schools can present environments where children can experience themselves differently and the brain remains open to new experiences that may help overcome early disadvantage.

Schools influence children's emotional lives. Schools place academic demands and expectations on their children that many will experience as stress, which, in turn, affects their ability to learn. Bullying can devastate a child's confidence and give a child severe difficulties in other areas of their lives. At the very least, schools should bear in mind the motto 'Primum non nocere' (Above all, do no harm).

We also have emotional problems at the societal and global level. Inter-racial and inter-group conflict is still a major concern for modern society; prejudice and fear of difference in other groups is apparent in all parts of the world. Although it may always have been and possibly will always be so, we also always strive for betterment and cooperation. Empathy and compassion can help increase our understanding of difference and aid communication.

We can help to make a difference

The better news is that there are so many things that can help to make a difference. Schools provide structure, support and opportunities for new experiences and successes that can positively develop children. Findings from the fields of mental health and education have demonstrated that children can overcome problems with benefits for their self-esteem and learning. This can be done through the development of emotional intelligence. This is not to suggest that teachers extend their role to become therapists or social workers, rather that we are learning more about how schools can facilitate children's learning and wellbeing. Also, emotional intelligence is not just for those having problems learning or who are hard to educate. It is for everyone. Young people with good coping and social skills can benefit from learning more about how to manage their feelings and empathising and relating to others. The skills required in the workplace are more and more about providing services to others and this means high levels of social skills are wanted. The qualities of high performing managers and leaders are often linked to being able to form relationships quickly and to understand what others need. Children will also go on to be the carers in tomorrow's society. Young people learn valuable skills when they learn how to communicate, cooperate and to confidently assert themselves; when they can overcome strong feelings of anger, aggression or fear and learn that these feelings are the essence of humanity and the foundation for living together.

> I believe that if one can help children continually to understand themselves, their desires and their fears, their hates and their loves; if one can help them to realise that these are shared by all; then one can lay the basis for a truly just and happy society.

Anthony Rodway, headteacher and educationalist

(*The Guardian*, August 15th 2002.)

Teachers are leaders in the classroom and, as many teachers know, effective leadership involves complex interpersonal skills that respect the child's integrity. Some of these skills necessary in people management that apply both to adults and children and applied to the classroom are:

- accessibility, understanding and responsiveness

- clarity about what the goals or learning objectives are and assisting in helping to achieve them

- awareness of a child's concerns especially related to learning

- genuine interest in a child's wellbeing

- a collaborative approach in dealing with problems.

These skills are about excellence in emotional literacy in the practice of teachers. How easy these skills are to learn and apply will vary. The primary school setting of working with one class regularly every day is very different from the secondary school where a teacher might only see a child once a week. There are as many different challenges as there are schools but the task of how to help all children feel connected to their school is important. There is no doubt that many teachers and schools have been practising the art and science of emotional intelligence and emotional literacy with great expertise before these terms were ever coined. What these concepts can provide us with is knowledge and information about why it is important and skills that can help us to do it better.

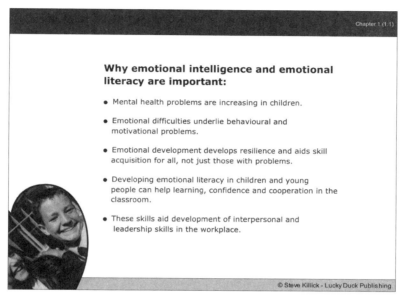

Slide 1.1

19   See Exercise One – Rating Emotional Literacy and Slide 1.2

20   See Exercise Two – Defining Emotional Literacy and Emotional Intelligence and Slide 1.3

21   See Exercise Three – Leaders of Motivation and Slide 1.4

Defining emotional intelligence and emotional literacy

Emotional intelligence and emotional literacy are terms becoming increasingly used in management, organisations, psychology, psychotherapy and education and they have both been defined in different ways. These terms are sometimes used interchangeably as if they refer to the same thing. But are they different and if so, in what ways? These are new areas and it is not surprising that researchers and practitioners have provided different definitions. This section explores a brief history and proposed definitions of these models.

Emotional intelligence

Emotional intelligence is a relatively new concept in the field of social science and is still undergoing definition and redefinition in an attempt to fully understand this concept. The idea that emotional function affects cognition is a very old idea. Plato wrote, 'All learning has an emotional base,' (Sharp, 2001). However, in the field of human science, although recognised as important, emotions were not always at the centre of scientific investigation until more recently. In psychology, a greater emphasis was placed on the rational, cognitive functioning of abstract linguistic and mathematical skills. Over the last few decades this has changed to an increasing recognition of wider aspects of learning. Howard Gardner (1983) broadened the concept of intelligence from the narrow set of skills that were measured by IQ, the traditional concept of intelligence. The areas of intelligence he identified are illustrated in Slide 1.5.

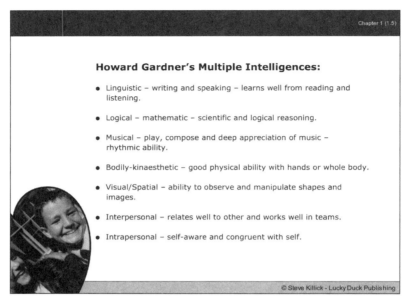

Slide 1.5

The traditional notions of cognitive intelligence and IQ that focused on academic ability were starting to be seen as too limited a view of our mental capacities and abilities. In 1990, Peter Salovey and Jack Mayer used the term 'emotional intelligence' and first defined it as:

> ... the mental capacity for processing emotion – the ability to monitor one's own and others' feelings and emotions, to discriminate among them and to use this information to guide one's thinking and actions.

Their definition combined two of Gardner's types of intelligence, intra and interpersonal, in this construct.

Daniel Goleman's book, *Emotional Intelligence – Why It Can Matter More Than IQ* (1995), brought the concept to a wider audience. The book had a tremendous impact. It brought to the attention of many the need, possibilities and evidence for valuing emotional development in the fields of education, health and work. He argued that education might have over-privileged the development of academic ability to the neglect of personal and social development. Although welcoming raising academic standards, the focus of academic abilities measured through examinations reflected traditional notions of intelligence yet lacked an emotional dimension that was critical to learning. Goleman defined the term as referring to:

> the capacity for recognising our own feelings and those of others, for motivating ourselves and for managing emotions well in ourselves and in our relationships (1998).

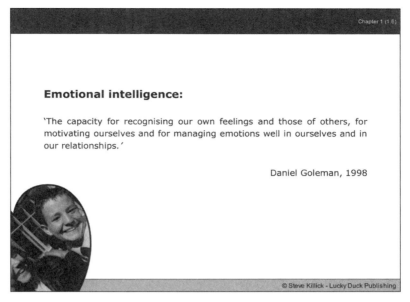

Slide 1.6

Goleman's argument was that the focus in the traditional concept of intelligence on cognitive abilities such as verbal and numerical skills, concentration, attention and memory was too narrow. A measure of these abilities delivered an intelligence quotient (IQ) used frequently in occupation selection and still used in education to determine special educational needs, and, occasionally, for school selection. However, IQ, although predictive of academic ability, is not predictive of how successful, effective or happy a person may be. Emotional intelligence may be more influential in this area. Further, our emotional abilities influence how we are able to use our thinking skills. The term emotional intelligence denotes the need for a much broader view of what intelligence is. As we understand more about the nature of emotion, we learn that there is much we can do to facilitate the development of emotional intelligence in children. This knowledge will have gains for their mental and physical health and help unlock their potential in living and learning fully.

Reuven BarOn, another pioneering emotional intelligence researcher, described emotionally intelligent people as those:

> … who are able to recognise and express their emotions, who possess positive self-regard, and are able to actualise their potential capacities and lead fairly happy lives. They are able to understand the way others feel and are capable of making and maintaining mutually satisfying and responsible interpersonal relationships, without becoming dependent on others. These people are generally optimistic, flexible, realistic and successful in solving problems and coping with stress, without losing control (BarOn, 1997, pp.155-6).

Goleman's book drew upon Salovey and Mayer's work, especially the ideas that there are five 'domains' or 'pathways' of emotional intelligence. These areas are significant in that they can be seen as skills that can be learnt and developed. All these skills exist on a continuum of development.

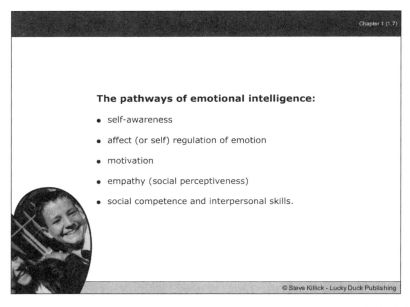

The pathways of emotional intelligence:

- self-awareness
- affect (or self) regulation of emotion
- motivation
- empathy (social perceptiveness)
- social competence and interpersonal skills.

© Steve Killick - Lucky Duck Publishing

Slide 1.7

Self-awareness

This is to know one's own emotional state, to be able to recognise what feelings are being experienced at any one time and being aware of the thoughts that are involved in this. It is to know one's self and to have a positive, integrated sense of self. We grow in sophistication in our ability to do this. The child in his first year of life can only be aware of bodily sensations. As he grows he is able to give names to these experiences and his emotional vocabulary is constantly extending. As he gets older he is able to recognise the causes of his feelings. We develop this capacity throughout life as we gain greater insight into the multiple, complex and often conflicting feelings we experience.

Affect (or self) regulation

This is to be able to manage one's emotions, to be able to respond and handle strong feelings such as fear or anger appropriately rather than to act them out. For instance, the angry child who hurts another or the anxious child who avoids playing with others is not dealing well with his strong feelings. The child has to learn effective ways of dealing with strong feelings that may meet rather than deprive him of his needs. The critical skill is being able to calm or soothe oneself and this develops throughout life.

Motivation

This is the ability to motivate oneself to achieve one's goals and is essential for us all. Children may search out the approval of others, peers or adults, or be motivated by internal drives or 'willpower' to achieve meaningful and desired outcomes. At some point there may be recognition that greater rewards may come through delaying gratification. Motivation is needed to work towards exams where the benefits of one's efforts may not be reaped immediately. Some children are struggling to find the motivation to get themselves out of bed.

Empathy (social perceptiveness)

This is the ability to see how another person is feeling or seeing the world, that is, social perceptiveness. To empathise is to understand another person's frame of reference. Not only is this a critical skill in helping others, it is fundamental for human relationships. As she grows, the child can increasingly recognise that others think differently from how she does and can develop the capacity for understanding what and why other people are thinking and feeling. The child (or adult) who is aware of how their actions affect others gains confidence in herself as well as being better able to get on with others.

Social competence

Beyond empathy, there are interpersonal and social skills we need to get along with others and this involves being able to manage strong feelings in others and to manage relationships. Children need to know when they have upset others or made them angry and how they can help to rectify the situation: to be able to repair relationships. They also need to know when things are going well and experience joy in relationships. Children learn social skills in all their interactions but even well-skilled children may benefit from learning high levels of assertion and conflict resolution skills. Some children will have particular difficulties and need additional help. These skills are critical for our self-esteem and wellbeing. Good friends can be a great help in life and possible relationships the source of great satisfaction.

It is through developing these skills in these five domains that emotional intelligence is facilitated. They develop throughout all of life but it is during childhood and adolescence that learning is accelerated; this is the hothouse period of emotional growth. All our interactions with children, provided that they are respectful and valuing, offer the opportunity for children to develop and strengthen these skills. These pathways to emotional intelligence are discussed more fully in Chapter Three.

The success of Goleman's book triggered a phenomenal interest in the area of emotional intelligence, in the areas of organisational work settings and in education. It also generated considerable academic interest including important criticism.

Personality or IQ?

Petrides et al (2004b) argued that the abilities that make up emotional intelligence are more to do with personality than intelligence. It is personality and personal characteristics that determine one's ability in the area of emotional functioning. However, although personality and temperament certainly influence one's emotional make-up, it is important to see emotional intelligence as the practice of thinking about feeling and that it is more changeable than personality (Maddocks, Cooper & Sparrow, 2005).

It has also been claimed that Goleman's theory that emotional intelligence is more important than IQ has been overstated. The process of thinking about feeling involves the thinking skills involved in intelligence. A further criticism is that some people feel that a scientific-rational perspective is incapable of offering a full understanding of the complexities of our emotional experience (Freshwater & Robertson, 2002). Another difficulty has been the almost evangelical zeal with which some have taken up emotional intelligence. The concept of emotional intelligence has been seen as something that could 'change the world' can be off-putting for some, possibly leading to claims that it is a buzzword, a passing fashion or just a 'bandwagon'. Emotional intelligence, it should be remembered, is a relatively new scientific idea and its potential and limits are still being examined and defined.

Emotional intelligence remains a new 'model' for thinking about human functioning and behaviour and as such is still in the process of being understood. That it has become so well-known so quickly perhaps reflects the experience of many that how we feel affects how we learn and think.

Emotional literacy

At the same time as emotional intelligence was having such an impact the term emotional literacy was also being increasingly used, particularly in the field of education. Emotional literacy has been seen as being able to positively impact upon academic performance, wellbeing and behaviour and drew on a long tradition of child (or person) centred education. Claude Steiner first used the term 'emotional literacy' in 1979. More recently, the writer and psychotherapist, Susie Orbach, has promoted the importance of emotional literacy in society. Her argument was that we live a culture that is emotionally illiterate, afraid of what happens when emotions can get out of control.

Orbach wrote in 1999 that emotional literacy was:

the capacity to register our emotional responses to the situations we are in and to acknowledge those responses to ourselves so that we recognise the ways they influence our thoughts and actions.

She also described it in much more straightforward terms:

Emotional literacy is making it possible to ask the question, 'How are you?' and to be able to listen to the answer.

Antidote, an organisation promoting the need for emotional literacy, was in part set up by Susie Orbach with the aim of encouraging emotional literacy in all aspects of society including education. They offer a definition of emotional literacy:

… the practice of thinking individually and collectively about how emotions shape our actions, and of using emotional understanding to enrich our thinking.

Emotional Literacy Handbook (Parks, Haddon and Goodman, 2003)

Emotional literacy:

- 'People are able to recognise, understand and appropriately express their emotions.'
  Peter Sharp, 2001

- 'The practice of thinking individually and collectively about how emotions shape our actions, and of using emotional understanding to enrich our thinking.'
  Antidote, 2003

© Steve Killick - Lucky Duck Publishing

Slide 1.8

Also in the UK, Southampton Local Education Authority have promoted emotional literacy widely, describing it as when, 'people are able to recognise, understand and appropriately express their emotions' (Sharp, 2001).

The authority has developed a strategy for the promotion of emotional literacy in schools across the area and their work is attracting wide interest. Their model identifies similar dimensions as that identified by Goleman. These are the personal competencies of self-awareness, self-regulation and motivation and the social competencies of empathy and social skills (Faupel, 2003). Closely associated with the Southampton project, Jean Gross, with funding from the Gilbukian Foudation, produced a teaching and resource showing emotional literacy provision in Bristol: *The Emotional Literacy Hour* (2000).

So, emotional intelligence and emotional literacy are terms functionally referring to the same general idea. The distinction is that emotional intelligence remains a scientific construct. Emotional literacy, as Simon Baron Cohen (2003) wrote, is a metaphor and one that is both apt and useful.

Emotional literacy is of course a metaphor. It depends on the analogy with reading words and suggests that when we look at faces we read the person's underlying mental states (their thoughts, intentions and feelings). But by the same token, this metaphor can be extended to suggest that there might be people who suffer from emotional dyslexia – for whom reading a face is not easy.

Peter Sharp (2001) felt that emotional literacy may be preferable to the term emotional intelligence as 'intelligence' is a word with negative connotations. That may, albeit incorrectly, lead to it be seen as a stable and fixed quality rather than being fluid and dynamic. The word 'literacy' implies that this is something that can be learnt and has relevance particularly for schools.

Emotional literacy in schools also has its critics. Some people feel that emotional literacy is in effect a form of social control, an attempt to make teachers amateur therapists that intrudes into a child's privacy (Furedi, 2004). Most of these criticisms appear to be based on misinformed conceptions of emotional literacy or, possibly, on poor practice in this area. Emotional literacy is concerned with mutual respect, effective communication and thus an increase in choice and responsibility. This would preclude making a child expose thoughts or feelings against his wishes. Having teachers as therapists is neither implied or seen as helpful. As has always been the case, there will be children who will need access to counselling services within the school or mental health services outside the school. What might be improved through emotional literacy is increased mutual understanding and shared expectations of what might be achieved between services. Also, emotional literacy may have a role in prevention of mental health problems but this no more makes teachers therapists than teaching about physical health or biology would make them doctors. Some of these criticisms may be based more on the anxieties many have about emotions rather than informed knowledge of emotional literacy in action.

A worldwide movement

Emotional literacy is becoming a worldwide movement in education, promoting teaching in 'the Fourth R – Relationships'. This movement is still in its infancy (although growing quickly) and yet it calls upon a long tradition in education. Its concern is to find a language for talking about emotions in the classroom and has the potential for a tremendous impact. Not only is there evidence that focusing on emotional development improves academic performance, but that it provides the basis for learning 'skills', rather than of learning knowledge, and of improving 'people skills' – both of which are essential in the workplace in the 21st century. Perhaps most importantly, these skills, (which were previously seen as unteachable) not only can be learnt in school settings but can also provide the key to helping people live more meaningful and satisfying lives, reaching their full potential. All over the world there are increasing numbers of programmes that focus on interpersonal skills and mental health promotion.

Common themes – the bridge between thinking and feeling

So, emotional intelligence and emotional literacy both refer to the same central idea. 'Emotional intelligence' is used more commonly in the US whereas 'emotional literacy' is more commonly used in the UK (Weare and Gray, 2003). In this book the terms are used interchangeably. However, emotional intelligence is used when referring specifically to thinking and emotional literacy when referring to practices within schools. Both these terms refer to:

the capacity in individuals (and groups) to perceive, understand and manage emotions in oneself and others.

For children and young people this means the skills that can be encouraged based on the five domains outlined by Salovey and Mayer:

1. To know one's self.

2. To have self control.

3. To have persistence.

4. To empathise.

5. To relate well with others.

Emotional intelligence is not just about our emotions. It is more about our capacity to think and reflect on our feelings rather than to act on impulse. It is a way of 'increasing the space' that exists between feelings and action (See Slide 1.10).

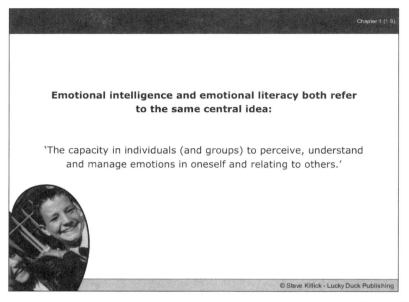

Slide 1.9

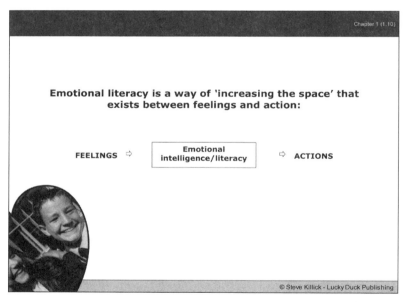

Slide 1.10

Our capacity to think about our feelings can determine how we use our other abilities to concentrate, to remember, to imagine, to predict the future and to evaluate our courses of action. These abilities may be over-ridden when we feel emotionally overwhelmed, either through fear, shame or anger amongst others. It is about how we can use and develop our thinking skills to understand and learn from our emotional impulses. This is because it is: '... not events per se which determine our feelings but the meanings that we attach to these events' (Neenan and Dryden, 2004). Emotional literacy is 'a bridge' between our thoughts and feelings (Antidote, 2003). It works in relation with cognitive intelligence to enable us to reach our full potential. This quality develops over time and changes throughout life and grows with experience. As Goleman said, '… we need to harmonise thought and feeling, not separate them. It is about using our emotions intelligently' (1995).

Perhaps most significant is that it is our capacity to think about others' and our own emotional lives that influences our state of wellbeing. It is related to our mental health, the ability to deal with stresses and problems that life brings. Emotional literacy is the key to mental health and wellbeing. We can practise the skills and develop our potential in this area in that same way that we can take steps to improve our physical health.

How can children bring intelligence to their emotions?

Children need to learn how to gain a degree of self-control over their feelings: to overcome worry rather than avoid challenges that may face them, to express anger by standing up for themselves assertively rather than aggressively and to cope with sadness, loss, disappointment and frustration. Also, they need to be able to motivate themselves to achieve longer-term and constructive goals rather than seeking out immediate gratification. These skills have traditionally believed to be unable to be taught. Rather children are often told to 'pull themselves together', 'be responsible' or 'think of others'. They are not often told *how* to do this. Comments that deny a child's emotion and experience can be an assault on self-esteem. This might mean the child may react through anger to fight back or, which may be worse, they may agree with the unconscious message that they cannot trust their own feelings. The seeds of self-doubt are then being sown. This doesn't mean that a child should not experience negative feelings about themselves or be allowed to behave as they want, but it places an emphasis on respectful communication with children that acknowledges and develops their emotional abilities.

Measuring emotional intelligence and emotional literacy in children

There are difficulties in trying to measure the fluid and fluctuating qualities of emotional intelligence as it cannot yet be done through objective measures like IQ or standardized attainment tests. However, some measures have been developed, the majority for adults, which attempt to measure this quality. These are based on self-report and the observations and judgement of others that, although cannot be seen as fully objective or reliable, are still of value. Reuven BarOn developed a measure that has become a well-used tool for adults and organisational development. More recently he developed a version for children, The BarOn Emotional Quotient Inventory: Youth Version (EQI:YV, 2000). This measure enables children (aged between 7-18) to be compared against other children or young people of the same age to assess their emotional functioning (norms based on North American children). The measure consists of five scales: intrapersonal, interpersonal, adaptability, stress management and general mood. The score gives an Emotional Quotient that is useful in evaluating needs and the success of any intervention to develop emotional functioning.

The Southampton Psychology Service developed a measure of emotional literacy (Faupel, 2003) comprising the five core pathways. This measure uses 360-degree feedback, that is, they not only rely on self-report but judgements of parents and teachers to give an all round view. This has been designed to aid interventions to improve emotional literacy in individual children, class and whole-school approaches. Scores can be compared to norms based on children in the UK. They can be administered quickly and are able to assess and aid in planning of how to intervene. There are measures for age groups 7-11 and 11-16 and the manuals contain considerable information for intervention.

A comparison between these two measures was conducted (Rendall & Robinson, 2005) with young people with emotional and behavioural difficulties. Little consistency was found between the measures and it was the Southampton Checklist that gave the most useful information to guide interventions.

Evidence for emotional literacy

Weare and Gray's report, *What Works in Developing Children's Emotional and Social Competence and Wellbeing* (2003), summarised their review of the available evidence of educational interventions to promote emotional and social skills. They noted evidence, mainly from the US, that demonstrated strong positive gains from interventions aimed in facilitating emotional development. However, despite such evidence, they argued that there is a strong need to develop a high quality empirical evidence base (see Slide 1.11). As much of the applied development of strategies promoting emotional intelligence and literacy are still in their infancy, the evaluation process is also at a very early stage. The evidence often tends to be qualitative rather than quantitative. Although rigorous evidence is hard to gain it is important to know what interventions work best.

In the US there has been a longer tradition of evaluating this area of work. In 1983, Carl Rogers summarised seventeen years of research into applying person-centred principles (empathy, congruence, positive regard) to education. He said:

> the findings can be briefly summarised in one statement: Students learn more and behave better when they receive high levels of understanding, caring and genuineness, than when they are given low levels of them. It pays to treat students as sensitive and aware human beings.

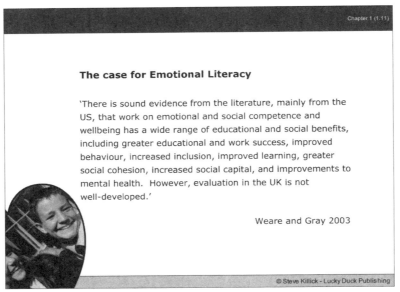

Slide 1.11

Goleman (1995) included the results of several projects focusing on social and emotional learning and found evidence that children developed in the five key competency areas of emotional intelligence:

1. *Self-awareness* Students improved in recognising and naming their own emotions and became better able to recognise the difference between feelings and actions and to recognise the causes of feeling.

2. *Self-regulation* Better frustration, tolerance and anger management skills were found. Also, fewer verbal putdowns, fights and classroom disruptions. Students were better able to express anger appropriately, to have more positive feelings about self, friends and family, and handle stress at school. Lower levels of loneliness and social anxiety were found and there was increased resilience against depression.

3. *Motivation* Improvement in concentration and motivation towards goals and decreased impulsiveness.

4. *Empathy* Increased levels of social perceptiveness and improved ability in reading emotions and in sensitivity to others' feelings. They are also better at listening to each other.

5. *Social competence* Better able to handle and understand relationships, resolving conflict and disagreements. Improvements in social problem-solving and cooperative behaviour.

Emotional literacy programmes have also claimed other benefits. Reductions in the number of suspensions and improvements in academic achievement were found in some studies (Goleman, 1995). Such evidence supports the beliefs that such programmes go beyond raising levels of emotional literacy and can also aid school improvement. A study by Petrides et al., (2004a) on 650 secondary school students in the UK, found those with higher levels of emotional intelligence less likely to have unauthorized absences and less likely to be excluded. High emotional intelligence was associated with better academic performance. This suggests that if schools can develop interventions in improving emotional intelligence there are potentially many benefits. However, difficulties in both the concept and measurement of emotional intelligence must be borne in mind when making definite claims about the potential for emotional literacy.

A review by Zeidner, Roberts and Matthews (2002) found that many intervention programmes had not been designed to alter emotional intelligence specifically, and did not demonstrate that emotional intelligence had any more predictive validity than general intelligence or personality. They concluded that whether school interventions could influence emotional intelligence is still undetermined. There is, most certainly, a need for further research as Weare and Gray (2003) suggest, especially as the potential gains are so high. There are now more and more schools providing an emotional literacy curriculum and there is also scepticism about the values of doing so. Yet if improving emotional literacy can, as many believe, help young people deal with the many obstacles they face in life – relationship difficulties, abuse of alcohol and drugs, vulnerability for mental health problems – then there is a need for an education that values emotional development.

Emotional literacy in the context of the school

Commentators have been clear that in considering raising levels of emotional literacy in schools, it is not simply a manner of just teaching with the aim of changing the child. A child's emotional life does not exist in a vacuum but is determined by the relationships and environment in which she interacts with others. In education, this means considering the context of the organisation – the school as a whole. We can teach a lot about emotions, and bring this into the curriculum but it is the values of the school and the behaviour of the teachers in which the values of emotional literacy are 'lived'. They are demonstrated and modelled and so they more 'caught rather than taught'. The values of respect, cooperation and consideration of others need to exist within the structure of the school. This means developing emotional literacy on multiple levels. The relationship between the school, the teacher and the child is illustrated in Slide 1.12. This demonstrates the many areas where emotional literacy may be usefully applied in the school that are explored throughout this book.

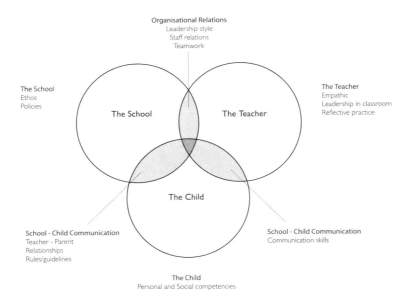

Slide 1.12

Introducing emotional literacy into schools is about the whole-school ethos, the school's relationship with the outside world (for instance, the often complicated relationship that can exist with parents and other agencies) and relationships between staff. Just as the emotional intelligence of an individual can be defined, so can the emotional intelligence of a group or team. A team needs to be able to work towards shared goals and to be able to reflect about its own processes and progress towards those goals.

Change at the organisational level is often difficult to achieve yet there are many examples of good practice. Developing high-level interpersonal skills is a key starting point; it is how the teacher communicates with students on a day-to-day level to build thinking and emotional skills from which more profound changes develop. Also, small initiatives in working with others can begin to prepare the ground for organisational change.

The importance of placing emotional literacy within the context of the whole school is explored throughout this book. The foundations of creating change at this level are rooted in our understanding of the emotional lives of others and ourselves and our ability to bring that understanding into our interactions.

Summary of Chapter One

- Emotional intelligence and emotional literacy are two related but distinct terms that relate to the capacity in individuals (and groups) to perceive, understand and manage emotions in one's self and in others.

- There are five key areas in which emotional development can be encouraged: self-awareness, self-regulation, motivation, empathy and social competence.

- Approaches that develop emotional literacy in schools are aimed at all students, not just those with difficulties.

- The benefits of emotional literacy are in academic learning, enhancing wellbeing in both children and adults and improving behaviour.

- Although there is evidence for the effectiveness of developing emotional and social competence there is a need to develop a greater evidence base and evaluate initiatives designed to promote emotional literacy.

- Emotional literacy is not just about raising levels of emotional and social competence in children, it is equally concerned with improving relationships between people in the context of the school.

Exercise One – Rating Emotional Literacy

This exercise, presented on Slide 1.2, can be helpful to do at the beginning of any training to gain an idea of individual participants' beliefs about the importance of emotional factors in education. As well as giving an indication of the group's beliefs, repetition of this rating at the end will enable an evaluation of the impact of any training.

It also introduces, for those who may not be familiar with it, the concept of the 10 point rating scale which can be used in many ways in helping people rate feelings, motivation and other factors.

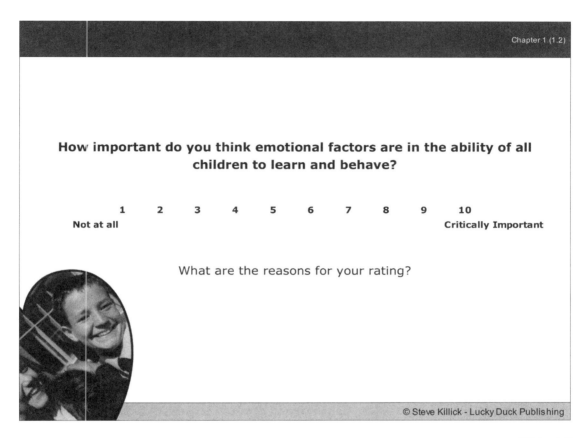

Slide 1.2

Exercise Two – Defining Emotional Literacy and Emotional Intelligence

The purpose of this exercise is to help participants to start talking about the subject and, if introduced early, can help make participants feel they can contribute to the discussions. The aims are to get people talking about their knowledge, expectations and preconceptions about emotional literacy and emotional intelligence. The facilitator asks the group to split into pairs or small groups to discuss 'what they think of when they hear the terms emotional literacy and emotional intelligence' (see slide). Even if the group is completely unfamiliar with the terms then they could be asked what they think the terms might mean to help initiate thinking about the subject.

This exercise gives the facilitator information about the group's level of knowledge and attitudes about emotional literacy that can help in ensuring further information presented is at the right level. It is not important that participants know what the terms mean or are correct in their answers. Answers can be recorded on a flipchart and briefly discussed highlighting the points where participants are making accurate or insightful points.

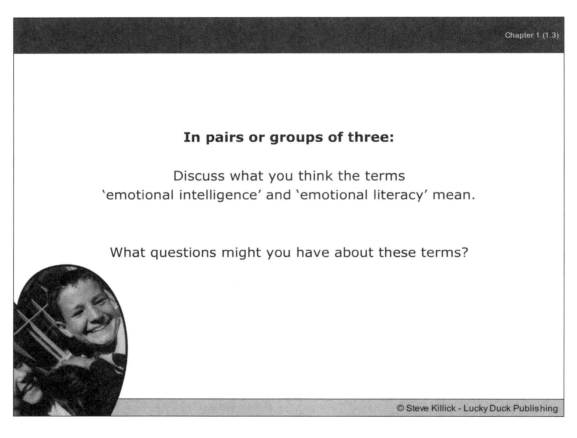

Slide 1.3

Exercise Three – Leaders of Motivation

This exercise aims to help adults recall their own childhood and how other adults, especially teachers, influenced and motivated them as children. By viewing the characteristics of teachers who inspired and motivated them, adults are made aware of how personal characteristics such as empathy, understanding and a sense of warmth have a dramatic impact on a child.

Individually ask participants to think back to their own schooling and to remember two teachers, one who was liked and one who was disliked (see Slide 1.4). Participants can be asked to spend a minute or so to think back and recall these moments from their own childhood.

Then, in small groups of between five and ten with one person to write down what is said, ask the group to describe the characteristics of the liked and then the disliked teacher. From each of the lists of characteristics, invite the groups to discuss the influence of these teachers on how they influenced them as children especially in terms of their interest and motivation towards their learning and behaviour.

Facilitative Inquiry:

What were the features that distinguished or characterised these teachers?

What effect did these teachers have on you especially with regard to your motivation, behaviour, and feelings about them and yourself?

What similarities and differences do you have with these teachers?

Remember two teachers from your own education and schooling:

- one who had a positive effect on you or who you liked
- one who had a negative effect on you or who you disliked.

© Steve Killick - Lucky Duck Publishing

Slide 1.4

Chapter Two

An Impulse to Act – the Nature of Emotion

Emotion is something we are at once familiar with. After all, everyone has feelings all the time. Yet our emotional life is also mysterious; we may not be aware of some feelings, or understand why we feel a certain way, or why others may feel the way they do. Our emotional life is rich and complex. Our feelings play a part in intuition (or in-tuition), the 'inner teacher' that comes from within. Emotional literacy is about how one learns to identify and communicate about emotions from the basic foundations through to the complexities of our experience; the more we understand the more we can exercise wisdom in choices and communicate with others. Our potential to learn is such that it is a lifelong process.

Knowledge about the nature and qualities of emotions is a sound starting point.

- The complexity of our emotional life is a product of evolution and is necessary for survival.

- Our emotions have purpose and function – they motivate us and are essential in communication.

- They are universal and physical, psychological and social in nature.

- They vary in strength and we can feel multiple, conflicting and complex emotions. We experience mixed and ambivalent feelings often and 'pure' emotion more rarely.

- They are developmental – increasing in sophistication throughout the life cycle.

- Strong feelings will peak in intensity and then diminish and pass.

- We have psychological processes or 'defence mechanisms' that help from us being overwhelmed by strong feelings.

- There are important gender differences.

- Emotions may be positive and negative in their effects on us. This is not a feature of the emotion itself but how we understand and act on it. They may give us pleasant or uncomfortable physical sensations or they may lead to emotional problems such as depression, phobias and others.

What is emotion?

The affective aspect of consciousness; a state of feeling; a psychic and physical reaction (as anger or fear) subjectively experienced as strong feeling, and physiologically involving the body in changes preparing for strong physical action.

Miriam-Webster Dictionary

This definition tells us that emotion has both psychological and physical components. For instance, a person experiencing anger might have thoughts about hating someone or wishing him or her ill. These thoughts have a physiological accompaniment. The person might feel extremely tense, his heart racing; he may have a sensation that his 'blood boils' and feel unable to relax. The experience may be so intense that it is like a feeling of being about to explode. It may be so fierce that a person may lose self-control and hit out, although moments later he may regret it. The strong thoughts and feelings are a powerful motivator for action. Goleman described emotion as 'an impulse to act'. The Latin origin of the word 'emotion' is 'that which sets in motion' and the word 'motivation' has a similar root. We may talk of being 'moved' after a powerful emotional experience. Emotion has the function of motivating us to act and this function has been critical in human development.

Beyond emotion lies 'mood' and 'temperament'. Goleman (1995) described mood as being more muted and longer lasting than emotion, although our moods are influenced by feelings. For instance, the rage of anger may not last long but a grumpy irritable mood may last some time. Temperament refers to a personality characteristic towards particular emotional states such as sadness, happiness, worry or anger.

Evolutionary development

The parts of our brain involved in the regulation of emotion are, from an evolutionary perspective, amongst the oldest structures in the nervous system. These emotional centres predate our higher cognitive abilities and remain critical in organising brain function. Emotions are linked with human development and are necessary for survival, both to deal with danger and to form relationships with others. Humans are social animals that have always lived in groups and been dependent on each other, so we need to assess risk, form attachments and to be able to stand up for ourselves. We need to know who we can trust and who we can't. It may be that our brains have had to develop their immense problem-solving skills to be able to form and evaluate relationships quickly, as to be able to work with others and communicate well gives an evolutionary advantage. We have needed to be able to calculate quickly whether we can trust others and continually make sophisticated social judgements. Our ability to empathise predated and laid the foundation for the development of language. Yet humans take longer to fully develop then any other creature. Therefore, the child needs longer periods of care than other mammals to become independent of the carer, time necessary for the development of complex cognitive and emotional skills. Although our emotional and social development matures in early adulthood it continues to develop in sophistication over the lifecycle.

Our basic emotional make-up is universal to the human race. Cultural and ethnic differences will exist but what makes us most human is the universality of emotional experience. Different communities and societies will develop their own ways of communicating which will include rules of social and emotional functioning. Such differences often lead to a lack of understanding or empathy with resultant anxiety and prejudice. An attitude of respect and curiosity, as opposed to stereotyping, may enhance communication and understanding between communities and it will always be important to foster this in the education setting.

> Over and over in my travels I've found that beneath the infinite variety of human complexity, beneath the cultures and nations, beneath the religions and rivalries, beneath the differences, we are profoundly alike... And more and more I am seeing that emotions are at the heart of this similarity. A universal language that bonds us and liberates us – if we will only find the courage to learn it more deeply, and use it more carefully.
>
> **Josh Freeman**

The functions of emotions

Emotions can be positive and negative in their effect on behaviour. However, it is not the emotion itself that determines its effect but how it is understood and managed. For instance, a child might feel a degree of jealousy towards another person whom she sees as being cleverer than she is. That jealousy might motivate a person towards finding ways of being aggressive towards the target of her emotion, perhaps openly by mocking or attacking the target, perhaps more subtly, through talking negatively behind the target's back. These actions may aggravate the situation and worsen any relationship these two young people may have had. Alternatively, feelings of jealousy may motivate the child to work harder, maybe to positively compete with that person and produce meaningful achievements. So jealousy is neither positive nor negative in its nature but can have positive or negative effects depending on how it is perceived and thought about. It is how we think about what we are feeling that gives us choices about how to respond. This is emotional intelligence and it lays the ground for responsibility – the ability to have choices in how one responds. Steven Covey (1989) described that understanding what responsibility is really about is by looking at the word itself: 'response-ability'. Responsibility is commonly seen as a desired attribute in children, but what this often means is that children do what is expected of them by adults rather than helping them become more able to make choices for themselves and to be aware of the consequences of their actions.

For children, the experience of shame is an important emotion that can have both positive and negative effects. The experience of shame in a young child makes an important contribution to the socialisation process. The young infant may experience shame as a result of experiencing the displeasure of the caregiver. This acts to make him change and correct his behaviour to please his caregiver. This enables the child to develop pro-social behaviours and will also help with the development of guilt, a sense of remorse and awareness that he has acted incorrectly. The development of guilt is an important part of moral development: how one should act towards others. Often 'shaming' a child, for instance to call a child a 'silly boy', is done with the intention of helping motivate him to correct his behaviour. The problem may be if the child experiences an intense feeling of shame or humiliation; he experiences such a profound sense of worthlessness that he becomes disabled. The strength of the emotion is such that he must shield himself from this perceived attack. The child may be overwhelmed emotionally or deny any responsibility for his behaviour. This is one important reason that invoking negative experiences in children in an attempt to motivate them is, at best, a high-risk strategy.

Emotions, then, are not fixed as being positive or negative; it is the effects of the emotions that can be either. Also, emotions can produce both pleasant and unpleasant physical experiences. Anxiety, for example, is an uncomfortable feeling and it is meant to be so; it cannot be easily ignored. Anxiety is a response to danger, a perceived threat of some kind, perhaps a problem that must be solved. The discomfort is relieved when the problem is solved which might come through a process of thinking or finding someone who can help. However, avoidance of something that is difficult might become a problem in its own right or repetitive worry about feared consequences that may never happen. A child may worry that when speaking in front of a class she will make a mistake, will be seen as stupid and be socially shunned. The opportunity to master the anxiety and to face our fears is not found. If anxiety was not uncomfortable we may not attend to the possible threat. The experience of the emotion then has a capacity to motivate our thinking and actions. It is also linked to physical arousal; strong feelings interact with hormones that place a person on a range of high or low arousal. High arousal prepares us for action but may make us less reflective or thoughtful. Emotions interact with our physical state. Physical and emotional wellbeing go hand in hand. Crying is a powerful physical and emotional reaction to help us deal with strong feelings of upset where stress-combating hormones are released to help calm us.

The foundation of our emotional lives is laid in our early attachment relationships. It is increasingly understood that in our early relationships we need to consistently receive affection, care, interest and commitment from our carers. The attachment relationship hard-wires our brain to be able to deal with emotions and relationships throughout life. It will influence our sense of self-worth, safety and security and personal styles in managing emotions, whether we may become anxious or dismissive in certain situations. This foundation is critical but we remain open to development throughout life.

Motivation

All emotions have a capacity to motivate. We may be motivated towards pleasant feelings (for example, relaxation, intimacy) and motivated to avoid unpleasant feelings. Emotional highs of excitement or euphoria are attractive. Drug induced states have an addictive quality. Equally, we may wish to avoid unpleasant emotions such as anxiety or fear. However, if we become avoidant of situations that are important (such as school or work) or that might give opportunities for growth, for instance to meet new people, then our quality of life may be impaired and opportunities to gain confidence avoided.

We are also capable of experiencing mixed emotions or different emotions at the same time. Indeed, it is rare that we feel a pure emotion and more likely we are in a state of ambivalence, for example, excitement may contain both strong feelings of euphoria and also apprehension.

How we think about our feelings also influences them. The child who feels that she may succeed in facing a physical challenge feels energised and confident. A child feeling unable may make a judgment that she cannot succeed and feels dispirited. The stronger our feelings are, the more difficult it can become to apply our rational thinking abilities to them. Our rational thought processes are contained in a different part of the brain to the emotional centres and both our 'head' and our 'heart' coexist in a complex system; our thoughts influence our feelings and our feelings influence our thoughts. The implication of this is that if we can change our thoughts we can change our feelings (and vice versa). Knowing that this is so is of the greatest significance. Thought and feeling are intertwined in their influence on each other.

There are mental processes that allow us to block out or repress feelings we find particularly disturbing or unpleasant. These 'defence mechanisms', particularly against anxiety, may prevent the experiencing of the emotion but it can still influence thought and behaviour. If feelings are particularly frightening or overwhelming the mind may cope with this by placing them out of consciousness, that is, the feeling is repressed and the person is unaware of it. In such cases, someone may deny to themselves the feelings they are experiencing or project those feelings onto others. When the behaviour of a child leaves an adult feeling frustrated and hopeless this may give that adult important information about how the child is feeling: that she too is experiencing frustration and hopelessness and the only way she can express it is through her behaviour.

Social processes of emotion

Emotions are not located solely in the individual, they are also intensely interpersonal or social in nature. They are the glue that binds us together with one another. Many emotions are physically expressed through non-verbal communication, while some we can hide or conceal. We can act to convey different feelings that we are experiencing. However, even when we hide our feelings they may still 'leak out'.

Again, the physicality of emotions has a purpose. For instance, when we are 'surprised', our eyebrows are raised and pupils expand. This simply enables us to take in more visual information, a useful precaution if we are experiencing something we did not expect. It also alerts others straight away that there is something unexpected. Another basic emotion is that of 'disgust'. Something seen as offensive, such as rotten food, might produce a response that has been 'hard-wired' in and our repulsion makes us avoid contact. Our face makes clear signals of repulsion that are communicated to others, giving warning signals to others of something repugnant. When someone looks sad this can trigger another person to look after him and offer comfort. Our emotions expressed in non-verbal communication can be 'care-eliciting' behaviours that trigger responses in others. These emotions and the responses in others are (generally) hard-wired into our systems. In our close relationships we may become attuned to the emotional needs or messages and our emotions are part of the bonds of attachment between us. Another interpersonal feature of emotion is that of 'contagion'. One person's feeling may affect another's feeling as people may unconsciously echo each other's physical stance. Anger begets anger as laughter begets laughter. Emotions are contagious and infectious in the way they can spread between people. People affect how other people feel all the time. Indeed our emotional systems are continually designed to be on the look out for the feelings of those around us. We can be influenced both positively and negatively and are constantly influencing others, even if we are trying not to. In this way a class or staff team, or even a school, may develop a collective mood that is both influencing and influenced by the individuals in the group. Emotional intelligence involves paying attention to the signals that are always being sent and received between us.

There are gender differences in emotional processing ability that have been summarised by Maines (2003). Females, on average, have greater empathic ability that may in fact be linked with linguistic ability, and focus more on feelings than actions, in contrast with boys, and place greater value on friendships. These differences exist in childhood and adolescence and will be familiar to most teachers. Boys may, on average, be slightly behind in their cognitive development than girls, with subsequent differences in their emotional development. However, the range within each gender exceeds the differences between the two sexes but boys may need more guidance in emotional literacy than girls, particularly understanding social rules and cues. Differences between the sexes may reflect the different learning styles that are often observed between boys and girls in the classroom.

Emotions are parts of a complicated cognitive, physical and social system and these components interrelate with one another.

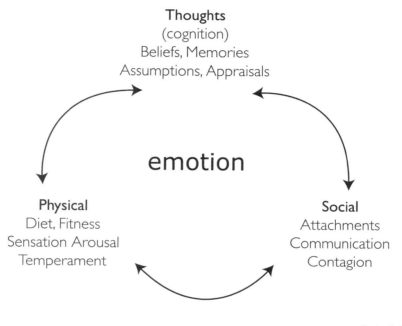

Slide 2.3

Our thoughts, physical state and our relationships influence, and are influenced by, our emotions which set up patterns of behaviour and help define who we are. While some of our feelings are communicated openly, they are often hidden, sometimes even from ourselves. Our innermost thoughts and feelings are what is most personal, but also what is most universal. We are all capable of experiencing feelings. The richness of our emotional life is universal across the human race. It is our emotional experience that can make life seem worth living or not. Managing our emotions can present us with our biggest challenges; problems of depression, anxiety and panic attacks, managing anger and relationship issues can cause considerable distress.

The language of emotion

We all have an emotional life, at all times, regardless of ability, age, gender or race. This is our mood which can comprise multiple or ambivalent feelings. Our mood affects both our perceptions and physical feelings, most notably our level of arousal. The complexity of our emotional life is reflected in the richness of language that has so many words to express different feeling states. We can experience emotions both positively and negatively and they are necessary for us to function most effectively. All emotions have value but we need to experience positive affect to be able to function at our best and to overcome negativity. When we are feeling good, we think more creatively, we are better able to work cooperatively and to relate with others. When we are overwhelmed with feelings such as frustration or anger, our capacity to think clearly deteriorates. Emotions are at the very core of our existence and there is an enormous vocabulary in our languages to reflect the complexity of emotions we feel. Many of these emotions can be classified into groups due to the similarities between them.

A major research project led by Simon Baron Cohen at Cambridge University found that the English language has at least 1512 emotion words. From this, 412 discrete emotional concepts were recognised which could be classified into 24 emotional groups. Our recognition of emotion and sophistication in language increases with age but even very young children have a rich emotional vocabulary and recognition rate that might surprise many.

Afraid	Angry	Bored	Bothered
Disbelieving	Disgusted	Excited	Fond
Happy	Hurt	Interested	Kind
Liked	Romantic	Sadness	Sneaky
Sorry	Sure	Surprised	Thinking
Touched	Unfriendly	Unsure	Wanting

Table One. The 24 emotion groups identified by Baron Cohen (in alphabetical order)

Biddulph (1998) and Goleman (1995) referred to anger, sadness, happiness and fear (or anxiety/afraid) as the 'primary colours' of emotion. These primary colours each contain a 'spectrum' of hues and shades reflecting the strength of feeling. They also mix with each other to produce more sophisticated and subtle emotions. For instance, jealousy or shame could be considered as mixtures of anger and fear, disappointment could be a mix of sadness and anger. It is these emotions that we all need to be able to manage at least to some degree and to be able to work with in children and young people. They are often referred to in more straightforward terms as 'mad, sad, glad and scared'.

Although there still continues to be debate as to whether these emotions are the only 'primary' colours or 'families' of emotions, these four groups of feeling will now be considered in more detail. These emotions are not completely independent of each other and there remain different theories about their relationship.

 See Exercise One

Anger

The greatest remedy for anger is delay.

Seneca, De Ira

Anybody can be angry – that is easy; but to be angry with the right person, and to the right degree, and at the right time, and for the right purpose, and in the right way – that is not within everybody's power and is not easy.

Aristotle, Nicomachaen Ethics

We need anger to help us meet our needs, to assert and stand up for ourselves. We need it to combat perceived oppression, abuse or injustice. We express our displeasure at others with the intention of influencing their behaviour and it can lead to us being better able to understand each other. We need it to defend ourselves but we can also use it to attack others. Anger has a strong physiological aspect. We become aroused and our body prepares itself to be ready to fight, the heart starts pumping blood to the muscles, and adrenaline is released into the nervous system readying us for action.

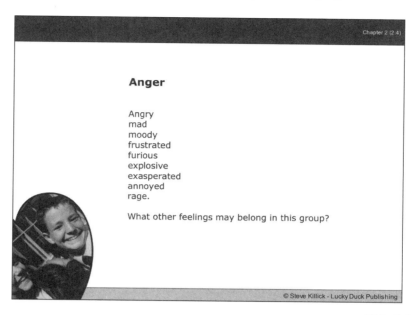

Slide 2.4

Anger is an emotion that many people find difficult to manage; it can lead to aggressive and destructive behaviour and can lead to violence. Many children and adults have problems with managing their anger both in controlling it and expressing it effectively, and who never loses their temper? Adults' appropriate expression of anger in response to inappropriate behaviour in children is a powerful way to help children correct their behaviour. Used inappropriately it may humiliate and harm and lead to resentment. Anger is not the problem but the aggression, in a physical or more subtle form, to which it may lead, certainly is. Anger can lead to violence, something that a large proportion of children will have experienced or observed at home and which may deeply trouble them. Learning how to express anger assertively, in a way that respects both oneself and others, as opposed to expressing it aggressively or passively, is a key life skill.

Children have to learn at an early age that rages or tantrums are not the best way of meeting their needs, and that aggression is not a way to solve problems. All of us have to learn how to deal with frustrations that life presents without being overwhelmed with rage. Some learn this developmental task easily. For others, it is much harder.

The management of anger is a critical skill that children need to learn and that can be helped or hindered by interactions with adults. Properly managed, after expressing anger we are able to repair the relationship. Some children will have experienced inappropriate anger from their parents, leading to disproportionate or overly punitive consequences for their actions, or denial of their feelings ('Don't you get angry with me!'). Many will have experienced physical punishments some of which may be abusive. The child's response may be that which is being modelled for him – to become angrier back; another response invoked may be of fear. Some people may express anger and frustration by being dismissive of the feelings of others. Anger and frustration will underlie many behavioural problems seen in the classroom. One central principle in helping children recognise, manage and appropriately express and channel their anger is that the emotion of anger is acceptable and can be expressed, but behaviour needs limits. For instance, the young person who kicks the door in rage after an argument

29

may not learn much from just the intervention of sanctions. Punishment may only maintain resentment. Children are more likely to learn when the message they receive helps them realise that it's OK to be angry but it is not OK to be destructive. An intervention that might begin with, for example, 'I can see you are angry but it is not OK to do that. Find a better way to tell me what you are feeling,' may be an invitation to a discussion that may lead to solving of the problem that has led to the outburst and to a more appropriate expression of his upset. Limits on destructive behaviour are still set. Anger is, in itself, not a bad thing and its expression in arguments in relationships can be one way that partners get to express some bottled up feelings that can, once understood, make them closer again. Inappropriately expressed it can lead to increasing resentment and miscommunication. The emotional issues are not addressed.

Teachers will deal with behaviours that will make them angry and children will behave in ways that will need appropriate consequences. There will be times when an effective reprimand is appropriate, where feelings are respected and limits are set constructively. How this can be done is explored further in Chapter Eight. Inappropriate expressions of anger when children feel criticised or told what to do may be ineffective. Both children and adults may have strong emotional reactions to such interventions and to retain their integrity and self-control, they may also get angry. Strong feelings of shame, hate, rage and fury can be extremely difficult to manage when the impulse to act is extreme. As anger rises, our empathy can diminish. An absence of empathy is a factor in young people and adults who exhibit very aggressive behaviour. This is a powerful reason for encouraging the development of empathy in children. Empathy, the understanding of another's perspective, inhibits aggression. It is also important to have the self-control not to succumb to the immediate impulse for action. One of the most powerful anger management strategies to learn is to wait. Senaca's quotation, that, 'the greatest remedy for anger is delay,' is born out in the familiar adage of 'count to ten before you act.' The impulse can pass and thinking can start. With thought may come the ability to take another perspective and perhaps the willingness to give up resentment, to be able to let it go and to forgive.

Sadness

> Give sorrow words; the grief that does not speak whispers the o'er-fraught heart and bids it break.

William Shakespeare, Macbeth, IV, iii, 209.

> You cannot prevent the birds of sadness from passing over your head, but you can prevent their making a nest in your hair.'

Chinese proverb

Sadness is a response to loss. This maybe something actual, such as the temporary or permanent loss of someone we love; the loss of a friend following an argument or something anticipated and imagined; the loss of a desired future through failing an exam or a relocation of a family. Sadness makes us feel low in mood and energy: we might want to isolate ourselves and lose enthusiasm for activities we might otherwise enjoy. It can be expressed through crying, a highly visible sign that something is wrong, or a period of withdrawal where it can be hard to think what to do. This might give time to think things through, to understand and adapt to the change. Sadness is an important and necessary process in helping us adjust to loss, to adapt to changed circumstances. Through this process the person emerges able to cope again. This process can take an instant or considerable time where sadness is the predominant mood.

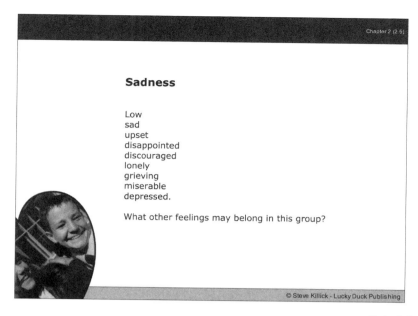

Sadness

Low
sad
upset
disappointed
discouraged
lonely
grieving
miserable
depressed.

What other feelings may belong in this group?

Slide 2.5

Children have plenty of opportunities in their lives for dealing with loss and sadness and learning how to do so is an important life task. From an adult perspective, a loss of a favourite toy or a pet hamster may seem insignificant, something that might be replaced. But the child is losing something he cared about and was attached to and needs the learning opportunity to deal with this loss, to grieve and then to carry on.

There are powerful interpersonal aspects of sadness. A younger child particularly can send strong non-verbal signals of their mood; crying, doleful eyes or a down turned mouth send powerful messages that can produce in others a strong feeling of compassion, a desire to help. Sometimes it can be difficult to know how to deal with strong expressions of sadness in others. 'Sadness' is actually becoming a term of derision for children. The expression, 'You're sad,' is now a derogatory one. More and more the term 'depressed' is used by people when they usually are referring to something less intense such as feeling sad or de-spirited. It can be hard to accept sadness and there may be a response of 'least said, soonest mended.' Sadness in others can make us feel uncomfortable or we can have a strong urge to make the unhappiness go away. We may wish to remove an unpleasant emotion by not attending to it or distracting ourselves but this may not give the child the opportunity to express her feelings and have them validated. Talking about feelings can often help to bring them to a place where they can be thought about more easily. This is not to say that that a child should be made to talk or never be distracted but a judgement may need to be made. The process of empathy can do much to transform strong and upsetting feelings into being more manageable and this means the acceptance of feelings of upset. Sometimes, simple acknowledgment can be enough. Boys, particularly, may find it so difficult to allow themselves to be vulnerable that they will not be open to experiencing comfort, a valuable medicine for sadness. Yet if we cannot name or experience our emotions they become much harder to deal with. If we are not allowed to have an unpleasant feeling, how can we feel safe when we experience such a feeling? Respect and tact are critical skills in deciding to intervene but children do not always offer us the chance to discuss how they think about these feelings.

Sadness can take extreme forms, such as grief resulting from bereavement and that of depression. This can affect students in schools. A bereavement of a parent or close family member is an event schools will inevitably have to deal with. Sometimes a member of a school may die. Grief is the process by which the loss (or bereavement) is adjusted to but it presents considerable challenges to children. Some will feel particularly isolated and there may be too much to deal with. Worden (1996) found that as well as the enormous emotional aspect to deal with there can be other challenges; the child may feel isolated from peers, academic work can suffer and some will develop learning problems that may not become apparent for some years. Schools can help such students but sometimes it can be difficult to know what to say, so nothing gets said. Schools can offer structure and extra support but often lack the confidence to know what to do. There are packages for helping schools manage such problems appropriately (for example, Killick & Lindeman, 1999) and the importance of bringing ideas of loss and change into the curriculum (for example, Ward, 1996).

Depression is becoming increasingly common among young people and should not be dismissed as just a normal phase in adolescence. Depression can lead to inactivity and withdrawal from social relationships and give problems in concentration and academic functioning. It may lead to self-harm and suicidal acts. Central to depression are feelings of helplessness and hopelessness where self-esteem is lowered. There is a loss of faith in one's self, the world and no optimism for the future – no hope that things may change for the better. How a young person thinks about himself, how he judges himself negatively and negatively evaluates what he thinks others think of him can help to maintain depressive mood. Depression is often maintained by negative thinking. Self-harm, strangely, is often ignored whilst simultaneously being described as an attention seeking behaviour. However, for young people, self-harm is a often a way of managing strong distressing feelings through finding short-term relief; others may find relief through the use of alcohol and drugs. However, this relief is often short lived and may exacerbate rather than solve the problems they are facing. Depression is clearly a difficulty that can be helped by emotional literacy interventions in schools especially in considering prevention. Help with emotional management and social problem-solving skills can help the young person engage, experience success and find ways of overcoming depression.

Happiness

When we are happy we are always good but when we are good we are not always happy.

Oscar Wilde, *The Picture of Dorian Gray*

Not what we have but what we enjoy, constitutes our abundance.

Epicurus

It is one of the most beautiful compensations of this life that no man can sincerely try to help another without helping himself.'

Ralph Waldo Emerson

We need to experience positive affect. Feeling good means we are more creative, more open to the world and more curious towards new ideas and those of others. When we feel good we are in our natural state, of being ready and open to learning. Positive emotional states like happiness are deeply linked with our finding meaning in our lives and, ultimately, our spiritual development. Feelings of relaxation, love and laughter are the physiological opposites of anger and fear. So, developing and bringing these positive states forth is a method of managing more negative states. This creates resilience in children, the capacity to deal with life's problems that also safeguards against the development of emotional problems. These skills are important for those who work with children, especially challenging and disturbed children who are capable of provoking strong reactions in adults. These positive emotions are also interconnected with our capacity to love and to care. When we are feeling good we naturally do many of the right things in our relationships: we appreciate and value, we attend to the 'good' in others. Under these conditions, relationships thrive. Under stress, we can easily do many of the wrong things and a vicious cycle develops. We overly criticise and this may be met with defensiveness. When we are feeling good, we are able to enjoy our successes and achievements and those of others, we are able to look forward to the future with confidence and hope. A virtuous circle that maintains wellbeing is developed.

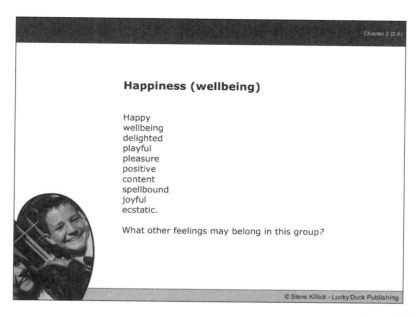

Slide 2.6

Another term for happiness is 'wellbeing' (Seligman, 2002B). It makes life worth living. In the field of Positive Psychology there has been a focus on particular strengths and competencies as a way of increasing our levels of happiness. Seligman (2002A) identified a number of character strengths, which if developed increase our wellbeing. We all possess these strengths but they will be developed to different degrees. These 24 strengths, categorised into six groups, are listed on page 28. These strengths appear to be more influential to our level of happiness than to our life circumstances. Seligman's work gives scientific evidence to help in the pursuit of happiness and in valuing what has a long tradition in education – the importance of moral and personal development.

Strengths such as an inquiring mind, a sense of fairness and optimism are apparent in children. Schools can facilitate and value these strengths through encouragement and support. Teachers can help develop these strengths in children through noticing, labelling and appreciating, even celebrating, these strengths. They can, as they often are, be incorporated into the school's own values and ethos. Emotional intelligence is listed as one of these strengths, but many of these qualities link with the key skills of emotional intelligence. These key skills can help develop qualities such as open-mindedness, integrity, kindness and optimism, amongst others.

Seligman's Classification of Character Strengths

Wisdom and Knowledge Cognitive skills in learning and using knowledge	Creativity – originality & ingenuity	Ability to find new ways to do things including artistic skill
	Curiosity – interest, openness to experience, interest in newness	Find new subjects fascinating, exploration and discovery
	Thinking things through from differing perspectives	Thinking things through from differing perspectives, changing one's mind in the light of new information
	Love of learning	Mastering new skills
	Perspective (wisdom)	Ways of looking at the world that make sense to self and others
Courage Emotional strengths that exercise will power to accomplish goals	Bravery (valour)	Acting on convictions even if unpopular
	Persistence (perseverance)	Completion of tasks, persistence in face of obstacles
	Integrity (authenticity)	Presenting oneself genuinely
	Vitality (zest, enthusiasm)	Feeling alive, seeing life as an adventure
Humanity Interpersonal skills involving attending to others	Love	Valuing close sharing and reciprocating relationships
	Kindness (generosity, compassion)	Helping others through taking care, doing favours and good deeds
	Social Intelligence or emotional intelligence	Aware of one's own and others' motives and feelings, socially skilled
Justice Strengths that underlie community life	Citizenship (social responsibility, loyalty, teamwork)	Working well with others', being loyal to the group and doing one's share
	Fairness	Treating others according to notions of fairness
	Leadership	Helping a group achieve goals and keep good relations
Temperance Strengths that protect against excess	Forgiveness (mercy)	Giving others further chances
	Humility (modesty)	Not seeing oneself as more special or deserving than others
	Prudence	Caution in choices, not taking undue risks
	Self-regulation (self-control)	Controlling one's appetites and emotions, discipline
Transcendence Strengths that give connection to the larger universe and provide meaning	Appreciation of beauty and excellence	Noticing and appreciation of beauty and skill in all areas
	Gratitude	Awareness and thankfulness of all good things in life
	Hope (optimism)	Belief that a good future can be brought about
	Humour (playfulness)	Seeing the light side, bringing laughter to self and others
	Spirituality	Beliefs of purpose and meaning that shape conduct and provide comfort, faith

Children experience emotional states with intensity. A healthy child absorbed in creative and imaginative play is in a state of 'flow', a state in which time stops and the reality of the present is transformed into endless imaginative possibilities. We all have the capacity for imaginative thinking, or what Robert Holden (1999) described as 'possibility thinking'. This playful attitude towards thinking is a building block of humour and laughter, one of the most effective ways of dealing with stress and anxiety. Many of Seligman's character strengths might be seen as characteristics of personality but, especially during our childhood, personality is open to influence. These character strengths are based on our attitudes and knowing we all have the ability to choose our attitude towards the situations we find ourselves in. For instance, to see working with a difficult child as either 'impossible' or a 'challenge' from which one may learn and grow reflects an attitude we bring to the situation. This can determine the emotional experience we receive. Dan Hughes (1998), who has written about working with very disturbed children, described that effective workers need to continually bring the attitudes of playfulness, acceptance, empathy and curiosity to their work. That these qualities also facilitate our own wellbeing is significant. These qualities help combat stress at work and have benefits for adults as well as young people.

One of the most important qualities in dealing with adversity and developing resilience is that of optimism. This is a quality to foster and develop in overcoming anxiety and depressive related problems. Seligman in his book, *The Optimistic Child* (1995), described and evaluated a successful project that helped children to think differently about how they evaluated social situations and themselves and to think more optimistically. The short programme lessened children's vulnerability to depression and provided important evidence for the effectiveness of education into the emotions. It is described more fully in Chapter Ten.

Anxiety

Our whole life is taken up with anxiety for personal security, with preparations for living, so that we never really live at all.'

Leo Tolstoy, *My Religion*

Neither comprehension nor learning can take place in an atmosphere of anxiety.

Rose F. Kennedy

Anxiety comprises a group of emotions from worry through to terror and fear. Anxiety gives caution and helps us assess risk, it makes us aware of danger and act accordingly. It can prompt us to seek safety and reassurance. It is an uncomfortable emotion physically and psychologically motivating us to act to solve the problem but it can paralyse us or so concern us to avoid danger that we never learn to overcome and gain mastery over our fears. Anxiety can debilitate; worry can be the cortical interference that prevents us from experiencing the infinite joy that exists in any given moment. Anxiety, at its most extreme, can be unbearable.

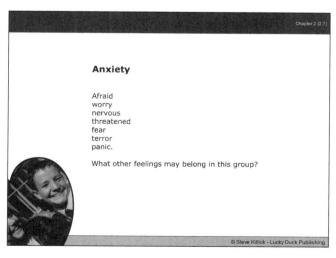

Slide 2.7

Anxiety is useful to deal with danger or threat. More accurately, it is about managing perceived threat: what we believe may be dangerous to us. This may include a threat to our sense of identity, that we may do something that will makes us look ludicrous or different, even to be criticised – real sources of worry to many children. For example, one child who had dyspraxia, a difficulty in coordination, had a history of absconding from school. It was discovered that the root cause of his absconding was the wish to avoid situations where he worried that he would fall over and be laughed at. He only felt comfortable in situations where he felt safe and would go to great lengths to avoid new or testing situations. His worry often stopped him from being able to work in class.

Anxiety lies at the heart of much behaviour seen in the classroom. It can prevent children from being open to new experiences and leaving the security of their 'comfort zone'. It can present severe problems in the shape of phobias, including school phobia. Young children particularly can experience tremendous anxiety in entering school and separating from home. Often the impulse, laid in the attachment relationship, is to seek out the person with whom we feel most safe. We need to seek out a place of safety. When we are anxious we can need help from others. Some theorists see anxiety as underlying all other emotional states such as anger and loss.

The physiological state of fear, like anger, is one of high physical arousal and our 'fight or flight' response is activated. Our body becomes physically prepared to either fight or run away; our heart pumps faster, we sweat, our pupils dilate. We may also feel jumpy or restless and start breathing quickly. Often we get a feeling in the pit of our stomach or of feeling sick (a sensation induced as the brain 'turns off' the digestive system as resources are needed for action at that moment). Our thoughts may start racing but we become less able to think clearly. We can become fixated on thinking about 'catastrophic' outcomes where the worst thing imaginable will happen. If these problems become extreme, for instance, in the case of phobias, an accelerating cycle between thoughts, feelings and behaviour can increase to lead to a panic attack, an overwhelming and debilitating feeling of dread.

A child with a fear of spiders who sees one becomes flooded with catastrophic thoughts that it might bite her, and if it did she will die as result. Her physiological system responds to the danger and she feels sick which causes her more worry; her distress is so acute she has to run away to a place where she feels safe and only after time can begin to calm herself down. Her fear of spiders remains so acute that she cannot even tolerate thinking about them let alone possibly learn that they are not something to be feared. But it is not the spider that elicited the fears but her beliefs about the danger of the spider.

A psychological response that can be activated in high anxiety is to become frozen so we cannot think or decide what to do. In the case of trauma, a person is often constantly interrupted by thoughts or flashbacks to the traumatic event. This is constantly replayed in her mind disabling her from being able to think in the present. Conversely, all thoughts connected with the terror may be pushed out of the mind. Our thoughts and feelings become 'disassociated' from the event.

When the child experiences a worry or uncertainty it often triggers a need to find someone who can reassure and help. The ability to manage anxiety is rooted in the early attachment relationship and behaviours learnt at this early stage may reappear throughout life. The child seeks comfort, the emotional opposite polarity of stress, and reassurance. However, problems in this early attachment may lead to difficulties in dealing with feelings and of accessing help later.

Childhood is full of experiences that teach how to master anxiety, to use it to recognise danger and assess risk accurately. Overcoming our fears lays great foundations for confidence and competence, but children need to be kept safe and have their learning experiences in ways they can manage successfully. Too much anxiety is not helpful for learning. One reason that child abuse is detrimental to the development of the child is the sense of fear and trauma it can produce. Such abuse, especially in the early years, can affect the physical development of the brain. The child can be acutely sensitised to danger, unable to feel safe or trust others. He can become preoccupied with thinking about danger, often responding with aggression or avoidance. For all children, the desire to avoid fear can have a big impact and they will do much to avoid the fear of humiliation, failure and shame. Children may have serious worries about themselves or their family, perhaps concerns about health or safety. If children experience excessive anxiety it can contribute to behavioural and academic problems. Excessive shyness often reflects many deep social anxieties about how they are seen by others. Events that can cause trauma, serious accidents or illness, can also give a child too much anxiety to manage well.

Children with severe anxiety problems may benefit from additional help but schools can meaningfully help all children in understanding these emotions of anxiety that we all face. We face anxiety provoking situations constantly, particularly in the shape of managing failure. One Year 4 child believed she needed to understand everything the teacher said. If she didn't her fears grew that she wouldn't understand what was said next, then she would get everything wrong and look stupid and feel embarrassed. Her worries stopped her from listening and that, in turn, made it harder to understand. Rather than seeing getting things wrong as a opportunity for learning and understanding she, like many children, feared it.

Dealing with social problems can also be a worry for many children: feeling not liked and not knowing what to do about it, knowing how to respond to teasing or bullying or what to say to other children who are upset or angry.

Laughter is the physiological opposite of anxiety and has a strong relationship with it. Comedians understand the power of a joke in dispelling anxiety. If we can laugh at something we make it less frightening. Humour and laughter are powerful tools in managing emotions but they can be used both positively and negatively. Using humour to laugh at is very different to laugh with someone. It can be used to mock, to attack and belittle. It can also be used to heal and to overcome fear. Humour can change perceptions from something terrifying to something ordinary.

Managing anxiety means learning to know when to face our fears when we need to and when we should act with caution. The fundamentals of emotional intelligence are about helping children to recognise and label these feelings and to find ways of coping with these feelings, to be able to be calm and relax themselves: thinking skills, such as being able to give personal positive self-instruction (or positive self-talk, see Chapter Ten) and problem-solving skills to decide how they deal with situations that worry them. Valuing forms of relaxation and pleasure-giving activities helps overcome excessive worries. Formal teaching and everyday interactions give opportunities in helping children overcome anxiety in ways that are appropriate to their age, development and the education context.

 39   See Exercises Two and Three

Summary of key points

- Emotions are physical, psychological and social in nature. Our emotional life is complex and has evolved as part of our central nervous system.

- Our emotions have purpose and function and are connected with motivation and communication. Emotions can be positive and negative in the effects they can have on our functioning.

- Feelings can be overwhelming and affect our capacity to think. We have many ways of dealing with strong feelings but the task is often to manage them appropriately. If extreme, they can lead to mental health difficulties.

- As children grow, their understanding of emotions greatly increases and their emotional vocabulary grows.

- Four groups or 'families' of emotions are anger, anxiety, happiness and sadness. These key emotions form the 'primary colours' of our emotional life and can mix and blend in combination.

Exercise One – The 'Qualities' of Emotion

Divide the participants into small discussion groups of four or five and invite them to discuss the nature and qualities of emotion. Use the question presented in Slide 2.1 as a starting point for a discussion for about ten minutes. Ask each group to briefly present back some of the things they discussed to the whole group.

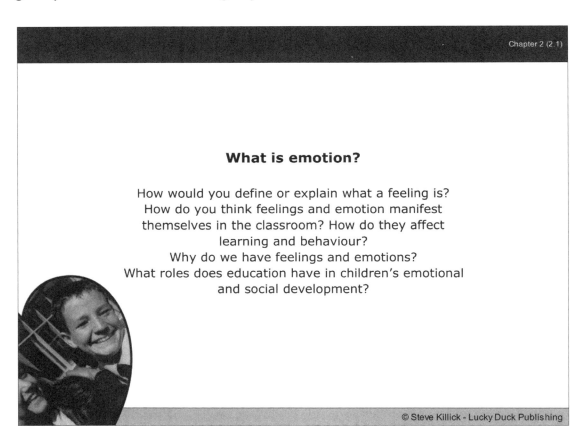

What is emotion?

How would you define or explain what a feeling is?
How do you think feelings and emotion manifest
themselves in the classroom? How do they affect
learning and behaviour?
Why do we have feelings and emotions?
What roles does education have in children's emotional
and social development?

© Steve Killick - Lucky Duck Publishing

Slide 2.1

For some groups, this question may be enough of a stimulus; others may need further prompts as a starting point. The questions listed on slides 2.4 to 2.7 may help or the group may wish to define their own question. The best question may depend on what kind of group it is and their stage of thinking about emotional literacy.

The purpose of the exercise is to draw out some of the ideas about the nature of emotion described in this chapter. Slides 2.2. and 2.3 summarise some of the issues and, if appropriate, can be used following the presentation to add more information, validate some of the issues raised and prompt further exploration.

Exercise Two – Emotions in the Classroom

Divide the participants into four groups and allocate each group one of the four emotion groups – happiness, anger, fear and sadness.

Ask each group to discuss how that emotion manifests itself in the classroom and school setting. Emphasise the importance of considering the small everyday examples of emotional life as well as more dramatic or, perhaps, distressing examples. For instance, how a child new to a school might feel anxious because they do not know where to go, where the toilets are or how to organise their homework.

Ask each group to consider how these emotions may impact on learning and behaviour, what things are easily managed and what may throw up dilemmas or disagreements in what to do.

Further prompts, if necessary, are, 'What positive and negative effects may these emotions have?' or to ask participants what emotions arise in them in teaching and learning situations.

Discussion can last for between ten and 20 minutes and each group should feed back something on their discussion to the whole group.

Exercise Three –
What Makes a School Safe Enough for Children to Learn?

This exercise may follow directly on from Exercise Two or just be done in its own right. It may be conducted as a whole group discussion or as an exercise done by small groups who then feed back to the group as a whole.

The question above, 'What makes a school safe enough for children to learn?' is then posed to the group. They have the task of exploring what they can do to make the classroom or school environment safe enough for children to participate in learning together.

It may be useful to point out that no environment could be made completely safe, as there is always the element of risk. Rather, what constitutes a safe enough environment and what happens if that environment does not meet that standard?

Chapter Three

The Five Pathways to Emotional Intelligence

Salovey and Mayer (1990) identified five key areas of emotional intelligence, illustrated in Slide 3.1. These formed the basis of Goleman's (1995) model of emotional intelligence and are also significant in Faupel's (2003) model of emotional literacy. They represent the five developmental pathways of emotional intelligence.

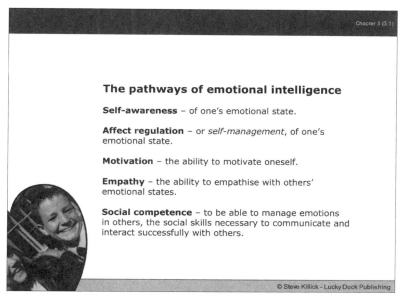

Slide 3.1

These dimensions have traditionally been seen as attributes of personality. In emotional literacy they are seen as areas of skills, competencies or areas to develop. When viewed as attributes of personality they are often seen as dichotomous characteristics: a person either has or does not have these characteristics. A child may be described as 'not motivated', 'empathic' or as having 'no social skills'. In emotional intelligence these dimensions are not seen from this black or white perspective but rather as areas of skills that exist along a continuum. These are areas that continue to develop over the lifespan and in which one can achieve high levels of expertise. High levels of emotional intelligence might mean a very high degree of insight into one's own emotional wellbeing and motivations, or to be a highly effective and skilled communicator or negotiator. Personality, or innate temperament, is influential in the development of emotional intelligence and early experience and attachment relationships also contribute significantly. Another critical factor is the context in which one operates at any particular time. The dimensions are related to each other; for example, self-awareness influences one's ability to empathise with others. Yet they can also develop independently of each other, such as, one may be very empathic to others but have poor management of one's own feelings.

Expertise in these areas develops throughout life and this development can be enhanced through emotional literacy programmes and positive relationships. This chapter explores the fives domains of emotional intelligence in detail and discusses some of the influences of the development of emotional intelligence in individuals.

Self-awareness

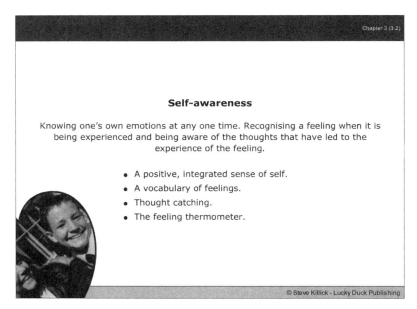

Self-awareness

Knowing one's own emotions at any one time. Recognising a feeling when it is being experienced and being aware of the thoughts that have led to the experience of the feeling.

- A positive, integrated sense of self.
- A vocabulary of feelings.
- Thought catching.
- The feeling thermometer.

Chapter 3 (3.2)

© Steve Killick - Lucky Duck Publishing

Slide 3.2

Self-awareness, or insight, is, 'being aware of our mood and aware of our thoughts about why we have that mood' (Goleman,1995). We all have a mood at any particular time and we develop in self-awareness throughout life. However, there are differences in people's ability to be aware of their own thought processes. Self-awareness involves attention to our inner state and exists in degrees. We may have good insight into some of our feelings, less so to other aspects of ourselves. Without awareness of our emotional state we are less able to change our mood and calm ourselves and are more likely to become engulfed by strong emotions and to act on impulse. It is about being able to monitor one's own emotional state. The ideal is to have developed a positive, integrated sense of self.

Self-awareness of our thoughts and feelings exists along a continuum of awareness of ourselves as separate from others through to an awareness of our deepest motives: a bringing into consciousness of what may be hidden from us. The newborn will gain awareness of himself as a separate being in the first year of life. Along the way the child learns that there will be similarities and differences between how he and others feel. He will become able to evaluate the risk of what is dangerous and what is safe.

A newborn child is only aware of emotion as bodily experiences of comfort or discomfort. With time these experiences can be named. The process of self-awareness is aided by developing a vocabulary of feelings. To be able to recognise that you are feeling angry, humiliated or lonely you need to know that such an emotion exists and that there is a word for that experience. The child in his first year of life can only be aware of bodily sensations. As he grows he is able to name his emotions as his emotional vocabulary is constantly extending. This vocabulary is usually learnt in the family and social environment and, as he grows older, school, friends and the outside world are important influences. It is important for the child, at an early stage, to experience that uncomfortable feelings can be soothed. If a feeling is experienced as unacceptable, such as anger, then the child may try to suppress the feeling that makes it harder to manage. Having an emotional vocabulary that reflects one's emotional life is one of the building blocks of emotional intelligence. The Mind Reading project (Baron Cohen, 2003), described in Chapter Two, has charted the emotional vocabulary of children as they grow older. Their findings reveal that children often have a far larger emotional vocabulary than many adults might suspect. As the child's cognitive ability grows he becomes better able to recognise what thoughts he is having about his feelings, which enables insight into the causes of those feelings.

However, some children may have particular difficulties in learning the names of these basic emotions. These children may be able in other areas but not able to be aware of their own inner states or how they impact on others. Social or neurodevelopmental difficulties may also delay the development of self-awareness and they may need additional help in developing skills in this area. However, naming and acknowledging feelings and encouraging children to reflect upon what they are thinking and feeling can facilitate the development of self-awareness.

Adolescence can present particular problems with the development of self-awareness. Teachers will be familiar with how limited some teenagers can be in emotional expression, being able only to label their experiences as good or bad, or their feelings as happy or sad. The expression of anger is restricted if only swear words can convey the strength of feeling. Some young people's emotional expression may be limited to only being able to respond with saying, 'Alright,' when asked how they are. Unusual or complex feelings may only be described as 'weird'. Encouraging emotional expression can be enhanced across a wide range of subjects, particularly the arts.

Rating scales can be used to help a person monitor her mood more effectively and be able to make finer discriminations in the strength of feeling. Rating a state of relaxation or happiness is more easily gauged when placed on a one to ten scale. One may be, for example, very relaxed and ten very excited. Rating feelings in this way enables graduations of feelings to be made. The feeling thermometer (Stallard, 2002) can give a visual aid in helping monitor mood.

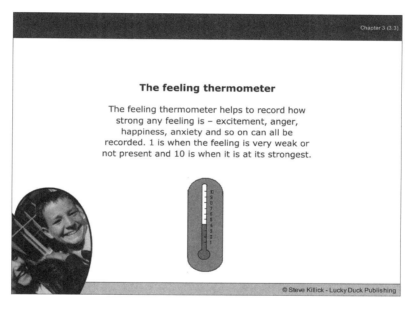

Slide 3.3

Cognitive psychology has discovered how the many 'automatic' or involuntary thoughts that we continually experience influence our moods and our behaviours. Adults and children, when learning a skill for the first time in a public setting, may have thoughts that rush through their heads such as, 'I'm going to mess this up,' or, 'I will make a fool of myself,' which produce feelings of anxiety. A key skill in developing a capacity to identify these thoughts is known as thought catching. When these thoughts are recognised they can be evaluated more accurately.

Self-awareness plays a part in decision making. Often a decision can be made on our intuition or 'gut feeling' – a valuable source of information – yet these decisions may be better helped by thinking why we have these feelings in the first place. The highest degree of self-awareness could be considered as reaching a spiritual or transcendental quality. It is an awareness of one's connectedness with a greater whole and of what constitutes our sense of self.

Affect-regulation

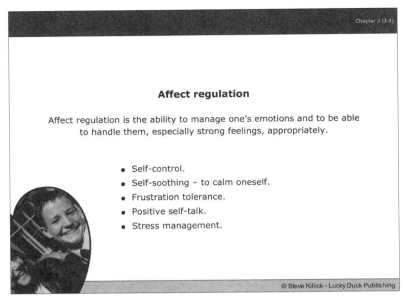

Slide 3.4

Being able to manage or self-regulate one's own feelings is a critical ability to develop. The ability to calm strong feelings rather than act on impulse is a necessary skill to develop. For example, if a child is so angry at another that he may hit that child or if a child who is so anxious at having to talk in front of a whole class feigns or becomes ill to avoid the situation, little is learnt about controlling aggression or overcoming the fear. Unproductive ways of managing emotions can lead to avoiding or disrupting both academic and social learning situations. Young people without these skills are more likely to resort to excessive risk-taking, alcohol and substance abuse as a way of managing feelings.

A necessary skill is to be able to calm ourselves when we experience strong or disturbing feelings (self-soothing). The learning of this skill begins in the primary attachment relationship. An infant learns to soothe himself by treating himself as a caregiver treats him. The infant is able to internalise these actions. In the classroom setting, being able to settle one's self is necessary to be able to learn, to concentrate and focus.

We need to develop a sense of self-control, to recognise that strong feelings will peak and pass and some actions are best not taken in the heat of the moment. There are a number of ways to respond to any given situation when one can think more calmly about the situation. It is this sense of having an ability to respond to situations that lies behind the meaning of being able to take responsibility – that one is able to choose how to act. Central to impulse control is to wait, even for a few seconds (while strong feelings pass and the rational mind can think more clearly) before action.

Temperament is another significant factor in any individual's ability to deal with strong feelings. Some children have a very low threshold for tolerating frustration and will explode in response to such frustration. Tolerance of frustration is a skill that needs to be learnt and this is harder for some than others. Ross Greene (2001) described the inflexible-explosive temperament in his book *The Explosive Child*. This temperament is often associated with children who may have ADHD, Autistic Spectrum Disorders or other developmental difficulties as well as existing in its own right. These children may need particular help to learn the important social skills of flexibility, compromise and negotiation to be able to adapt and adjust to the constantly changing environment of the busy classroom.

Skills in dealing with emotions are often about being able to reflect upon and evaluate our thoughts. Self-awareness is therefore a fundamental building block of self-regulation. For example, in a classroom, one child brushes past another and accidentally knocks against him. The thought comes into the second child's mind, 'He tried to knock me over.' If this is followed by a series of thoughts that instantaneously flash through the mind such as, 'He's trying to hurt me... He did that on purpose... He's always doing that... I know he hates me,' the mind is then filled with rage and a desire for revenge. He may act this out by attacking the other child. These thoughts can flash through the mind in a second. However, after the first impulsive thought, if the child is able to stop and think about alternatives, there might be different emotional reactions. Different ways of thinking about the situation might include generating such thoughts as, 'He must be in a hurry... I don't think he saw me there, he can be clumsy sometimes.' This explanation will lead to a different emotional response. What is wanted is an ability to consider one's response. In dealing with anger, one of the most important skills is waiting for the intensity of the feeling to pass.

Managing anxiety often involves evaluating the causes of anxiety and, if appropriate, facing up to and mastering the fear rather than avoiding anxiety provoking situations. Managing sadness may involve being able to treat oneself kindly or to seek others who can give care.

Emotional regulation is helped by curiosity or an 'open mind' towards situations rather than a fixed or dogged belief in what we think must be true. It is mainly in our interactions with others that strong feelings are evoked and we need to be able to calm ourselves before we can clearly think and bring our problem-solving skills into focus.

Another important skill used with children to calm strong feelings is positive self-talk (or self-instruction). This is the ability to think calming, reassuring and positive thoughts to help regulate strong feelings, such as, 'It's going to be alright... It's understandable to feel worried but I'll soon be alright and work out what to do. I can handle it.' Helping children to learn how to think both positively and realistically can help them find productive and useful ways of managing feelings.

Problems at home or at school, including working for examinations, can contribute to stress. For some children this may develop into emotional difficulties such as anxiety problems or depression. These emotions can all contribute to stress, and we all face stresses in life so we all need at least basic stress management skills. Many of these skills are associated with promoting good learning skills and can be integrated into the teaching of such skills. These skills may include identifying and focusing on priorities, time management, being able to relax and enjoy pleasurable activities.

The ability to motivate oneself

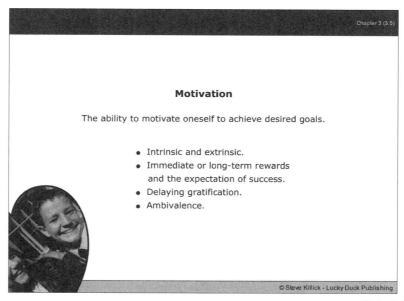

Slide 3.5

The young child, dependent on adults, is motivated through the approval he receives. As he grows he must be able to find internal motivation to achieve his goals and meet his needs, and to be successful. There is always a balance between external (or extrinsic) and internal (or intrinsic) motivation. Extrinsic motivation refers to rewards or gains, such as praise, recognition, stickers or prizes. Intrinsic motivation refers to one's own feelings of success, mastery or satisfaction. This may come from developing skills, satisfying curiosity. It may also come from avoiding something seen as undesirable such as a rebuke.

The child also needs to be able to generate the persistence and determination to embark on a project that may not yield benefits immediately, for example, to work towards an exam. Motivation provides the resilience to resist the impulse of instant gratification, to play or to watch TV rather than to work first and enjoy later.

Motivation is a familiar area for schools. A central task for teachers is to encourage motivation for learning and this much-debated area could fill many volumes in itself. For many teachers the problems of dealing with motivation in children are so overwhelming the result maybe to feel de-motivated themselves. Motivation is intertwined with emotion. The word itself has the same root as the word 'emotion', that is, to move and to act.

The belief that one can achieve is nurtured by both family and school cultures that firmly believe that the child 'will amount to something'. However, many children are not motivated towards the goals of learning, of making an effort to work towards long-term goals. They are instead motivated to avoiding failure and humiliation that they expect to experience in learning and often their best form of defence against these feelings is to attack the learning situation. Ginott (1972) said that for positive motivation for learning to exist it must be safe for children to risk failure. Obstacles to learning include feeling or appearing stupid. Children who receive persistent criticism will soon learn it is easier not to try than to risk failure. Positive praise will often not be enough and may even be perceived by the child as disingenuous. Effort needs recognition above achievement and mistakes can be celebrated. Life cannot be lived fully without making mistakes. The most valuable learning is often gained from painful errors and this learning is more likely enhanced if one is not left feeling attacked, humiliated, or 'defensive'.

With young children, adults are usually focused on the encouraging of positives and disregarding of errors. When a child learns to walk, his first steps are vigorously reinforced by the reactions of adults. The success of the effort is talked about and no critical comments are made when the child falls, such as telling him that all he needs to do is to put one foot in front of the other. Rather the adults applaud; they tell their friends and relatives. They know that the natural process of learning will continue, that the child will learn to walk despite repeated failure; indeed the child learns from the failure. However, the child also gains satisfaction from his mastery of the skill of walking. It is also strengthened by the fact that his world expands; he can more easily explore his environment. Children grow in sophistication but an approach that recognises effort not achievement and is on hand to help when things go wrong is important across the lifespan. External encouragement and reward is helpful to 'kick start' and can tail off as more internal motivation develops. Use of token systems can be extremely effective in rewarding effort and encouraging motivation. A sound knowledge of why they work and of their limitations helps in maximising these approaches. Also how we give feedback, that is knowledge to children about what they are doing both in learning and behaviour, both positive and negative, can play a key role in enhancing motivation.

Faupel (2003) identifies motivation as being concerned with our choice of goals and our determination to reach those goals. Developing and setting clear goals is a critical aspect of motivation and this involves being able to conceptualise the gains involved in reaching that goal. What motivates us may be the hope of success, anticipated rewards (both internal or external), or it may be the removal of something undesired or unpleasant. A young child may be motivated to learn to read through the encouragement of adults. For the child to continue reading she needs to discover the enjoyment through the act itself. Having a clear goal that is seen as achievable brings an expectation of success that is essential for motivation.

To be motivated towards something it has to be imagined. Children can be helped to 'paint pictures' in their mind's eyes of the benefits of their effort. It is important to be able to visualise the success of achieving goals that can help this process. Creating visual images in the mind can also help with dealing with change such as making transitions, changing schools and so on.

We are also motivated by our emotional states. Emotions can be pleasant or unpleasant. We can be motivated to avoid situations where we might experience unpleasant emotions such as anxiety or fear. Alternatively we may be motivated towards feelings of success, achievement or happiness. We may be motivated by a sense of a fear of failure, and even a fear of success. Another key aspect of motivation is to feel optimistic, and possess hope that effort will bring benefits. Martin Seligman's (1995) work has demonstrated that optimism, although influenced by temperament, is learnt and can therefore change.

Motivation requires the ability to delay gratification. Research suggests that children displaying a greater capacity to delay gratification at a young age were, in their teens, more socially competent, confident and had higher self-esteem than those who were less able to delay. Again, the ability to motivate oneself is interconnected with intellectual ability and temperament but it is not fixed and varies over situations. Another term for motivation is 'willpower'. Willpower is not something that we do or do not possess. It is based on a conviction of, 'I can and I will, and I am determined to do so.' It is a choice, although for some this is not an easy or clear choice.

Our emotions underlie our motivations, not only whether we anticipate whether we will succeed or fail, but also the importance we place on any particular action. When considering whether to do something, such as make an effort for work, or change a behaviour such as giving up smoking, we often find we are in a state of 'ambivalence', that is, we have mixed and often conflicting feelings about changing what we do. Developments in the field of Motivational Interviewing (Miller & Rollnick, 2002) may have great relevance for education. Motivational Interviewing is a counselling technique that can be used to help change people change health related behaviours such as smoking, drinking or exercise behaviours. The approach challenges the traditional approach of persuasion as a way of trying to convince people of the benefits of a particular course of action. Rather, helping people explore their natural state of ambivalence and then by providing information about their concerns may help them make their own proactive decisions about what they do. If we just insist, persuade or direct, we may encounter resistance and opposition. Guiding people in making their own choice may be far more motivating for them. To feel motivated towards something also depends on two key beliefs: our confidence in being able to achieve that goal and the importance of achieving that goal. A child may really value the goal of being able to read better, or to get along with others, but may not feel she can achieve this. Conversely, she might think that she could do it but not value it. This may mean she does not see it as being worth the effort. Assessing these two areas of confidence and importance can again help us to think about how to intervene.

Other aspects of motivation are the social process of competition and cooperation. Competition can be both positive, through creating motivation, and destructive. Those who see themselves as having a chance of success may be motivated further but those that see themselves as having no chance may lose motivation altogether. Competition becomes positive when it is applied to oneself and not encouraged with comparison with others. To 'beat your own best' is a goal that is both achievable and motivating.

The highest achievers in such fields as the arts or sports are at the highest end of the motivational pathway. They describe a state where learning and performance becomes effortless. The state is known as 'flow'; the awe and engagement as performance and concentration becomes almost unconscious. Using 'flow' is the one of the healthiest ways of learning that exists and can be experienced by learners at many levels. When you are really engaged in an activity, learning comes without effort.

Motivation is a complex area but central both to the task of learning and of emotional intelligence. It is in this area, especially in working with poorly motivated children in the classroom, that the fruits of developing emotional literacy in schools can be most valuable.

Empathy (social perceptiveness)

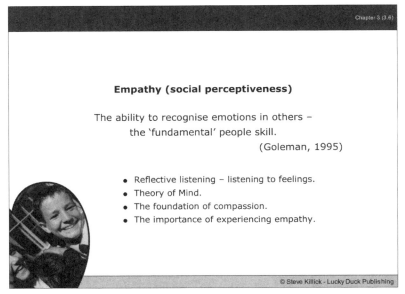

Slide 3.6

The ability to empathise lies at the heart of emotional literacy. Empathy moves beyond one's awareness of one's own feelings to be able to feel with and for others. It is about accurate insight into the motives and feelings of others and being able to communicate that understanding. Empathy also gives insight into how others see us – and they might see us in a different way to how we see ourselves. Being able to empathise with others is critical in communicating with others and thus building and maintaining good relations. Empathy gives the ability to see another person's point of view and is the basis of caring and compassion; to feel for another is to care. Identifying distress in others leads to helping behaviour. The roots of morality, kindness, compassion and generosity are found in empathy. It also inhibits aggression. Girls tend to exhibit higher levels of empathy than boys but empathy training has been found to reduce this difference considerably (Cotton, 2001).

Empathy is social perceptiveness: to perceive the internal frame of reference of another accurately and to be able to communicate it to the person. An empathetic response acknowledges the way a person feels and states it in a way that helps the person to see it differently, perhaps more clearly (Rogers, 1987). It is at the heart of person and child centred education with gains for both learning and behaviour. Cooperation is gained when feelings are acknowledged and accepted, developing positive relationships and communication.

Teachers and childcare workers develop empathy in children and young people best by offering them empathy continuously. This is done through 'reflective listening', going beyond the content of what is said and 'listening to the feelings' expressed both verbally and non-verbally. It is to see the world through the child's eyes. To do this needs flexibility and imagination. A child does not need to say what he is feeling in order to receive empathy; he expresses his feelings through posture and behaviour. Bringing feelings into words can enable them to be thought about. Responding to the feeling underlying behaviour can mean the child no longer needs that behaviour to express himself. This is critical in dealing with many behaviour problems.

A child with severe emotional and behavioural problems ran out of school, a special unit where he had help but at times it was still too stressful for him. He went to a deserted house nearby and began throwing stones at the windows. When a teacher caught up with him, the teacher may have reprimanded or ordered the child to return but this may have inflamed the situation. Instead he used empathy to connect to the feelings, 'It feels useless, it's all broken and it might as well be smashed some more.' The teacher's comment linked the child's behaviour and feelings and communicated an understanding. The behaviour ceased, a conversation could begin. The issue of consequences and how the young person could make amends was still addressed but was done so in a climate of understanding rather than punishment.

There are many advantages for schools in developing and valuing empathy. Being empathic is a characteristic of being a good learner and is also a prerequisite for pro-social behaviour. Cotton (2001) has found that improved academic outcomes with greater levels of critical and creative thinking followed programmes that aimed to develop empathy. Altruism relies on empathy and having the ability to take the view of another increases altruistic behaviour.

Therefore developing empathy in schools is a desirable goal. Our capacity for empathy is innate. Some evolutionary theorists believe that the human ability to empathise evolved before the development of language and was necessary for the development of verbal communication. The ability to empathise increases with age and it is not always seen as something that can be taught. However, the development of empathy in individuals, as with the other domains of emotional intelligence, begins in the primary relationship of carer and child in early infancy. The carer responds to the child's emotional state and lets the child know that they know what the infant is feeling. This is known as attunement and is vital for healthy child development. The carer is able to listen to the child's feelings, accept them however destructive they may be and can offer some understanding back that makes the emotions manageable.

From age three onwards the child can increasingly recognise that others think differently from how she does and she can develop the capacity for understanding what and why other people are thinking and feeling. These children have developed a 'theory of mind'. This theory of mind is a critical building block for the development of empathy; the child needs this to be able to infer the intentions of others, to know when they are pretending, or perhaps, deceiving. Without such an internal map of others it is hard to know when others can be trusted. It is also important for imaginative play. Conditions such as Asperger's Syndrome or Autistic Spectrum Disorder are associated with poor development of theory of mind. Children with such disorders are less able to accurately read the mind of others especially with a degree of sophistication. Children with Asperger's Syndrome may have strong intellectual abilities but lack critical social skills in understanding how others are thinking and feeling. These children may need particular help in reading emotions in others. There are special programmes to help develop these skills, for example Howlin, Baron-Cohen and Hadwin (1999) and the computer-based programme Mind Reading (2003).

There will be children who will have particular difficulties in learning about empathy for other reasons Children are not always able to explain and name their emotions fully. We live in a culture where it is sometimes seen as acceptable to discount children's feelings. Abuse and violence in the home inhibits empathic development, as can authoritarian, punitive and non-responsive attitudes towards children both at home and at school. An absence of empathy in older children is associated with criminal tendencies and sexual aggression. Those with poor empathy are not always aware of their own feelings making it easier to deceive themselves. This makes it possible to justify hurting others, for example, the rapist who may claim that their victim enjoyed it or the parent who justifies excessive discipline by claiming it is good for the child.

Developing empathy in children and young people

A review by Kathleen Cotton (2001) of studies investigating the development of empathy found a number of significant ways of doing so. There are specific empathy training programmes, however, it is through interpersonal empathic communication that has the most effect.

In our communication with young people we need to ensure we, 'listen and attend to feelings in a way that articulates and validates the person's experience.' This helps the child gain self-awareness of himself and empathy for others. The way that the child learns empathy is to continually experience empathy from others. Poor early experiences can be re-mediated through contact with adults who are able to communicate about emotions. Reflective listening, described in Chapter Seven, is key in helping children develop not only empathy but all the critical skills of emotional intelligence. It is also an important component in behaviour management where the principle of, 'try and understand before you try to be understood' (Covey, 1989) helps encourage cooperation rather than defiance. Statements of understanding should precede requests for behaviour change. As Ginott points out, such statements are also in adults' interests as they diminish the child's feelings of resentment.

Statements of understanding can also helpfully precede explanations of learning processes. This is an important principle of both Carl Roger's and Hiam Ginott's approach to education. To acknowledge how difficult it is to learn something assists in helping someone learn and be more able to listen to explanations.

Within a climate of responsive non-punitive and non-authoritarian approaches and continual modelling of empathic caring behaviour there are a number of specific techniques which can be introduced into a variety of subject areas that help develop empathy. Cotton (2001) described the following techniques as contributing to empathy development:

- Encouragement of children to discuss feelings.

- Focusing on discussing similarities and differences between self and others. This can range from taking different perspectives in the classroom to considering other cultures.

- Repeated practice in imagining and perceiving another's perspective. This includes the use of role-plays or debates to encourage seeing and evaluating different points of view.

- When children hurt others they are helped to understand the hurt they caused and to learn how to make amends.

- Exposure to emotionally arousing stimuli in a way that helps children be moved rather than overwhelmed. This might be through stories or discussion of current affairs.

- Studying empathic individuals such as Gandhi, Martin Luther King Jr. or others (including religious figures or people in the news). Characters in stories, literature and fiction can also be explored to examine the internal emotional world and intentions.

- Feedback on considerate actions that comments positively on personality characteristics. For example, 'I noticed you shared that with Robert. Making people happy seems important to you'. The goal is not to produce a given behaviour but help the child see himself as a person who is thoughtful of others.

Managing emotions in others (social competence)

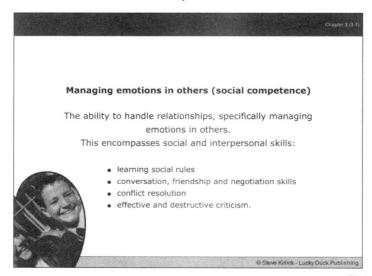

Slide 3.7

We need social skills to be able to get along with others. This involves being able to manage strong feelings in others and being able to calm oneself rather than escalate situations. A child needs to be aware of how he effects others, to stand up for himself assertively and to let others know if he is being annoyed or hurt. The child needs to know how to do these things without hurting others' feelings in acting in retaliation. Growing up is about learning these interpersonal skills in the trial and experience of relationships with siblings, peers and adults. If this goes well he learns to get along with others, feel secure in friendships and to give and receive care. These abilities enhance wellbeing. Some children will have particular challenges in this area that may be linked with specific or general learning difficulties such as Attention Deficit Disorder (yet some children with these difficulties may also excel in these areas). Some children may become unpopular which, in turn, may lead to being excluded from social groups or becoming victims of bullying. They then miss valuable learning opportunities. These children may need additional help but all children can benefit from experiences in thinking about how to get along with others.

To gain competence in relationships we need to be aware of the impact we have on others and to know what others may be feeling and trying to communicate with us at any given time. If a young person understands that they may be doing something that makes another person upset they may be able to adjust their behaviour accordingly, if not they might get hit or bullied and not understand why. Learning assistants can play a particularly useful role in providing some children with feedback about how their actions are affecting others. Brief descriptive comments that are given immediately help children become aware of their action. For example, 'You've just grabbed Gary's pencil out of his hands. That will make him angry,' gives the child information about his actions to which he can them make amends.

Even young children display a degree of empathy and attunement that can lead them to help other children who are in distress. Young children can be observed to display a high degree of skill in organising groups, negotiating solutions and to have a high degree of insight into others' feelings, motives and worries. Development of high levels of social skills will benefit children and young people in their social relationships and, later, when they move into the workplace. For those children with difficulties in this area the costs may be high. Often, specific children are described as lacking social skills, yet often this assessment is not helpful. There are many social skills that they do possess and it is rarely specified which skills they need to develop. Specific skills, which must be assessed appropriate to age, include the following areas:

Conversation skills:

- ability to initiate a conversation.
- listen to the other person.
- wait for the appropriate moment to speak (turn-taking).
- keep a conversation going and end a conversation appropriately
- to empathise.

Negotiation skills:

- share possessions or objects
- join a group already embarked on an activity
- to compromise
- to handle teasing and rejection
- say no to peer pressure
- express one's own views and listen to others' opinions
- able to disagree
- to mediate and resolve conflict.

Friendship skills:

- to accept and receive compliments
- to apologise
- to ask for help
- to take part in games or group activities
- to introduce themselves to new people.

Helping children learn social skills requires high levels of social skills in the helper. Correcting inappropriate behaviour can offend and create resentment. Criticism is best when it is constructive as opposed to being critical.

In effective criticism it is clear that the 'action' is the problem not the child. It gives specific information about the effects of the action on others and may offer a suggestion about what the child might do that would have a better effect. There is no suggestion of fault or blame and the focus is on more effective communication. For example (to a child talking too much), 'It's good to hear what you think but it's important to listen to what other people are saying as well.' In effective criticism there is also suggestion of what to do.

Destructive criticism criticises and attacks the person leaving them feeling blamed or disliked such as, 'You're staring, don't be rude.' Sometimes, this is expressed not only through words but also through body language showing contempt.

Social skills can be developed through positive interpersonal skills on the part of the teacher and also through activities such as games and Circle Time – indeed any situations, especially those involving cooperative learning. Children will learn best from brief frequent comments that give information about what to do rather than from comments about what not to do. Brief cues and prompts are often all that is needed to help the child work out for herself what to do. Teachers will be familiar with the continual task of correcting children's behaviour and this is eased when the child also hears recognition and feedback about when they are doing things right. Feeding back appreciations strengthens positive behaviours and constructive criticism is more likely to be received and respected when children know they are getting things right as well. This helps the child feel their actions are recognised and appreciated.

Highly socially skilled people understand that complex social rules exist in any given situation. Learning that different situations have different rules is an important step in helping children learn appropriate behaviour. Effective teachers will make clear their expectations of how children interact in the classroom and continually model these rules. If these expectations are clear, positive and achievable they will not only develop social skills but they will facilitate better behaviour. Rule setting is discussed further in Chapter Five.

Learning Support Assistants (LSAs) and ancillary staff can also play a vital role in helping children develop social skills. LSAs, as previously discussed, are able to provide immediate and useful feedback often discreetly and effectively. Ancillary staff are able to intervene in the important learning environments in the playground and dining hall. Training for these groups in facilitating social problem-solving skills can enhance their effectiveness and confidence in helping children learn. Visual cues can be effective also. Posters stating positive rules can also help give children prompts for how to develop and strengthen social skills.

That children develop high levels of social skills is increasingly important for success in the workplace. Schools do not always prepare young people to work in teams yet most workplace environments involve teamwork. Effective teamwork needs good people skills and the ability to relate and communicate effectively with others.

 See Exercise One (Including Slide 3.8)

The core competencies of emotional literacy

All children possess the capacity to develop in these five key areas. These areas also develop throughout adulthood as well – emotional development is life-long. Individuals will differ in their stages of development. Many factors influence the development of emotional intelligence: temperament, early attachment relationships in the family, the quality of our environment and relationships. These all affect our how we see ourselves and others and how we manage our emotional lives. Although the child arrives at school with the foundations of their development in place, schools can develop these areas both in the culture of the school, a climate that respects and values the emotional life of the community, and through facilitating learning in these areas.

An emotional literacy curriculum can address many of the skills in the five areas. Defalco (1997), Goleman (1995), Elias and Clabby (1992) and Weare and Gray (2003) have all identified key areas that may be addressed in such a curriculum. However this should not be seen as an exhaustive list nor, as Weare and Gray point out, as a 'blueprint for a perfect person'. There may be some debate as to whether they can be seen as skills or competencies at all. If these features are seen as attributes of individuals we might only forget they may also be features of interaction, a product of how people respond in certain situations rather than a feature of their selves. With these cautions in mind, consideration of these skills levels can assist in knowing how to intervene.

The Emotional and Social Competencies checklist has been compiled from some of the core competencies that have been identified, particularly those relevant to the five pathways, and can act as a method of assessing where a young person may be along those pathways and what interventions then may assist in their further development.

 See Emotional and Social Competencies Checklist

 See Exercise Two (including Slide 3.9)

Emotional and Social Competencies Checklist

The checklist on page 56 itemises some of the key skills in each of the pathways of emotional literacy. This checklist, when completed by someone who knows the child, can identify strengths of the child and areas to work on. It is not intended to provide a numerical score, rather as a way of quickly identifying strengths and problem areas. As this is a brief checklist, the skill areas that are enquired about cover a wide area. If areas to work on are identified then consideration could be given to finer aspects of that skill.

This questionnaire can be completed by an individual teacher or a group, including parents, who knows the child. A judgement should be made about the extent the child has learnt each skill in comparison with children of the same age and a tick placed in the box which best describes the child's level of skill.

Summary of Chapter Three

There are five key areas, or pathways, which contain the key social and emotional competencies of emotional literacy.

1. Self-awareness – knowing one's own emotions at any one time. Recognising a feeling when it is being experienced and being aware of the thoughts that have led to the experience of the feeling.

2. Affect-regulation – the ability to manage one's emotions and to be able to handle them, especially strong feelings, appropriately.

3. Motivation – the ability to motivate oneself to achieve desired goals.

4. Empathy – or social perceptiveness, the ability to recognise emotions in others.

5. Social Competence – the ability to handle relationships and manage emotions in others. This encompasses social and interpersonal skills.

Exercise One –
Debating the Pathways

Divide the group into three smaller groups. Allocate one group to advocate for the above proposal, the second group to debate and argue against the proposal. The third group is given the task to listen to both sides of the argument and evaluate the arguments given fairly.

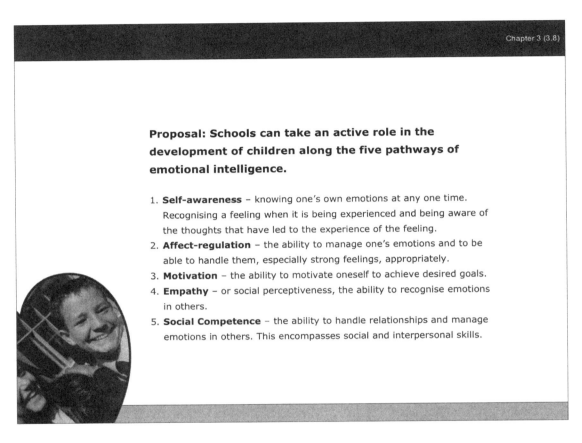

Proposal: Schools can take an active role in the development of children along the five pathways of emotional intelligence.

1. **Self-awareness** – knowing one's own emotions at any one time. Recognising a feeling when it is being experienced and being aware of the thoughts that have led to the experience of the feeling.
2. **Affect-regulation** – the ability to manage one's emotions and to be able to handle them, especially strong feelings, appropriately.
3. **Motivation** – the ability to motivate oneself to achieve desired goals.
4. **Empathy** – or social perceptiveness, the ability to recognise emotions in others.
5. **Social Competence** – the ability to handle relationships and manage emotions in others. This encompasses social and interpersonal skills.

Slide 3.8

Give the two debating groups ten to 15 minutes to prepare their arguments. During this time the evaluation group can consider what evidence they would want to consider and how they can take a position where they can evaluate both arguments. Each group presents their case and the evaluation group can ask questions to clarify. After this the third group have a 'goldfish bowl' discussion to evaluate the strengths and limitations of each argument. They do this whilst the two other groups observe and listen to the evaluation group's discussion. Finish with a whole group discussion on what has been learnt.

Exercise Two –
Using the Emotional and Social Competencies Checklist

Ask individuals to complete the task given in Slide 3.9. Inform participants that if they find themselves unable to evaluate and particular item they can either leave it blank or consider how they might gain evidence to be able to evaluate it or make a 'guesstimate' of what they believe it to be.

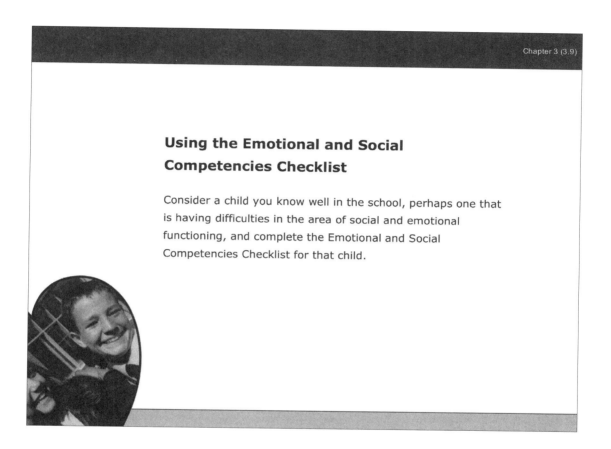

Using the Emotional and Social Competencies Checklist

Consider a child you know well in the school, perhaps one that is having difficulties in the area of social and emotional functioning, and complete the Emotional and Social Competencies Checklist for that child.

Slide 3.9

When the participants have completed the measure they should form into pairs and discuss the profile they have completed and from that identify what may be priorities for intervention. When they have selected one or two priorities they can decide how they might intervene to help the child progress along that pathway.

This checklist has been compiled based on key competencies identified by Elias & Clabby (1992), Weare & Gray, (2003) and Goleman (1995).

Emotional and Social Competencies	Rarely demonstrates this skill (priority for learning)	Sometimes demonstrates this skill (learning)	Frequently demonstrates this skill (learnt)
Self-awareness			
Is able to say and/or express how she/he feels			
Can communicate needs and worries in words			
Is able to identify reasons for feeling emotions			
Has an emotional vocabulary for range of moods			
Has accurate sense of self-perception			
Self-regulation			
Is able to manage strong feelings appropriately including seeking help			
Knows the difference between feelings and actions			
Can problem-solve well when frustrated – can think of things to do and evaluate them before acting			
Can tolerate stress and high degrees of pressure			
Is able to control and resist impulses			
Motivation			
Is able to delay immediate gratification			
Optimistic of success in many endeavours			
Can weigh up conflicting feelings to evaluate decisions			
Evidence of intrinsic motivation, curiosity, pride, mastery			
Able to set goals to work towards			
Empathy			
Is able to read social cues both verbal and non-verbal			
Can listen to and appreciate another person's perspective/point of view			
Can recognise when another person is pretending or deceiving			
Can identify how others are feeling			
Able to show consideration and compassion to a person who is distressed			
Is able to experience and express, guilt, remorse or sorrow if he/she has upset another person			
Social competence			
Is able to take turns in speaking and listening			
Is able to start a conversation and enter into a group of people			
Is able to resist inappropriate peer pressure and assert own beliefs			
Can compromise and negotiate to achieve mutually satisfactory solution			
Is able to give compliments and express dissatisfaction to others appropriately			

Chapter Four

Calmer Classrooms, Safer Schools – the Emotionally Literate School

The organisational climate for learning

The pathways of emotional literacy do not apply merely to child development. Both children and adults continually develop along the dimensions. Teaching, however, may not best facilitate this learning for it is 'caught rather than taught' and it is developed in the context of relationships. The environment in which people operate assists this learning. Goleman wrote of the importance of the application of emotional intelligence in the workplace (1995, 1998) and this application applies equally to the workplace of the school. As with childcare, traditional authoritarian approaches are being seen as increasingly unacceptable and ineffective in the workplace. An approach that takes account of how people feel increases people's effectiveness in working together. Schools do not 'teach' emotional literacy, they need to practise it. It must exist in the organisational climate of the school.

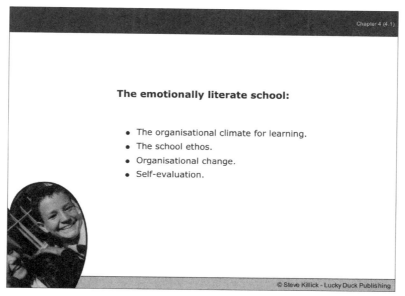

Slide 4.1

The school ethos

Some schools are now incorporating emotional literacy into the very fabric of a school's life (Goleman, 1995). Emotional literacy is not something that can be seen as placed solely in the individual. It is at the heart of how people relate to each other. Schools who want to create the context for emotional learning will want to place this as a core activity. Peter Sharp said that emotional literacy is not something that can be delivered through an 'emotional literacy hour'. It should flow through all the activities of the school. This means that the development of emotional literacy in schools is interlinked with the, often slow, process of organisational development.

However, schools are currently under continual pressures to change. Pressure from Government, parents and the continual demands of the curriculum are adding to the stresses and demands of the classroom. Many schools are dealing with so many numbers of children poorly motivated to learn and presenting considerable challenges that many teachers are under stress themselves. That a teacher's union in the UK felt it necessary to complain about a recruiting campaign for teachers that attempted to present a positive picture of working in school suggests the environment for positive emotional growth is far from commonplace in many schools.

Emotional literacy offers solutions to many of these difficulties but it is not something that can be achieved quickly or easily. To expect schools to change in response to Government directives to support children's emotional needs will not be easy and may even be counterproductive. However, schools can make positive changes by involving all staff and children in a process of working towards creating a safe and collaborative culture where everybody's views are sought and listened to. In so doing the school starts to evolve. Individual development can lead to organisational change. To do this, however, means placing emotional literacy at the heart of the school ethos. The support of the senior management team is critical in the achieving this.

Is there such a thing as an emotionally literate school?

Schools have always been concerned with the emotional, moral and social development of children so, in one sense, emotional literacy is not something new, rather it helps us focus on the importance and centrality of that task. It is therefore difficult and perhaps misleading to categorise schools as being emotionally literate or not (as it is also unhelpful to categorise children in this way). However, it is of great benefit to think about what organisational cultures are most helpful in creating a context that encourages and facilitates the development of emotional literacy. Many schools may be extremely emotionally literate in their practice without ever having heard of the term. Others may have an environment where thinking about emotional issues would be too threatening for both adults and children and such matters are often dismissed. Park, Haddon and Goodman (2003) described the features of a school that creates the context for emotional literacy to flourish. In their book, *The Emotional Literacy Handbook*, they give many different examples of how schools have developed emotional literacy through many different processes and projects. Emotional literacy is seen not as an endpoint or outcome but as a ongoing process, an activity. The 'ambitions' of schools wanting to create the context to nurture emotional literacy are different for the different stakeholder groups in the school setting. These ambitions for young people, all staff and parents are illustrated in Slides 4.2 to 4.5.

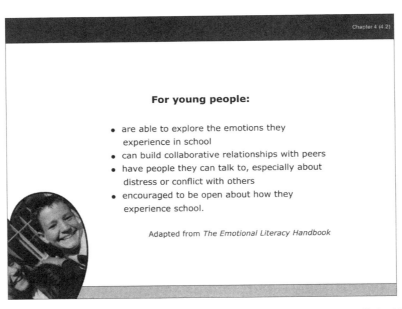

Slide 4.2

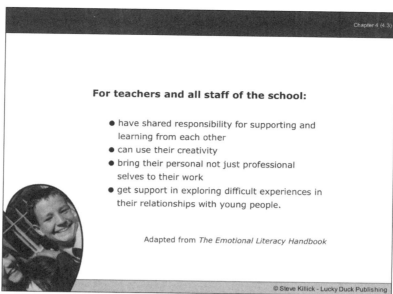

For teachers and all staff of the school:

- have shared responsibility for supporting and learning from each other
- can use their creativity
- bring their personal not just professional selves to their work
- get support in exploring difficult experiences in their relationships with young people.

Adapted from *The Emotional Literacy Handbook*

Slide 4.3

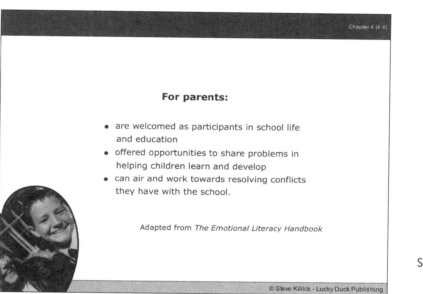

For parents:

- are welcomed as participants in school life and education
- offered opportunities to share problems in helping children learn and develop
- can air and work towards resolving conflicts they have with the school.

Adapted from *The Emotional Literacy Handbook*

Slide 4.4

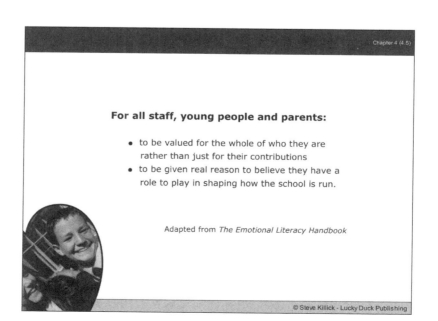

For all staff, young people and parents:

- to be valued for the whole of who they are rather than just for their contributions
- to be given real reason to believe they have a role to play in shaping how the school is run.

Adapted from *The Emotional Literacy Handbook*

Slide 4.5

The emotionally literate school is concerned with the democracy of the school, in creating a place where people can be involved and participate. Critical for this to happen is that the school is a place where people can feel safe. Tackling issues such as bullying, discrimination and other issues that threaten safety can be addressed through ways which also foster emotional literacy. This involves placing a focus on communication skills that enable people to listen to each other, accept multiple viewpoints and recognise that everyone in the school is capable of contributing towards solving the problems that arise in working together. Participation in schools means involving people – staff and students – in the decision making process in a way that they experience as having their voices heard and to feel that they have been offered meaningful choices.

So, emotional literacy is a whole school activity with its heart at the centre of how people communicate with each other. With a philosophy or ethos that respects an individual's emotional life and fosters collaborative working there are then a series of ways that the organisation can develop and also a number of strategies that can be used to promote emotional literacy. An emotional literacy focused ethos encourages staff to look for opportunities inside and outside the classroom to help students reflect on feelings. Moments of personal crisis can be transformed into learning opportunities. It can be taken further to be linked with what is happening in the child's home. To have most impact, emotional literacy strategies need to begin early, be age appropriate, run throughout the school years and can intervene in the school, home and the community.

Organisational change

Organisational change can be a long and difficult process. Change may be facilitated through taking on small projects which aim to use emotional literacy strategies to tackle issues such as bullying, or relationships with parents, or by developing certain activities through the school such as Circle Time or school councils. Special interest groups for staff can help give opportunities for staff to think and work together in practising emotional literacy. A key question will always be the involvement of the Senior Management Team of the school who do much to shape the culture of the school, especially of the staff team. Projects developed within the school can set a positive momentum for change.

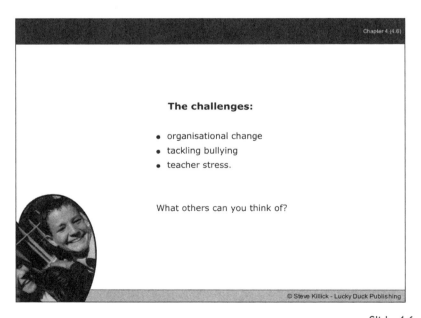

Slide 4.6

Tackling bullying

Bullying is an issue that faces all schools and should be an issue of central importance to any school concerned about the welfare of its children. Bullying threatens safety. It creates considerable distress for those who experience it and anger in adults when dealing with perpetrators. Applying an emotionally literate approach to the problem would involve helping of both students and staff to become aware of the effects of bullying and to explore possible solutions. Approaches to tackling the problem can happen at a number of levels that involve everyone in the school: staff, parents, governors and especially children themselves. A number of approaches have been developed to tackle bullying that might be developed into policies and procedures. Techniques such as Peer Support and Peer Counselling (explored in Chapter 12) or the No Blame Approach (Robinson & Maines, 2000) can be helpful. The No Blame Approach (now called the Support Group Method) helps perpetrators understand the effects of their actions on those they bully. By increasing their empathic understanding they become more likely to correct their actions than might be achieved through punishment. This approach also empowers the observers and others to be proactive in supporting the target of bullying. Ways of working with staff, students and parents help to create a safer school environment, are described in a training manual, *Dealing with Bullying in Schools* by O'Moore and Minton (2004).

Teacher stress

Given the demands on teachers, exploring and helping the staff group deal with and manage stress is an important area. Does the organisation of the school increase or decrease stress levels? Creating emotional literacy contexts involves encouraging children to talk openly. If teachers do not feel safe to do that amongst themselves it makes it harder to engender the openness necessary to be empathic and listen to children. Teachers, like any other group, need to have their own sense of calm and wellbeing before they are able to think of the needs of others. A climate of trust, respect and support is necessary in the staff group for it to permeate to the whole school. Even in well-functioning teams there will be issues and challenges that will affect staff morale, wellbeing and how they get on with each other. Teachers need to develop an understanding of emotional intelligence to be able to develop it in others. Tackling the areas that create staff stress and developing the staff team is an exercise that may have value in itself as well as being vital to bringing emotional literacy into the life of the school. The impact of school culture on teachers is just beginning to be recognised (Roffey, 2004). The atmosphere of a school affects everyone in it and is evident to the visitor on arrival. The staff room environment is also important. Is it a supportive, calm and positive environment or full of negativity? Exploring this area might be difficult and may benefit from outside assistance but here the foundations of emotional literacy can be well laid.

From this point we may be able to think about how all staff develop an attitude towards work that fosters emotional growth; one of infectious optimism, empathy towards others and curiosity, values in the workplace where the successes of all are celebrated and staff can collaborate together towards shared explicit goals.

Whole-school development

Bringing emotional literacy into the fabric of schools can be done in many ways. There are now considerable resources available to school to do this. *The Emotional Literacy Handbook* (2003) gives many examples of how emotional literacy has been introduced into schools. There are also other agencies such as specialist training providers and Local Education Authorities' support to help towards these goals. Other support includes voluntary agencies and, increasingly, mental health services who are increasingly working with schools as opposed to individual children. Such external support can help teachers gain confidence in talking about feelings. Training for teachers in imparting emotional education has not always been provided. Teachers, like many people, are not always comfortable talking about feelings. This is not something that comes easily for many people, as it is a sensitive area and it is easy to cause upset. Sometimes initiatives must start small and develop slowly. However, training can be provided to create a safe environment where teachers feel more confident in discussing emotional issues appropriately. Training can be provided both on and off-site and may be project based. There are advantages in using external sources to help schools develop new ways of working that may be more effective than one-off training.

The UK Government's initiative, Social and Emotional and Behavioural Skills (SEBS), emphasises the importance of schools being environments that foster warm relationships and promote participation. The political agenda will reinforce the need for placing emotional literacy on the curriculum. However, it will be how a school uses its own resources that will determine the extent to which it will succeed. A useful starting point is always seeing which one is already doing well and to identify areas for development. The Schools Emotional Environment for Learning Survey (SEELS) is an online emotional literacy audit developed by Antidote to help schools develop their emotional literacy strategy. It provides information about a school's emotional climate based on how staff and students perceive their school to be:

- Safe – That emotions are acknowledged as impacting on how they think.

- Accepted – How much individuals are allowed to 'be themselves' as opposed to simply complying with expectations

- Included – Encouraged to find a distinctive and valued role for themselves

- Listened to – That people can say what they think or feel knowing that this will have an impact on others and stimulate change

- Competent – That there is a genuine interest in enabling them to realise their potential in whatever field they choose.

The purpose is to provide a benchmark for whole-school emotional literacy that can then stimulate and monitor change through dialogue between members of the school to improve communication and relationships. The survey can be found on the Antidote website www.antidote.org.uk

Some schools have clearly taken emotional literacy to heart. Southampton Local Education Authority has made emotional literacy fundamental to school development (Sharp, 2001). Weare (1999) felt that emotional literacy can only be fully developed through a whole school approach as it is the school environment that is the most powerful influence on the capacity to think about feelings. So placing emotional literacy at the heart of the school ethos is critical and it may be expected that more and more schools will take the message to heart. However, there needs to be caution also. Key concepts such as 'ethos' and 'values' and terms such as 'collaboration' and 'partnership' are becoming frequently used, especially by governments, in trying to bring about organisational change but often leave people disengaged and cynical. The activity of emotional literacy needs always to be genuine and authentic. Insincerity is another form of minimising the importance of emotion. This work is about emotional honesty and integrity.

 68 See Exercise One

Developing an emotional literacy curriculum

To help facilitate the emotional and social competencies discussed in Chapter Three it is possible to construct a curriculum for emotional literacy. It is essentially through the communication that takes place that emotional literacy develops in both individuals and in the climate of the school. However, the continual pressure on teachers to 'deliver the curriculum' means there may not be the opportunities for the two-way process of talking and listening to students about their learning (Park, Haddon and Goodman, 2003). There are plenty of activities, both traditional and more recent, that can allow for an emotional literacy curriculum to be introduced into the life of the school.

Among the more widely used 'structures' are:

- Circle Time

- stories in lessons and assemblies to help develop values, empathy and ways of managing feelings

- games that foster cooperation

- peer led learning

- one-to-one sessions to reflect on and guide learning

- PHSE lessons including health, sex and relationship education

- parent support groups

- school councils and related ways of increasing school democracy.

This list is not exhaustive. There are also many ways within the national curriculum that allow for the emotional issues to be introduced beyond PHSE. Emotional literacy is critical to aspects such as 'speaking' and 'listening' – core skills for development.

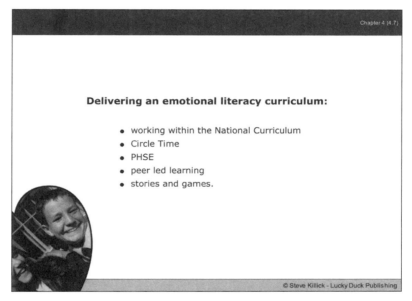

Slide 4.7

Working within the National Curriculum

All subjects may have entry points, topics which offer the opportunity to enter into discussions or exercises about emotional issues. These may be brief or more in-depth. Some subjects will particularly lend themselves to raising emotionally related topics. For instance, art, music and drama are ideal vehicles in which young people are able to reflect on personal issues and creating the context to do so directly or indirectly can allow for safe expression.

English, where stories can be imagined, told and written, will offer plenty of opportunities for exploring emotional issues. Using stories that exist in young people's popular culture can be helpful. The Harry Potter stories, for instance, offer the opportunity to explore friendship, loss and fantasy. Poetry is particularly useful. Poetry allows for the expression of subtle and complex emotion and the development of the skill of expressing feelings through poetry has been linked with improved mental health. This opportunity exists in all the arts, visual arts and drama. Drama is an invaluable medium. Play, games and role-play will offer the chance to learn skills in recognising, expressing, dealing with feelings in self and developing empathy and interpersonal skills.

Opportunities to raise the subject of empathy, caring, persistence and perspective taking can often arise and can be tackled even in such diverse areas as religious studies or physical education. It is the constant, albeit thoughtful and sensitive, exposure to emotional thinking which will help to build up young people's awareness of the key concepts of emotional literacy.

Science also offers the opportunity to relate to emotional literacy. Biology offers the opportunity to explore the physiology of emotions in humans and animals. Thinking skills developed in science have a place in making sense of feelings (See Chapter Ten). Beyond this, as Parks et al (2003) state, science involves imagination, creativity and social and political values and emotional literacy can contribute to helping students become more interested in science.

 70   See Exercise Two

Circle Time

Circle Time is a key technique associated with emotional literacy and is now used in many primary schools. It is not so frequently used in secondary schools. This may be due to both practical obstacles such as finding the right space or the difficulties in creating the right 'mood' in the group. However, these obstacles can be overcome, as Circle Time is such an important vehicle for emotional literacy. The themes commonly explored through activities in Circle Time include self-esteem, relationships, spiritual and moral development and communication. There are a number of resources for Circle Time activities listed below to help plan lessons and activities and many of the activities in this book can be used in the Circle Time context.

The classroom is arranged so that chairs can be placed in a circle. Ideally there might be part of the classroom that is big enough for chairs, or even cushions on the floor, to be brought over. In Circle Time, feelings are listened to. Negative feelings are seen as important and discussed in class, especially feelings like upset, hurt, envy and disagreement, and might be discussed in relation to stories as opposed to directly enquiring about children's internal feelings. Many activities can take place in the circle. It symbolises that the class is in the round, a group of equals.

Setting boundaries of one person talking at a time and listening to the person speaking is important and for some groups this will take time. An environment where it is safe to speak or not speak without it disrupting or adversely influencing others needs to be created. It can be useful to give people the option to say, 'I would like to pass', which gives choices and encourages cooperation. Some Circle Time lessons are structured around three stages: warming up, main action and winding down. These stages can be used to explore themes on any subjects within the curriculum especially those relating to physical and emotional wellbeing such as friends, bullying, physical health issues and so on.

> **Warming up** – games are often used to help energise and focus the group. Games maybe adapted to fit the theme of the lesson. This might be followed by a 'round' where everyone is encouraged to say something about themselves, their feelings or attitudes related to the theme of the lesson. Often pair work may be used to get people talking and then each person may say to the whole group what she or their partner was saying. For instance:
>
> 'Something good that happened to me in the last week was...'
>
> 'Something that someone said to me that made me feel good in the last week was...'
>
> 'A helpful/unhelpful thing a teacher said to me was...'
>
> 'I think my diet is...'
>
> **Main action** – This is the main action of the lesson that might include activities such as devising role-plays or writing scripts, working on a poster and activity sheets in pairs . Any activity might be brought into this section such as telling a story and exploring some of the themes, group work exercises or using puppets and videos.

Winding down – This might involve reflecting on the lesson or looking forward to what is happening next. Compliments may be given and successes celebrated by the teacher or group members. This feedback may be given verbally or written down. There might be some closing 'ritual' such as a favourite game or again using unfinished sentences such as, 'Something I noticed about...' or, 'Something I enjoyed/didn't enjoy was...'

Nurturing Circle Time

In schools where there may be many children experiencing emotional and behavioural problems the focus may be on nurturing. This may also be useful for those finding difficulties in mainstream classes. Nurturing groups often take place with small groups with a high staff to student ratio and focus on creating a safe and trusting place. There may be greater use of games, songs or interactive storytelling. Trust exercises can be used to facilitate appropriate touch and an atmosphere of calm and safety. Nurture groups can be very useful in pre-school and early years in providing the nurture necessary for development, with additional gains for literacy and communication skills.

Games and stories

Games and stories are excellent entry points for talking about emotions, empathy, taking different perspectives and exploring relationships.

Games

Games, especially those that can be played in the circle, are a key way of learning social skills as they:

- build and reinforce interactive skills such as turn-taking
- involve listening and attending to others
- give the opportunity for feedback, positive and negative
- involve participation in groups
- allow ideas and behaviours to be tried out where people can 'take risks safely'
- utilise key issues of competition and cooperation
- give 'micro-experiences' of success and failure
- are fun! Learning often takes place best when it is enjoyable.

How games can be used to develop social competence is explored more fully in Chapter Eleven.

Competition or cooperation

Underlying the debate about the role of competitive games in schools is a view that competitive games are encouraging of competitive ethics and favour the winners, therefore such games should be avoided in favour of non-competitive games. However, it is not whether games are competitive or not but the spirit in which they are played that is important. Competition may allow for the safe expression of aggression and provide motivation to try harder. Feelings of competitiveness, like any other feeling, can have positive and negative consequences. Competition encourages motivation, success, focus and enjoyment. However, if one cannot see oneself as succeeding the outcome may be negative leading to de-motivation, avoidance of participation or destruction of the activity. Important principles are not to value winning over participation. If this means people 'drop-out' after losing, what happens to them? How are losers treated? Are their efforts still applauded? an they still be actively involved? Many games, especially involving teams, need both cooperation and competition – an ideal learning environment.

Storytelling

We all have a love of storytelling in its many forms – film, written, performed and of being told to us. The telling of stories is a universal and timeless human activity. The practice of telling stories may be seen as an activity more suitable for younger children yet young people and adults are all drawn to listen intensely to 'told' stories. Storytelling has many functions that help facilitate learning:

- They entertain and in so doing, captivate and capture the imagination, developing visualisation capabilities. They engage curiosity, we want to know what happens next.

- They inform: they tell us about different people, different cultures and about the world. They can tell us what to do and, perhaps more importantly, what not to do.

- They inspire and bring vision. They can lift the spirit and place in people's mind what is possible alerting the listener to the possibility that things can be different.

- They give meaning to events: they can enable the exploration of the inner mind, about feelings and motivations, and can thus develop empathy. Stories are metaphors.

- They help to deal with emotions. The fascination with scary stories helps in learning to deal with fear. They can deal with mystery, the unexplained and terrifying monsters. In stories these terrors and fears are overcome, helping us to understand that anxiety can be mastered.

- They engage our desires, our longings and our fantasies. They can involve love, intimacy, bravery and heroism. We can identify with the protagonists in the story and unconsciously learn of the importance of wisdom.

Stories are a way of talking about the personal but not the individual. They explore emotional matters at a distance and through metaphor allowing the listeners to project their own meanings onto them. They do not need to be interpreted or explained. Stories are extraordinarily versatile. They can be short, long, used in assemblies, interactively with children and in any context. They can break up the activities of instruction and didactic teaching. They can be pitched for every age and ability level. There are advantages of telling as well as reading stories aloud as eye contact can be made, encouraging interaction and engagement, and the story can be modulated in response to the listener's reactions. The skills used in telling stories can be quickly gained and mastered through practice. Children and adults can learn these skills through telling jokes, relating incidents or summarising their favourite stories.

Stories offer the opportunity to explore the inner world of the characters and problems in relationships. Such tales are best when they contain ambiguity and complexity rather than being simple moral tales in which the 'message' is obviously clear. Rather they can present characters with conflicts, dilemmas and obstacles that can be explored with listeners during or after the story, using questions to explore emotions and motivations in a non-threatening way.

What is that character thinking and feeling?

Why did he do that?

What else could he have done?

What would you have done?

Students can be asked to take on the role of characters and be interviewed or role-plays can be developed.

One emotional literacy course used stories to explore the theme of friendship. Two friends faced a series of different situations, conflicts and dilemmas in their relationship. Issues such as how does it feel to have a trick played on you, what is it like to share feelings with friend, what to do if a friend is sad or being bullied were dealt with. Another emotional literacy project used the folk tales from the Brothers Grimm to explore masculinity and the transition from child to adulthood with boys who were disaffected from education. The telling of traditional 'initiation' stories was used to develop listening skills. As they became engaged, they were encouraged to share their own stories and start developing them through writing and role-play. It then became possible to discuss their own values and beliefs about relating to others, justice and compassion and what it really means to 'do the right thing'.

Resources for Circle Time

Davies, G. (Ed.) *Six Years of Circle Time – A developmental primary curriculum.* London: Lucky Duck, Paul Chapman Publishing.

Mosely, J. & Tew, M. *Quality Circle Time In the Secondary School.* London: David Fulton Publishers.

White, M. *Magic Circles – Building Self-esteem Through Circle Time.* London: Lucky Duck, Paul Chapman Publishing.

Boxall, M. *Nurture Groups in School – Principles and Practice.* London: Paul Chapman Publishing.

On the Internet

www.circle-time.co.uk

Resources on Games and Storytelling

Games

Brandes, D. & Phillips, H. *Gamesters Handbook 1 & 2. Game for Teachers and Group Leaders.* Stanley Thornes Publishers.

Jennings, S. (1997) *Creative Drama Groupwork,* Speechmark Publishing Ltd.

Fisher, R. (1997) *Games for Thinking.* Nash Pollock Publishing.

Butler, S. & Rohnke, K. Quicksilver (1995) *Adventure Games, Initiative Problems, Trust Activities and a Guide to Effective Leadership.* Kendal Hunt Publishers.

Stories

Fisher, R. (1996) *Stories for Thinking.* Nash Pollock Publishing.

Fox Eades, J.M. (2005) *Classroom Tales: Using storytelling to build emotional, social and academic skills across the primary curriculum.* London: Jessica Kingsley.

Park, K. *Interactive Storytelling – Developing inclusive stories for children and adults.* Oxford: Speechmark.

Gerise, A. & King, N. *Storymaking in Education and Therapy.* London: Jessica Kingsley.

Summary of Chapter Four

- Emotional literacy applies to organisations as equally as it applies to individuals. Emotional literacy is applied through the communications and relationships of all the members of the school.

- Some schools are incorporating emotional literacy into the school ethos. It is at the very heart of their purpose.

- Making schools safe both physically and psychologically, for both children and adults, is key. Bullying and teacher stress are just two areas that can be addressed through emotionally literate approaches.

- A curriculum for developing emotional competencies can come through the National Curriculum. Circle Time, games and stories are also very useful vehicles for tackling emotional issues.

Exercise One – Perceptions of Priorities

Ask staff to complete the self-evaluation questionnaire, 'Perceptions of School Functioning'. Many of the items were based on Peter Sharp's work in developing emotionally intelligent teams (2002). Go through completed questionnaires looking for where there are high areas of agreement in the response (i.e. most people have responded in the same category: Almost fully, Getting there or Early stages).

As scoring the questionnaire will take a little time it is probably best to distribute the questionnaire at the end of a session and collect the completed questionnaire at this time also. The results can be presented back at a subsequent session and then used to facilitate a discussion about perceptions and then to begin creating an action plan for change.

To score the questionnaire, identify the questions with the highest areas of agreement and disagreement in how the group responded. In presenting back the responses, remember, that this questionnaire is about perceptions rather than how things may actually be. Disagreement reflects a wide range of opinions and these results can be used to facilitate a discussion around how the school operates, particularly on dimensions of emotional literacy. In the discussion, differing points of view are not a bad thing and can help lead to a discussion about how people's experiences are different. From these perceptions it can be then useful to move onto gathering evidence.

From the areas that emerge, both whether there is high agreement or high disagreement, what areas seem to emerge as a priority for the group.

When one or two areas have been identified, it can be useful to then ask the group to then work on an action plan to address the issue. If there are a number of issues, it may be more beneficial to divide into smaller groups to develop action plans, one group for each issue.

Action plans should specify:

- what needs to be done
- who needs to do it
- who needs to be consulted about developments in this area
- what timescale is planned for actions to take place.

Questionnaire – Perceptions of School Functioning

Please tick each box according to which box you think most accurately reflects how the school operates in this area.

The extent to which you believe the school is currently like this	Almost fully	Getting there	Early stages
The environment of the school is pleasant and well-maintained.			
Pupils' emotional wellbeing is a central feature of the schools purpose.			
We seek out the views of students, parents and others about what they like and don't like about our school.			
The ethos is clear and well-known by staff. It reflects our values and beliefs and we put it into practice.			
When outsiders visit the school they are made to feel welcome.			
Difference and diversity is respected within the staff team. Different viewpoints can be expressed and considered.			
Students, on the whole, feel engaged in activities they experience as enjoyable, worthwhile and meaningful.			
When staff take on new tasks they receive help and support whilst they learn new skills.			
The Senior Management Team are supportive and clear in their expectations.			
Parents are encouraged to be interested in their children's progress and talk to teachers.			
The School Rules are known by all and generally respected by staff and students alike.			
Staff have the opportunity to develop specialist skills and interests.			
A sense of satisfaction in both staff and pupils is seen as important.			
Parents really have the opportunity to get involved in the life of the school.			
If staff need particular help when they need it, it is safe to ask for it.			
Both staff and students receive regular positive feedback about how they are doing.			
When people get things wrong they are given specific and constructive feedback about that.			
Students have a sense of pride in themselves and their school.			

Exercise Two – Our Poem

This exercise aims to illustrate how creative methods can develop emotional literacy and also to generate some fun and laughter within the group as well.

Divide the participants into groups of four or five and give them the title of a poem. It is in fact the title of a poem they are about to write as a group; it may be something like...

Musings on Emotional Literacy

Our School

Or the title may be generated from what is topical or spontaneous for the group.

Each individual is then asked to think of two words that come to mind when they think of the title. They write these words down.

Then as a group they must compose a poem using all the words that have been generated; they can add other words or repeat words or do the poem in a particular style. The group should not be given long to do this, between five and 20 minutes maximum which will encourage them to be bold and spontaneous. They should also find a way to present their poem to the other groups.

Chapter Five

An Emotionally Intelligent Approach to Managing Behaviour

Good behaviour in the classroom is clearly a prerequisite for effective teaching and learning to take place and the teacher is constantly facing the challenge of maintaining order and discipline. Children will always be testing the boundaries of acceptable behaviour and in so doing inviting the adults in their lives to maintain an environment that is safe and enables them to learn the benefits of cooperation, and of knowing that actions have consequences. Modern approaches that take a positive approach to behaviour management are compatible with the goals of emotional literacy. Accepting and valuing the emotional lives of all does not mean that destructive behaviours can be tolerated. The teacher has a powerful role in responding to problem behaviour in the classroom. This is not easy; many teachers possibly feel powerless in the face of continual disruption and uncertain of the many effective communication skills they have at their disposal. Ideas from the field of emotional literacy and emotional intelligence can assist in the prevention and management of behaviour problems. Perhaps most importantly these ideas can help children become more effective in their communication and solve many of their problems that are leading to problem behaviours. These approaches are compatible with positive and assertive behaviour management strategies such as that of Bill Rogers (2002, 2004) and of effective teaching skills (Kyriacou, 1998).

Many children, particularly in secondary schools, will present particular challenges in being able to trust and accept help from adults and in attitudes towards learning. Problems at home or in school can manifest in behavioural difficulties of non-cooperation, disruption and defiance. There are often emotional factors underlying these behaviours. The teacher needs to have authority without being authoritarian to be able to tackle the many different aspects of managing behaviour: to create the safe and respectful environment that encourages cooperation, to be able to calm flashpoints and to intervene and give assistance to those whose behaviour presents particular and on-going challenges. The objective is to create a calmer, safer environment for learning.

Effective communication skills reduce the need to rely on sanctions and punishments. These skills and strategies are about helping children express emotions and solve problems appropriately within acceptable limits. It is often strong emotions that underlie many behavioural problems. Feelings such as revenge, anger, fear, guilt, shame or jealousy may underlie acting-out behaviour. Teachers can find ways of helping the young person deal with these complex emotions. It is through behaviour that these emotions are often communicated so it important to see challenging behaviours as having a function and a communicative aspect. This is helped by a climate where feelings and emotions are frequently discussed, yet in many schools it is surprising how little feelings are spoken about. Communication skills of reflective listening and effective feedback are as critical, if not more so, than giving praise or sanctions.

Beyond these skills, there are five key areas explored in this chapter that lay the foundations for effective behaviour management in school:

- A positive philosophy towards behaviour management that emphasises and encourages appropriate behaviour and minimises the inappropriate.

- Clear rules or expectations that help everybody understand what is and what is not acceptable and desired behaviour.

- To be able to calm crisis situations through having an understanding of the emotional aspects that underlie the visible behaviour, particularly when 'emotional hijacking' occurs.

- To be able to link actions with consequences in a way that helps the child learn how to communicate effectively, manage their own feelings and understand the effects of their actions on others.

- To help maintain the child's integrity and avoid 'reactance' through interpersonal skills and the avoidance of inappropriate commands.

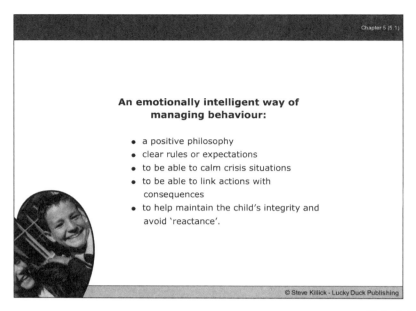

An emotionally intelligent way of managing behaviour:

- a positive philosophy
- clear rules or expectations
- to be able to calm crisis situations
- to be able to link actions with consequences
- to help maintain the child's integrity and avoid 'reactance'.

© Steve Killick - Lucky Duck Publishing

Slide 5.1

A positive philosophy

Many schools now have policies towards discipline and behaviour management that aim to, 'accentuate the positive to eliminate the negative.' This aims to encourage and reinforce positive behaviours by clearly stating expectations and promoting self-discipline. These standards of behaviour emphasise respect, consideration of others and responsibility. This positive approach is founded in the belief that children do best when given encouragement and support and that a safe environment is necessary for wellbeing. The emphasis is on 'catching children doing things right rather than wrong' and ensuring that appropriate and desired behaviours are acknowledged and recognised. It is accepted that limits need to be put on behaviour appropriate to the needs of children and by putting the primary focus on the reinforcement and celebration of what is appropriate, less emphasis can be placed on inappropriate behaviours.

The value of a positive, whole school ethos encourages consistency across the school and helps everyone know – staff, students and parents – what is expected. It also aims to minimise the negative effects of an over-reliance on sanctions that can create an atmosphere of distrust, fear and resentment as well as having a negative effect on relationships.

Creating such an environment is hard work. It can be easy to overlook or take for granted that most, if not all, children are behaving appropriately most of the time. It is also very easy to be drawn into addressing disruptive behaviour in the classroom whilst knowing that one's own responses may actually be reinforcing it. To balance appropriate responses to both positive and negative behaviour requires a great deal of skill, yet a positive approach can yield significant benefits as well as creating a much more positive atmosphere in schools. One headteacher, tired of constantly haranguing children for not wearing school uniform, decided on a positive approach. On random occasions she used the assembly to talk briefly about her appreciation of those wearing uniforms and to use the school's house point system to give all those dressed appropriately one point. Another teacher who was consistently yelling at children as they congregated around a stairwell blocking traffic and making noise tried a different approach. Instead of angrily shouting at offenders he stayed at the bottom of the stairs and thanked quietly those who came down the stairs appropriately. The effect of both these interventions over time was dramatic, not least in the teachers' own feelings of wellbeing.

Positive approaches have been effectively utilised in reducing behaviour problems in many different settings, including those that work with people who have exhibited high degrees of challenging behaviour. Particular tenets of such a philosophy might include:

- Every intervention with children is an opportunity to demonstrate care, reinforce or set appropriate limits and create opportunities for change and learning. 'Respect' is highly valued and such interventions can therefore influence emotional literacy.

- Behaviour cannot be understood without considering the emotional life of young people, that is, what they are experiencing and trying to communicate through their behaviour.

- It is important that the environment is 'safe' both psychologically and physically. If the school is not experienced as safe then people will have to defend themselves and understanding the emotions is less possible. If behaviour is not contained the emotions may be unbearable.

- Effort is aimed at preventing crises but should any crisis occur it is managed effectively with the objective of returning to calm as soon as possible.

- Children gain when the adults in their lives collaborate. Teachers can work with parents and others involved to overcome difficulties. Record cards provide clear feedback about how well a student is doing and if teachers and parents are supporting each other it sends a clear and positive message to the child. Conflicts between staff and parents are serious and need to be addressed quickly and effectively.

- In dealing with serious problems, the aim is not just to manage the problem but to think how it can be overcome in future. Many problem behaviours will endure, however effective the intervention, and so the effectiveness of strategies need to be frequently reviewed. Some strategies may be reducing the frequency of problem behaviour without eliminating it completely. Monitoring is essential.

- The individual is not seen purely as the problem. Managing behaviour is an interactive process of cooperating together. It is about relationships first; techniques are secondary.

- Children do well if they can (Greene, 2001). Our ethos should reflect our deepest held beliefs about what children need to develop to reach their potential. As Greene points out, a philosophy such as 'children do well when they can' reflects children's innate capacity to learn and to get on with others. If we contrast this with a philosophy that says 'children do well if they want to' then we may over rely on rewards and punishments to manipulate behaviour. There may be reasons stopping a child from complying and a continual focus on the problem may only reinforce it. It may be better to focus on the positive approach and what skills they need to overcome what they are experiencing as difficult.

The points are summarised in Slide 5.2.

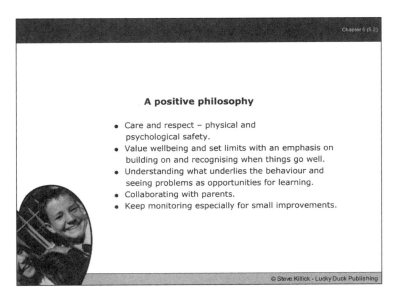

Slide 5.2

Guidelines, rules and expectations

Human beings are social animals and an understanding of the complex social rules that exist in different situations is necessary to know how to behave in those situations. Children particularly are guided in their behaviour by knowing what the rules in different situations are. If the rules are explicit and clear they are more likely to be acted upon than if they are not.

The purpose of rules should not be about attaining compliance but in helping children learn how to live and work alongside others and to know how to get their needs met. Rules reflect the values of the school as a whole and that of individual teachers in their expectations of what people should do and how they get along with each other. Rules are often referred to by a number of different terms such as guidelines, expectations, boundaries or limits. Rules are important for social order and how they are stated and implemented reflects social values.

Rules can either discourage or encourage motivation and cooperation as well as directly impacting on an emotional state. To help foster cooperation and wellbeing rules that tell people what to do rather than what not to do, and allow for individual responsibility rather than being a rigid set of regulations, are more effective. Rules can exist for the school as a whole, for specific settings such as certain classes and environments such as playgrounds or dining halls. Effective teachers will be very clear about the rules in their classrooms. It is often appropriate to involve children and young people in the negotiation and evaluation of the rules. Such discussion helps both understanding of the need for rules and adherence to them. It promotes an understanding of social justice.

The qualities of 'good rules'

Rules are not there simply to be obeyed, they are important in social development and cooperation. How the rules are conveyed and implemented can assist in achieving the objective of creating a calm, safe learning environment. School, class or other rules can be evaluated using the following dimensions:

- Are the rules clear and known to everybody?
- Are the rules positive in a tone that informs people what to do or are they negative and restrictive? A list of 'DO NOT...'s is not encouraging or enabling.
- If the rules include abstract terms like 'respect' and 'courtesy' are people helped to understand what these terms mean?
- Do students receive frequent feedback and appreciation when they comply with them?
- Do people have the chance to debate and, if appropriate, negotiate the rules?
- Do the rules mean everybody has to behave the same or do they allow for individual differences? If people have different rights and responsibilities, is it clear how advancements can be made?
- If rules are transgressed are the consequences proportional to the misdemeanour? Are students helped to think about why the rules exist?
- Do staff model the standards in their own behaviour?

 See Exercise One and Slide 5.3

Calming crisis situations

It is often when emotions get out of hand that problem behaviours can escalate into a crisis when someone may get hurt either physically or emotionally. Verbal abuse or physical violence can result when strong emotions are aroused that may set someone on a course of action they may regret when they are calmer. Strong feelings can erupt in both adult and child that can lead to 'a battle of wills' for control. Effective intervention can be made from an understanding of the arousal cycle (Breakwell,1997, Faupel, 2003).

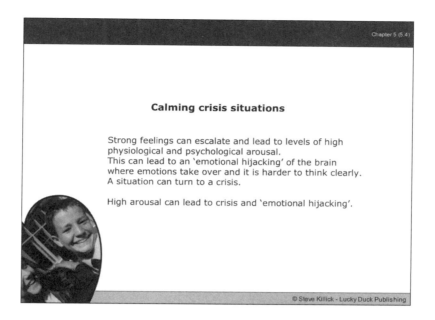

When strong feelings, particularly of anger or anxiety, are aroused they have very direct physiological and psychological components. They also affect how we interact with others. It can lead to what Goleman calls an 'emotional hijacking' where the emotional brain overrules our more rational cognitive abilities. The arousal cycle, illustrated below, demonstrates the stages a person may go through.

The Arousal Cycle

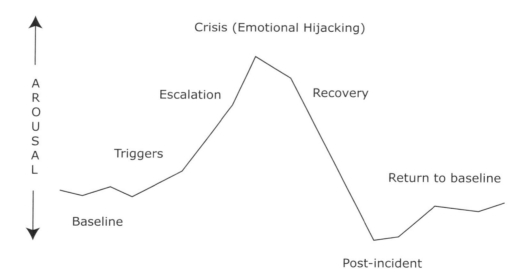

Slide 5.5

The stages of the arousal cycle are:

- **Baseline** – our normal 'everyday' emotional levels.
- **Triggers** – events that lead to stronger emotional reactions.
- **Escalation** – an increase in the strength of feelings when what is happening at that particular moment may either arouse one further or help one calm down.
- **Crisis** (or emotional hijacking) where internal control is lost.
- **Recovery** – strong feelings will inevitably peak and pass and there is a return to baseline.
- **Post-incident** – feelings of exhaustion or remorse and regret may surface.

The 'baseline' – our everyday levels of arousal

Most of the time our emotional level is that of 'baseline' level. That is, it may go up and down, with the daily interactions and events that happen to us, but remain within a certain range. This baseline level is different for all of us. Some individuals are very relaxed while others may be more excitable or more easily aroused. Our base-line levels may also vary over time, when under stresses caused by exams, problems at home or dealing with change and transitions; our levels of emotional arousal may be higher.

The triggers to an increase in arousal

Stronger emotional reactions might be triggered by internal or external events. Something may happen that triggers an upward movement in our level of arousal. This may be something that happens in the external world, like a frustration or someone who says something upsetting. Children will often 'wind another person up' in the hope of triggering some reaction – teasing or insults might be seen as some kind of attack that needs to be reacted against. However, a trigger may also be internal, a thought or a feeling that flashes across the mind that recognises some danger. This may take several forms; it might be some immediate physical danger or threat to our sense of security or safety. It may also be something that might threaten how we see ourselves, a threat to our identity. It is important to recognise that it is not the event itself that triggers the response, but the perception or interpretation of the event. When there are no observable reasons that someone's mood may have changed quickly it is likely that he was responding to internal triggers.

What is a trigger for one person may not be for another. It may be that there are many triggers that happen one after another and if we dealt with them singularly we would find it easier to cope. For instance, a child who is having a difficult time at home might get angry in response to what others may see as trivial. These triggers have a physiological effect as well. The autonomic nervous system that prepares our body to 'fight or flight' in response to danger is activated. Adrenaline is released into the blood and we become ready to act, possibly impulsively.

The escalation phase

It is often when emotions are escalating that a teacher has to intervene and it is his response that may determine when the situation de-escalates or escalates further. At this crucial point the teacher needs a range of interventions to be able to effectively calm the person. However the teacher may find his own emotional reactions triggered and may contribute to a 'vicious cycle' of escalation. Understanding the 'interactive' nature of this phase aids in helping the situation return to calm. Escalation can be observed in an argument that might take place between two people. One person might make a complaint to another who, in response to the perceived criticism, makes a complaint back. Emotions of anger may rise as each person feels the other is not listening or understanding. The tones in their voices may both gradually rise as each feels they have to make their point more firmly but in so doing they become less able to listen to each other. As emotions rise the initial trigger may even be forgotten as now personal attacks are being made. If the escalation continues it may result in hurtful insults, even violence. Often one person may 'storm' out. Anger has erupted. After a period of time, emotions have calmed and there may be regret at what was said or it may have cleared the air allowing a more rational look at the issues that were causing difficulty.

The teacher in a situation of conflict often faces a dilemma, either to prioritise taking control of the situation or to find ways to give the child choice and control in being able to calm. A secondary school teacher may often face the challenge of an angry student who swears at him and he may use the threat of consequences, or the expression of strong anger, in response. This may work yet the danger is it may escalate the situation further. Making the right choice can be a matter of great skill. An audience of other children looking on may also contribute to the escalation. Backing down may mean losing face that neither the teacher nor the young person feels they can afford to do.

As emotion rises, our bodies and minds start changing.

- Breathing and heart rate increases as does muscle tension and blood pressure to make muscles work more efficiently. We may start sweating which serves to cool body temperature, which is also a preparation for physical action. These changes can send signals to the other person to prepare for action.

- Our pupils dilate to take in more visual information. We may stare at the person who is upsetting us which may be perceived as a threat. However, we might narrow our focus only to the perceived threat and have less awareness of the wider environment.

- The ability to communicate and to think rationally diminishes. We may speak louder or look agitated. We become less empathic and able to be calmed. Indicators may be speaking louder or appearing agitated.

- As a person becomes more aroused, he becomes less able to distract himself or think about other things.

- Strong feelings can make it hard to think clearly, and so we become more likely to jump to conclusions or anticipate the worst. Our working memory may fail; we become less likely to think through the consequences of our actions. At this point our logical and reasoning abilities may be diminished.

Understanding that these changes may be happening to a young person and even to ourselves can help in intervening to calm the situation. At this point, a child may respond to threats of consequences with, 'I don't care,' or, 'You can't make me do anything,' so these kinds of interventions may only inflame the situation further. This is because the child may just not be able to think through clearly in that situation. The objective is to help the child return to calm when reactions can be more considered.

Many young people can be constantly caught up in creating confrontational situations from which it becomes difficult to back down. It is important to be able to calm oneself or the other person, to be able to take on the other person's perspective and to hear the emotion underneath. Helping the child regain self-control is paramount. Many children will have particular difficulties in controlling their responses to frustration and anger and need some additional help in learning these skills (Greene, 2001). Often the feelings that are invoked in adults by children such as anger, frustration or even powerlessness can tell us what the child is feeling but cannot appropriately express. He has communicated his feelings through his behaviour. We need to use this information to help the child to manage these feelings rather than act on our own feelings of dislike, avoidance or an over-reliance on sanctions.

The crisis – 'emotional hijacking'

A conflict can escalate to a point where something has to give. The situation may reach a crisis and it may lead to verbal or physical violence or fleeing the situation. 'Emotional hijacking' is the state when emotional thinking overwhelms our capacity for rational thinking. We become unable to 'think straight' and the experience is often described as 'losing it'. The emotional brain has become dominant and the balance between feelings and thought is lost. What is also sometimes lost is a sense of self-control over our actions. The 'executive functioning' of the brain has become hijacked by the emotional centre of the brain (the limbic system) and the ability to control aggressive impulses is diminished. So the emotional brain has overwhelmed the rational brain and we behave in ways very different from when we are calmer. Our functional IQ can fall 15 or 30 points lower and we just cannot think clearly. To see this in children can often be confusing. We may think that children are in control of their actions at this point, when it may be more accurate to see that they may have lost control. If we think they are in control, we might think they are acting this way because they want to, or that they are doing it on purpose or to 'wind us up'. It may well have that effect, as such behaviour can cause high arousal in ourselves but, in the case of emotional hijacking, it is not done on purpose. Also, if we have this belief we may respond with punishments that do not help the child who has lost control. What can be more helpful is acting in a way that does not further stimulate or inflame the situation. Later, the child can be helped to develop strategies or to assist in problem-solving. Punishment or the threats of such might only frustrate the child further. He is in a state of cognitive paralysis and cannot think about his consequences. Punishments imply intention and the child's sense of himself as bad may be only reinforced by such actions. The child may feel he has to justify his actions.

Although the immediate task is to calm the child it is not to say that incidents of violence or other extreme or unacceptable behaviours are ignored. Issues of helping the child take responsibility for his actions and to face the consequences of them are important. He may also need help in learning how to better control and regulate himself. This is a major objective of emotional literacy. However, in the heat of an emotional outburst the primary objective is the safety of all concerned. With children exhibiting aggressive or unsafe behaviour of immediate risk, this might even mean physical intervention done with the intention to make the situation immediately safe.

Children generally learn how to regulate feeling through experience. Unfortunately, experience is a contrary teacher. Temper tantrums of the infant are a phase of experiencing strong emotions that they may learn are not an effective way of meeting needs. It is not just anger that can lead to an emotional hijacking; all strong feelings are capable of 'tripping the system'. Young children will also experience these hijacks and have different ways of responding to frustrations; tiredness, not having one's needs met, fear, jealousy and so on can trigger a reaction which can lead children to hit out or act to hurt others physically or emotionally. As the child grows older the interpersonal nature of these outbursts becomes apparent; the adolescent arguing with parents can easily escalate to the point when someone gets hijacked. Developing a sense of controlling these outbursts is a key task for children and helping them to do so is a key task for those working with young people.

However, controlling such strong emotions can remain a task for many people throughout life. Greene (2001) describes the child with an inflexible-explosive temperament that may make handling frustration and rage harder. Traditional systems of reward and punishment will not help the child learn these critical skills. Other children may have had adverse early experiences that make them less trusting and more suspicious of others and more likely to feel threatened and respond aggressively.

How we can help children learn to calm feelings and communicate effectively is described in Part Two. Some immediate techniques to calm situations when children are in states of extreme agitation and aggressiveness are described in the box on page 79.

De-escalating Crisis Situations

Be aware – be one's **BEST** (adapted from Elias et al, 1999)

B Body posture

E Eye contact

S Speech

T Tone of voice

Body posture

Be confident but not aggressive or confrontational in your posture. To get too close can be threatening and may escalate the situation. Should the person lose control, you may also be more likely to be hit.

Eye contact

Keep eye contact appropriate; avoid staring as this can be confrontational. Keep looking around and making brief direct eye contact. Keep your eyes on what else is happening in the room. Eye contact conveys much of one's facial expression. Look attentive and assertive. Be aware that dominance is established through eye contact and looking down on someone can intimidate. Try to keep eye contact on the same level rather than looking down on the person.

Speech

Keep communication positive, brief and simple. Rationalisations, even long sentences, may not be understood and can even cause further stress to someone who is highly aroused. Say what you feel assertively but don't insult the person. If you ask a question wait for an answer and do not rush to fill silence. Keep listening and explore options or help to problem-solve. Humour can be very effective in defusing situations but not if it is used to belittle. If you have to be directive, help the child keep some sense of control by offering them a choice, perhaps of two alternatives.

Tone of voice

Keep it calm and confident. If it is raised for effect, be aware of raising it and try to return to a normal tone of voice quickly.

De-escalating Crisis Situations (continued)

Attitude problems!

Watch your attitude! If you find yourself thinking something like, 'He is not going to get the better of me,' or, 'I must be in control,' you may be falling into the vicious cycle of escalation. It can be more helpful to replace such thoughts with, 'What does she want?' 'What is he trying to communicate?' or, 'What 'works' for this individual?'

Observe and listen first – attend to the young person's frame of reference, 'How can their crisis be resolved? How can I help in this?'

What are possible triggers? What are their communication styles?

Hear what the person is saying.

Also, don't expect immediate compliance. If you make a request expect it to be followed even if the person doesn't do so straight away. They may comply after a brief token act of defiance.

Feel confident in your ability and have compassion in your authority. Ensure the person has physical and psychological 'exits' and that they can leave the position with dignity. Try to communicate a helpful, non-judgmental, non-confrontational attitude.

Try to avoid...

- Too many direct instructions, they might create 'reactance' (see later in this chapter). Rather offer fixed choices, 'You can get back to work now or we can sit down and talk this through together. What would suit you?' If a person has a choice they have to think, they also have some sense of self-control.

- Fighting fire with fire, 'Don't get angry at ME!'

- Rationalising – if giving reasons isn't working, give it up. Too many reasons sound like nagging and not listening to the person. They will probably stop listening to you and this could leave you feeling angry. If you want someone to listen to you, listen to them.'

- Planting suggestions for challenging behaviour – don't say don't. When we give 'don't' instructions we actually place a suggestion in the person's mind and then ask them to cancel that suggestion out. However, the aroused mind can act impulsively on the suggestion. Rather, say the behaviour you would like to see.

- Telling the child to calm down. If anyone has ever said this to you in an argument you may know how unhelpful it can be. Rather model calming down through your own behaviour.

- An audience effect. If people are watching, it will matter to both sides who looks like the 'winner'.

- Escalating to verbal abuse. Either respond to the feeling not the content, 'I can see you are angry with me. Can we talk about this?' or briefly respond in a way that makes it clear it won't provoke you, 'I don't respond to that kind of communication.' Responding to such inflammatory verbal attacks can always be dealt with later when both parties are quieter.

Recovery

Strong feelings peak and then pass. The level of arousal in an emotional hijacking cannot be sustained and with time there is a gradual return to baseline. Physiologically, noradrenaline is released to counter the effects of adrenaline. However, immediately after such an outburst a person may easily become aroused again and there is the risk of re-escalation. Immediately after an incident a person may feel exhausted and low in mood. At this point, they may experience remorse or regret for their actions. For some people, especially those who experience high levels of mistrust in others and may be vulnerable to frequent behavioural outbursts, there may be confusion. Underlying feelings of rejection and fear may surface alongside anger and resentment to those involved. Sometimes feelings of shame are invoked. Overwhelming shame is a very difficult emotion to manage. This remains a time for support and reflection rather than recrimination. Many children will not have experienced support during such times and only experienced criticism that may again provoke hostility. The experience of being listened to may be difficult for those not used to it but can lay the foundations for significant change. With time, there is a return to baseline levels of emotional arousal.

 See Exercise Two/Activity sheet and Slide 5.6

Linking actions to consequences

Helping calm moments of high tension through de-escalation does not mean that some unacceptable or undesirable behaviours are not addressed. Also, not all disruptive behaviours arise from high emotion. Children need to learn that actions have consequences and this learning aids motivation for appropriate behaviour. However, there can be problems with an over reliance on using reward and punishment systems. Punishments and sanctions do not always aid learning and may breed resentment. Rewards are often sensed by children as being manipulative. So, how can children learn about the effects of their actions especially upon others?

- One of the most significant effects of actions is on feelings. Helping children be aware that their actions have positive effects on how others feel helps their own feelings of competence. They feel they can make a difference. Verbal, non-verbal and written feedback can build on the positive aspects of behaviour. If children experience the pleasure of knowing they can positively influence others, they also are more likely to be concerned when their actions have a negative effect. The guilt experienced will motivate to correct actions.

- If behaviours have negative effects on others there will also be natural and logical consequences that might help the child learn to think about their actions. The natural consequence of, say, making a mess is to clear it up. Hurting someone's feelings might provide the consequence of understanding why the action was hurtful and to make amends by apologising in word or through writing. If homework isn't done as arranged then break time may be used to catch up on work not done. The principle of making amends in the way that follows logically from the offence is simple but in practice can take time to establish. It can be time consuming to ensure actions are carried out but the gains made may save time in the long run. Natural consequences should focus on safety and learning rather than trying to make a child feel bad about their actions in the hope that it will dissuade him in future. For instance, two young children who cannot play safely outside together may need to be supervised or restricted in their activities if they are not safe by themselves.

Bill Rogers has made the point that it is more important that inappropriate behaviours are followed up with certainty than that they are followed up with severity of punishment. As well as using natural consequences, consequences should be 'proportional' to the act. If there is an active philosophy of recognising and acknowledging appropriate behaviours then a more curious and learning approach can be taken to misdemeanours. As well as many of the communication skills discussed in Part Two it can be useful to use techniques that help the child think meaningfully about the action. For instance, if a child is continually uncooperative or inconsiderate it may be helpful to use the Follow-Up Review (adapted from Elias et al's Trouble Tracker, 1999).

In the Follow-up Review, time is taken to either have a conversation with the child about the problem or to ask her to complete the activity sheet. Working through the questions given on the sheet helps the child think about her actions and find other ways of solving the problems that underpinned the behaviour. The child may be involved in the process of deciding how to make amends for any actions. The incident or behaviour must be clearly defined for the child and discussions can use strategies of reflective listening, feedback, problem-solving and thinking skills discussed in Part Two. There is no harm in taking time to think through what might be appropriate 'consequences' especially as best decisions may not be made in the heat of the moment. On the other hand, any negative consequences should be over quickly. If they drag on over time, learning decreases and more negative feelings can predominate. Also, as soon as behaviour becomes appropriate again, there should be recognition and reinforcement of that. However, it is critical that there are consequences, both positive and negative, for this is an essential part of learning responsibility.

Follow-up Review

Name   Date

Where were you?

What happened? Did you break any rules?

Who else was involved?

What did you do?

What did other people do?

How did you feel? How did the other people feel?

How do you think you handled yourself?

1	2	3	4	5
poorly	not so okay	good	great	well

How upset were you?

1	2	3	4	5
mad	really upset	pretty upset but OK	a little upset	not upset at all

What are some other things you could have done?

What are some things you could do now to fix the problem?

What are some things you could do next time to prevent it from happening again?

Emotionally intelligent behaviour management is concerned with helping children learn about responsibility and offers more options than just rewards and punishments. It is based on relationships that give positive feedback when things go right. Often traditional methods tend to over-rely on methods that we might hope will shame the child into better behaviour but they usually only humiliate instead. Punishments are often ways of venting our feelings of anger. Positive programmes overcome many of these problems but one should always be mindful of how our desire to be punitive can become activated. One class was using a sticker chart to reinforce good behaviour in children who were experiencing difficulties. Even though it was rewarding good behaviour there was a more negative message sent as well which was probably more powerful. That was, 'if you need to have a good behaviour chart, then you are a naughty child.' Similarly, 'support' programmes can bear similar messages. An example of how feedback systems, such as stickers charts, can work effectively is given in Chapter 8. Whatever techniques are used it needs a commitment to a philosophy and ethos that reflects real emotional care as well as limit setting designed to keep children safe and help them grow. If children and young people learn that appropriate behaviour works best for them, this is recognised and acknowledged and there is greater motivation to think about negative feedback. If children learn that they will have to make amends for unsocial actions then they are learning valuable principles of restorative justice and restitution.

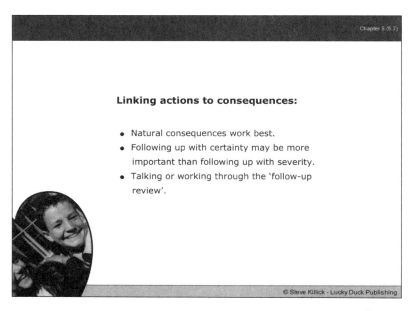

Slide 5.7

Understanding 'reactance'

Reactance (Brehm & Brehm, 1981) is a term used to describe a quality found in both children and adults. It refers to our intolerance and reaction against being told what to do and having no choice. In this situation many people become motivated to do the opposite of what is requested of them. Nobody likes to be ordered around. This quality reflects our strength, determination and autonomy. It can also lead to problems in the classroom. Children can lose their, often fragile, sense of dignity by having to do what is told of them. Some will not comply. Again, by having a wide range of communication skills the teacher can rely less on commands and orders and has a range of skills such as cues and prompts that give information and let the listener work out what to do. This lets the child show initiative and demonstrate it. When it is necessary to make a clear request, the child may demonstrate his autonomy by continuing the behaviour a moment longer before stopping. This is a way of saying, 'I'm not going to do as I'm told.' This way the child can keep a sense of autonomous dignity. A teacher who demands instant compliance may risk escalation as opposed to the teacher who makes a brief statement of the problem and moves on, confidently expecting cooperation.

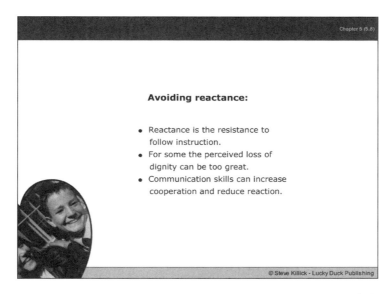

Avoiding reactance:

- Reactance is the resistance to follow instruction.
- For some the perceived loss of dignity can be too great.
- Communication skills can increase cooperation and reduce reaction.

© Steve Killick - Lucky Duck Publishing

Slide 5.8

Conclusions

Emotions underlie many behavioural problems in the classroom and attending to emotions offers the chance for children to communicate more effectively. They do not need to communicate with their behaviour because what they say is more likely to be listened to. Managing behaviour is a major challenge and the techniques of emotional literacy also require great effort. This effort may give great benefits especially in helping prevent or overcome many of the behavioural problems that children present. In managing behaviour it is critical to know how important it is to avoid causing shame, humiliation or reactance in children. These emotions rarely help create the cooperation we would wish to find in schools. When children find their sense of personal integrity attacked they may either accept that attack as evidence of their incompetence or fight back against it. Neither is desirable. Rather it is our ability to communicate what we expect, the respect with which we hold our children, ourselves and the task of learning and our confidence that children will positively grow and learn to cooperate with us and each other. This involves examining our deepest beliefs about what children need to grow, learn and change. It does mean that we lower our expectations of appropriate behaviour. The communication skills at the heart of emotional literacy are now explored more fully in the second part of this book.

Summary of Chapter Five

- Behaviour management should come from a very clear ethos that children need to learn and to behave well. An appropriate ethos might value emotional wellbeing and appropriate limit setting and ensure that appropriate behaviour is reinforced and inappropriate behaviour is seen as an opportunity for learning.

- Rules and guidelines contribute effectively if well known, positively stated and negotiated and debated. Such guidelines can prevent many difficulties from occurring.

- Strong emotions can underlie many behavioural outbursts. 'Emotional hijackings' can result from escalating interactions between students or between student and teacher. Knowing how to calm situations rather than inflame them can lead to more effective management.

- The emphasis is on thinking about consequences for behaviour rather than rewards and punishment. Consequences for negative behaviour should be natural and logical, help to make amends to the situation and be brief.

- Difficult behaviour is often trying to communicate something and it might be concerned with how we are feeling for instance, becoming angry at being told what to do or anxious about how we may be seen by others. A threat to identity can be as dangerous to our sense of self as a physical threat.

Exercise One/Activity Sheet – Evaluating Rules and Expectations

In pairs or small groups, discuss the school rules. Which of the school rules first come to mind? Try and remember as many of the rules as you can.

Using the following questions as a guide, evaluate the school rules. Be prepared to discuss your views in a group.

1. Are the rules positively or negatively stated, (that is, are they mainly DO's or are they DON'TS)?

2. Why have rules? Shouldn't people do as they like?

3. Are the rules well known by the members of the school? Are they clearly displayed?

4. Who made the rules? Do you know? Should young people be involved in debating and negotiating rules?

5. Do these rules get the balance between individual freedom and clear structure right? Are they too authoritarian or too vague?

6. Do rules mean everybody has to be treated the same? Is fairness the same as equality?

7. What do the rules say about the school's values and beliefs, what do they suggests the school stands for?

8. How are the rules put into practice? Are people who respect them appreciated, what happens when people transgress them?

9. Do you think any of the rules should be changed? What suggestions about rules would you make?

10. What makes rules respected? What are the qualities of good rules?

Exercise Two/Activity Sheet – De-escalating Situations

Scenario (you can use your own scenario if you wish)

A student is in a belligerent mood. He has been slamming his desk too loudly, he has been distracting others and rolling his eyes when you have been talking. Eventually you lose your patience and ask the child, in a sharp tone of voice, what the matter is. The child replies, 'it's nothing to do with you' and swears under his breath. You feel furious but you are aware the situation is escalating.

1. What other things might you have done to manage the situation to have prevented it from getting to this point?

2. Now the situation is at this point, what can you do to de-escalate?

3. What can you do after the situation has passed to follow-up on this event?

4. What good strategies do you have for de-escalating crisis situations?

5. Can you identify strategies that you would like to develop for handling crisis situations?

Part Two

Communicating Emotional Literacy

Chapter Six

It's All About Communication

Emotional literacy at its most fundamental level is about how we communicate with each other. However, some studies suggests that much of the communication children receive both at school and home may not be of the kind that best promotes motivation and a positive self-image. Murray White (1999) described studies that found that teachers spent less than one per cent of their time giving praise and estimated that some children would hear about 15,000 negative statements in school a year, and in many families children hear about 16 negative statements to every one positive. If these studies are representative then it is not surprising that many children have lost the curiosity to learn and the confidence in themselves to try. White argues that if children are to learn they need to receive much more positive feedback then negative. How we communicate and interact with children sends powerful messages. If we can communicate well with children we facilitate their academic learning and can boost their sense of confidence and competence. An overview of the areas discussed in this chapter is presented in Slide 6.1.

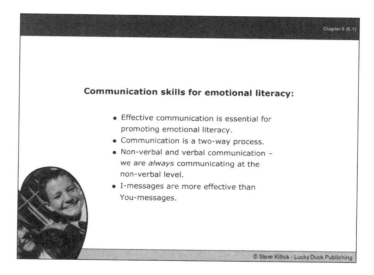

Slide 6.1

It is through our communication and our everyday interactions in the classroom that are always taking place that emotional literacy is facilitated. We practise many of these skills much of the time without always being aware we are doing so. Often we stop practising these skills when we most need to apply them. The skills described in Part Two of this book are illustrated in Slide 6.2.

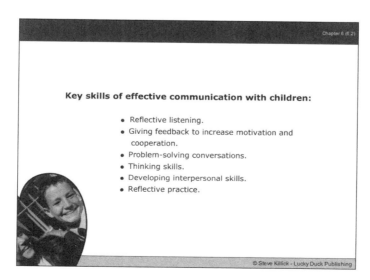

Slide 6.2

Many of these skills overlap with each other and can be used interchangeably with the purpose of encouraging emotional understanding and expression. These skills can be applied in the teaching of any subject and in the management of children in the classroom and beyond. Teachers will find that they use many of these skills routinely already but may be unsure of how they can utilise them fully or apply them in the classroom to facilitate emotional learning. These skills can also be taught to children and young people to aid their communication. However, these skills are not just about how the teacher talks to the child. Communication is a two-way process and non-verbal communication is as important as verbal communication.

Encouraging dialogue

As we hope our interactions will facilitate learning in children, we have to be equally open to learning from the children we interact with. The task is to be open to the emotions that are expressed in the classroom and exploring these. This is not to say it is about making children talk about things they don't want to or exploring their private lives. Rather it is about the 'here and now' interactions in the classroom which enable us to demonstrate that we are interested and can accept what children have to say. In so doing their feelings of self-worth and competence are validated. It is an ongoing process. Park et al (2003) describe how teachers can encourage dialogue through the following steps (also summarised in Slide 6.3):

- Attending to what happens between young people. How are they relating to each other? What ideas are they bringing to their work and where is their thinking coming from?

- Encouraging young people to give reasons for what they say and help them ask questions when they don't understand or want to know more.

- Relaxing control of the content of discussions and be ready to be taken in new directions by children's contributions.

- Be facilitative in a way that encourages dialogue and discussion and managing the class in such a way that some individuals do not dominate or others are sidelined.

- Being ready to encourage and explore controversial, damaging and sensitive statements. To be open to emotions rather than attempting to control them in a way that enables feelings to be reflected upon.

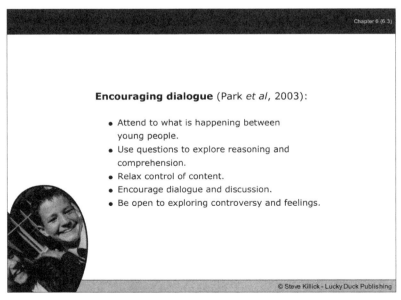

Slide 6.3

Non-verbal communication

Studies of communication have continually demonstrated that most communication that happens between people is non-verbal rather than verbal (Mehrabian, 1981). We communicate our attitudes and our relationships through our posture, facial expression, eye contact, tone of voice and physical proximity. We communicate our feelings through our actions far more than through our words and we can learn more about what someone is feeling by looking at what their body is saying. That non-verbal communication is far more powerful than verbal communication was vividly illustrated to a teacher who, for years, had dismissed her class from behind her desk. She prompted, asked and even shouted for her class to leave the room in an orderly and quiet fashion. This was something that rarely happened and the teacher would often comment that she was just wasting her time. Then she realised that, instead of talking, if she went and stood by the door the class formed an orderly queue, and then she opened the door and the class walked out much more quietly. Soon she did not have to speak at all, the non-verbal cues gave all the information necessary to manage a situation much more effectively than verbal requests. The power of non-verbal messages can easily be underestimated. In helping a child talk, such simple things as ensuring you are on the same eye-level can make a significant difference but awareness of such non-verbal elements of communication is frequently overlooked.

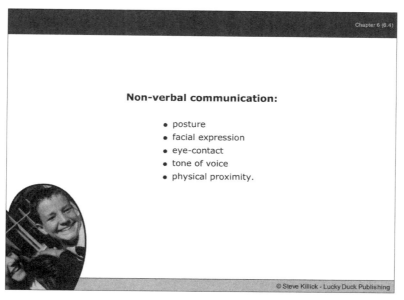

Slide 6.4

It is not just in classroom management that non-verbal communication is important. It is key in responding to how a child communicates how she is feeling and essential in offering understanding and compassion. Emotional communication is highly non-verbal in nature. Consider a child who might be looking tense and upset. A direct question such as, 'What's wrong?' might not elicit any more information from the child. A predictable answer may be, 'Nothing,' and there is nowhere the conversation can go. Similarly, a question like, 'How are you feeling?' might just elicit an answer like, 'Fine'. However, the child has already communicated much through their non-verbal communication and this can be responded to by the teacher's non-verbal communication. The teacher may not have to say anything to communicate that they have noticed. Comments based on this observation may more likely elicit what the difficulty may be. 'Looks like you're finding this exercise hard?' opens a door for a conversation. Even if it does not the teacher has communicated an openness and willingness that the problem can be examined.

Communication about emotional issues requires trust on both sides and awareness of what the child and teacher communicates non-verbally assists in the development of that trust. Non-verbal communication gives a constant flow of information about people's emotional states. Attending to this, without even having to comment upon it, can make our communication more effective.

- Posture – how we hold ourselves, upright and open or hunched up and closed.

- Facial expression – relaxed, smiling or more tense, frustrated or angry.

- Tone of voice – confident, enquiring or anxious, angry.

- Eye contact – appropriate, friendly or avoided out of anger or shyness.

- Physical contact – appropriate touch (a hand on shoulder or forearm) can send powerful messages of support and understanding.

As well as being aware of a child's communication we need to be aware of the messages we are sending. We are always communicating non-verbally. In looking at how people relate we can see that body language often mirrors or echoes each other's posture, and unconscious body language will influence how well people are experiencing the degree to which they are communicating or feel understood.

Listening and acceptance of feelings is conveyed through eye contact more powerfully than any other medium. It is through body language that it is easier to see the signs of escalating emotions and yet we may not always be aware of the messages we are sending and receiving. Discrepancies between what a person is saying and how they are saying it are also important. A person's body language may be the more accurate guide to what they are feeling.

In using the communication skills of reflective listening, feedback and so on, how we say it is as important as what we say, and attending to non-verbal communication not only provides important information it can guide whatever happens next.

 See Exercise One (which includes Slide 6.5)

Verbal communication

We want to put an end to talk that wounds the spirit, and search out the language that nourishes self-esteem. We want to create an emotional climate that encourages children to cooperate because they care about themselves and others, and because they care about us. We want to demonstrate the kind of respectful communication that we hope our children will use with us.

Adele Faber and Elaine Mazlish, 1999

Our verbal communication also sends important messages about our emotional life and the very language we use creates meanings that we can send, often without being fully aware of what we are communicating. The words we use can send messages of blame and judgement as well as praise and acknowledgement. One of Ginott's central principle's of effective communication was, 'Talk to the situation, not to the personality or character'. Consider the difference of these two responses to a child who repeatedly hasn't handed his homework in.

A: 'I've noticed you haven't given me your homework for a second time this term. I'm concerned that you might not be on top of your work. Can we think about how to make sure you complete your tasks for a minute?'

B: 'You have forgotten your homework again. You're very capable of doing well but you are lazy. I want it on my desk tomorrow or you will do it over lunch.'

There are several differences here. The first teacher described the problem specifically, their own feelings about it and was prepared to enter into a conversation about how to resolve the situation. The second generalised the problem, made comments about the child's character and prescribed the solution. This response is more likely to provoke resentment in the child. Even if he does his homework it will be done only grudgingly. One of the most specific differences between the two is the use of 'I' and 'You' messages (Ginott, 2004, Faupel, 2003).

I-messages and You-messages

The distinction of sending messages about a situation and talking about one's own feelings, in comparison with making personalised and generalised statements, represents a significant difference in attitude towards communication and motivation. I-messages involve the teacher taking responsibility for their own feelings and conveying them in such a way that the child can respond appropriately. You-messages are judgemental and can be blaming and put the focus on the fault being the person. Immediately they can create a defensive attitude as judgement of personality can be very emotionally charged or a way of unhelpfully ventilating our own feelings. Often such language is used to motivate, by making someone feel uncomfortable we might hope they will change their ways to be seen in a better light. Unfortunately, it is more likely that the child will feel resentful or, worse, accept the label. The language we use to a child influences the development of his identity. If he doesn't like how he is described, his response may be one of resistance.

Effective communication avoids using the 'predicate of being'; a child is not judged, evaluated or even described. Rather by talking about the situation we are being specific about the problem or behaviour. By talking about our own feelings we convey information about ourselves, we are letting the child know that they affect us, that they, like ourselves, are powerful people. We also convey that we take responsibility for our feelings. It models to the child how they can acknowledge their own feelings. As Faupel points out, using I-messages can be difficult and takes considerable practice. Some teachers may feel vulnerable talking about their own feelings but it does not mean becoming emotional or expressing weakness. We demonstrate our emotional literacy in giving feedback to others. This is the basis for appropriate and helpful ways of expressing anger without insult. It is equally important in giving feedback about positive behaviours. Children do not always like to be told they are 'good', they are more likely to feel patronised. But they do like to know they can please others or when their efforts are acknowledged.

Using I-messages helps us communicate more accurately and effectively and is fundamental to helping facilitate emotional literacy in the children and in the school as a whole. The language we use conveys important messages about our attitudes and prejudices and it is important that we are able to examine these to ensure we are sending the messages we wish to send.

When we communicate we use both verbal and non-verbal communication together. This means we can send strong messages about what we are feeling without describing an emotion at all. Indeed, language can be very non-specific. As Maines (2003) points out we can be very unclear about feelings even when we are talking about them. A comment could be made to a child, such as, 'I feel you are not listening to me.' This makes sense on one level but the person is not talking about what they are feeling, rather making an observation about the child's behaviour. The message is then much more complex and subtle. That we learn these complex ways of interacting demonstrates our natural ability for emotional learning. But we can assist this learning greatly through our understanding of how we communicate.

We are able to use language to communicate meanings way beyond what is actually said. Communication is about context and our brains are able to extract meanings about what is implied. A teacher or parent may make a comment to the child such as, 'Have you fed the rabbit?' knowing full well that the child has not. This comment serves as a prompt to which the child might respond, 'No, I will do it right now.' The child has applied meaning to the comment and responds accordingly. It should be noted that some children will have difficulties with the pragmatics of communication. They take the question literally and cannot see that there is an implied meaning in the question.

Creating the climate for emotional literacy involves an awareness of all aspects of communication. The goal is to find methods of communication that respect and value our emotional experience. As the quote from Faber & Mazlish that begins this section suggests, such effective communication utilises language that fosters self-worth and respect of others. It also aids cooperation and motivation. The following skills aim to encourage this effective communication but it should be remembered that it is a two-way process: one of listening and responding. There always needs to be an awareness of what is happening in this process; often the message sent is not always the message received and being reflective of what is happening in the process aids effective communication. This is so of all the relationships that can exist within the school beyond that of just teacher and students. It also includes relations between staff, teachers and parents and that between parents and their children. By taking care to communicate effectively we send an important message to others that they can do the same. The key points of effective verbal communication are illustrated in Slide 6.6. The rest of this book explores these skills in more detail.

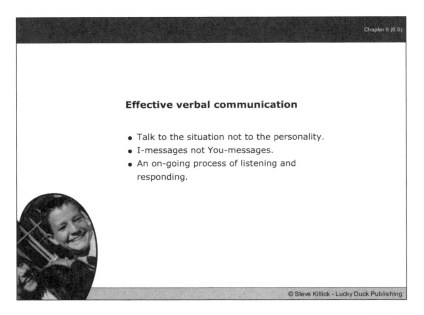

Slide 6.6

 See Exercise Two (including Slide 6.7)

Summary of Chapter Six

- Effective communication is fundamental to fostering emotional literacy. Emotional communication is not about the intrusion into the private lives of individuals but about how we communicate with each other in the here and now. It is a two-way process that is always ongoing.

- The two major elements of communication are verbal and non-verbal communication – what is spoken and what is communicated through our body, face and tone of voice. Emotional communication is highly non-verbal in nature.

- We are always communicating at the non-verbal level and we can use this information to improve how we interact with others. Eye contact and tone of voice are critical factors to be aware of in ourselves and others.

- I-messages are much more effective in developing trust in communication. You-messages can promote blaming and hostility.

Exercise One –
The Importance of Non-verbal Communication

This exercise aims to raise awareness of the importance of the non-verbal factors in the activity of listening. Divide the participants into groups of four to six and ask them to appoint a scribe. Present Slide 6.5 (below) and ask them to list the features of good and bad listeners. Some flipchart paper with two columns may be helpful for this , one for good listeners and one for bad. It may be helpful to begin with asking them to consider adult to adult situations in any context: home, friends or work settings, and then to focus on teacher and child situations – both how teachers and adults listen to children and how children listen to adults.

After five to ten minutes ask each group to feed back briefly and comment on the importance given to non-verbal factors especially.

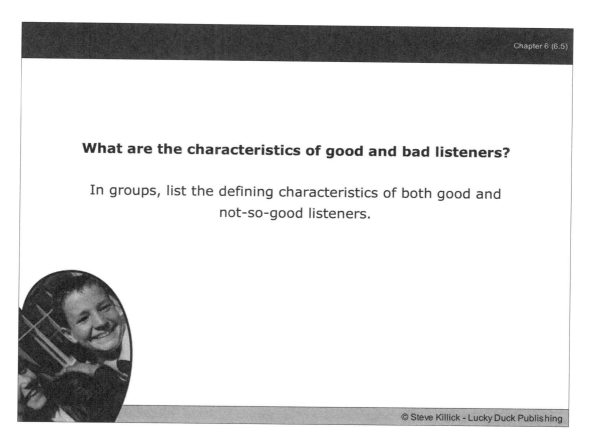

Slide 6.5

Exercise Two – What Are the Obstacles to Effective Listening?

This exercise aims to raise awareness of some of the difficulties in listening effectively. Active listening is a difficult skill to practise and there are many difficulties to giving one's full attention to listening. The purpose of this exercise is not to solve these difficulties at this stage but to highlight how many of the skills in the following chapters may serve to overcome some of these difficulties. However, if useful and positive suggestions are made, reinforce and explore these.

Again, divide the participants into small groups to discuss the question presented in Slide 6.7 for five to ten minutes and to then feed back to the large group to stimulate discussion.

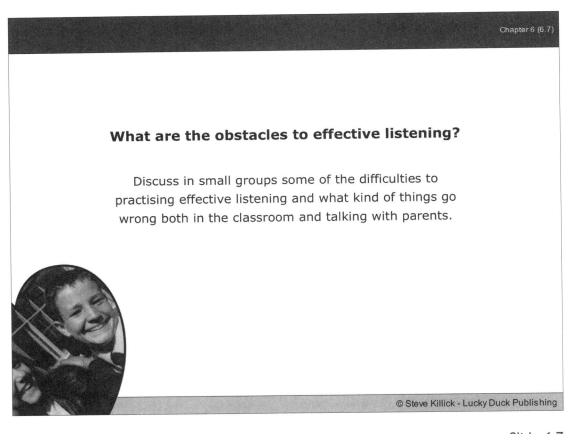

Slide 6.7

Chapter Seven

Reflective Listening – Attending to Feelings

When we are able to find an authentic language with which to express our feelings, we extend our experience of self. We then hold the complexity of feelings within our own person, where we have the choice to act on them rather than be pushed into expelling them.

Susie Orbach, Towards Emotional Literacy, 1999

When we attend to, and accept, the feelings of children we help them to understand their experience and to feel understood. This understanding may transform the feelings they are experiencing. This is often sufficient for the child to be able to manage their own feelings, to find solutions or perspectives that help them solve the challenge that is facing them. However, it is not always easy and adults may jump in with solutions to problems too quickly. It can be frustrating when children don't respond to adult's suggestions that are often given with good intention and based on experience. Worse, we can often end up denying or belittling feelings in a way that is not helpful. If a child who is afraid of something is told that 'there is nothing to be afraid of' her fears may increase not decrease. She might feel her feelings are something to be ashamed of, that she cannot trust her own judgement or that she might not be able to hide the 'shameful' feelings. Denying the existence of feelings doesn't make a feeling go away.

Unpleasant or negative feelings in a child, such as a disappointment, anger or sadness, can create in adults a feeling of wanting to help, or it may activate similar feelings. Anger begets anger, fear begets fear. We become anxious about how to respond. Yet attempting to take away unpleasant feelings, to minimise or divert attention away from them, may not always be the most helpful response. Giving attention and respect to the child's emotional state is sufficient for the child to make sense of the experience for herself. We do not need to try and change the feeling that person is experiencing. Empathy facilitates a young person's own ability to recognise and manage emotion. Empathy from an adult can offer a new perspective to the child on his own feelings. This process can be as simple as just naming the feeling that is being experienced or perhaps validating or acknowledging the experience for that person. The aim of offering empathy is to acknowledge what the person is feeling and facilitate that person's own emotional management or problem-solving skills.

Empathic, or 'reflective', listening can help a child in the process of self-awareness and self-regulation but it has another important advantage as well. It is through the experience of receiving empathy that a person grows in their ability to empathise with others. What is communicated to the child is an understanding of their 'mind' and through this process the child becomes able to understand the mind of others.

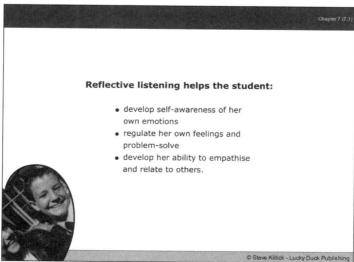

Slide 7.1

Reflective listening

Reflective listening is actively listening to feelings and to the thoughts expressed about those feelings. That an adult is willing to engage in a conversation about feelings communicates that emotions are important and to be valued and respected. For the listener it means being open to what is being expressed rather than trying to make the person feel better too readily.

Children may not openly say what is on their minds and their worries are expressed indirectly. A Year 5 child was upset when a trip out had to be cancelled due to poor weather. He was taking his frustration out by banging the table and being boisterous. The teacher might have responded with a direct instruction to behave differently or, as it was clear what the source of the upset was, to rationalise the situation by pointing out that it will be rearranged. Instead she decided to attend to the feelings underlying the behaviour.

> Teacher: You seem disappointed about the trip.
>
> Child: I am.
>
> Teacher: You were really looking forward to going.
>
> Child: I was. I'd brought my camera especially. I was going to take pictures.
>
> Teacher: Then the weather changed everything.
>
> Child: Yeah, I can't wait for when we can go.

The child's disappointment was transformed and his anticipation was renewed but this did not happen because he was reminded of what he already knew by being given sensible reasons. It happened because he felt understood and his feelings were acknowledged.

Statements of understanding – the difference between reflective listening and reasoning

Such statements of understanding that the teacher used above can have a transformative effect upon the child. They communicate that we understand and respect the experience of the person. They can often be used in place of instructions or commands to great effect as the following example illustrates.

A teacher noted that one of his Year 3 children was finding it hard to leave the classroom to join with others at break time. Some days he was asking to stay inside or spending a long time putting things away. Prompts did not seem to help and the teacher was becoming increasingly impatient as he needed his own (well deserved) break. One day, the teacher asked, 'You don't look like you want to go out and play. What's the matter?' The boy replied, 'Everybody hates me. I haven't got any friends'. The teacher replied by arguing what he knew to be true. 'Hey, you've got plenty of friends. Yesterday, I saw you were playing with Luke. He's a good friend of yours.' The boy did not respond to this accurate observation and the teacher felt more frustrated and the child was looking more sullen. Further appeals to reason didn't help. Eventually, the teacher found himself saying, 'Now don't be silly, everybody likes you, now go out and play.' The child walked off, giving the teacher an angry stare. His body language displayed a child defeated and the teacher was left with the feeling that although he tried to help, his intervention had made things worse.

The incident bothered him and he reflected on the conversation. When he thought about his statements he realised that he had not been accepting the child's comments about himself and had immediately offered alternatives and solutions. It wasn't that his suggestions were inaccurate; the child did have good friendships that the teacher had observed. He hadn't helped because he hadn't accepted the child's view of the world before offering his own. In fact, he had sent a message that the child couldn't trust his own feelings. He realised, in telling the child not to be silly, he had really implied that he was being silly in what he was feeling and that he should stop it. He knew this situation would arise again and he resolved to take a different tack.

It was not long before the situation arose again and he found the child was lingering in the classroom. 'Looks like you don't want to play today.' The child looked at the teacher, 'No one wants to play with me.'

'That sounds lonely,' offered the teacher tentatively, 'It's really hard when you feel no one wants to play with you.'

'Some days nobody talks to me. I wish I didn't have to go to school.'

'It must feel really horrible to feel left out like that,' said the teacher and as he did this he had the recognition that sometimes he had a similar feeling when he entered the staff room. However, the child went on to say. 'Yeh, but some days aren't so bad,' and he went to leave and rushed out into the playground with a smile on his face.

The teacher thought about this exchange often and kept his eye open on what was happening for the child. In accepting and naming the feelings, the young person himself had transformed them. Indeed when the teacher tried to articulate the feelings he thought the young person was experiencing, he himself was transformed. He realised that he too shared that feeling. In his observations of the child he realised that the child was struggling with the hardships of the playground. Yes, he had friends who he played with well, in one-to-one situations, but group situations were just too overwhelming for him. He was becoming frightened and at times avoiding the rough and tumble that free play presented. But, he was also learning how to deal with it. Over a period of months the teacher observed the child gain confidence. The child learnt the important social skill of being able to enter a group. Had the child failed he might have become a victim, vulnerable to bullying or scapegoating in the class. All children are afraid of the anxiety of isolation. The teacher realised that the child could not describe or evaluate accurately what was happening. He couldn't articulate, 'Yes I'm fine in one-to-one situations, it's just group situations that I find difficult.' However, the teacher had found a way of acknowledging some of the feelings and let the child find his own solution to a universal problem. Reflective listening had created different solutions than reasoning alone.

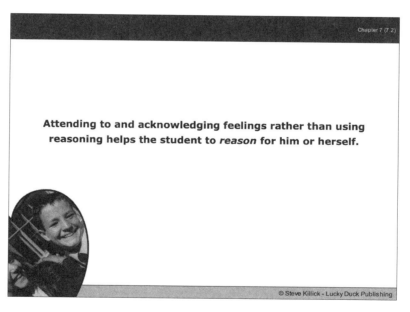

Slide 7.2

Accepting and denying emotions in children

We might like to think that we always accept the feelings of others, especially children, all the time. Unfortunately, listening to conversations adults have with children we find that it often just not so, especially if a child has a complaint or is not complying with what is being asked of her. At points like this attention is often not given to feelings but to having something imposed on the child – a short lecture, advice or instruction. At best, this loses an opportunity for learning. At worst, it insults the child who reacts by not listening. The adult who is hoping to instruct by talking is then frustrated. The denial of children's feelings is commonplace in their interactions with adults in their life. Faber and Mazlish (1995) identified a number of ways that children's feelings are often discounted, denied or minimised in everyday interactions.

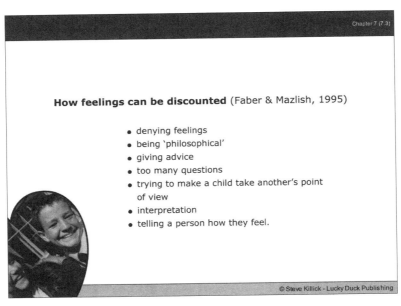

Slide 7.3

- **Denial of feelings** If a child is frustrated with a task, comments like, 'This is easy,' discount what the child is experiencing and can de-motivate. If a child is finding something hard and being told that it is easy, then they are likely to feel very discouraged and not motivated. Common statements might include, 'There's nothing to worry about,' or, 'There's no reason to feel like that.' Comments like this do not reassure a child, only inform them that they cannot trust their own feelings. It is more helpful to acknowledge difficulty rather than deny it.

- **Being philosophical** If a child doesn't want to do something they are often met with responses that generalise about all of life's experiences, 'We all have to do things in life we don't want to,' or, 'You are no different from anybody else'. When adults say these things they often hope to inform but these comments may patronise or enrage. Children learn early that everyone has to do things they might not choose to do but having this continually pointed out does not help.

- **Advice giving** Sometimes we offer advice and solutions too quickly, 'I know what you should do...' or, 'Don't let things get you down. Why don't you...' Telling children what to do when they have not sought advice short-circuits any opportunity for them to develop their own problem-solving skills.

- **Too much questioning** Too many questions, especially if they have our own assumptions embedded within them, can be unhelpful as they are often another disguised way of telling someone what to do. Questions have an important role in facilitating thinking but too many can sound inquisitorial.

- **Trying to make a child take another's point of view** If a child has a complaint about somebody else, we may rush to defend that person's point of view before fully exploring how the child sees things, 'You should listen to what Mr Williams was telling you. He was saying that for your benefit.' This robs the child of finding his own way of perceiving another person's point of view.

- **Interpretation** An adult can make their own amateur attempts at therapy by commenting on inner motivations without respect or even evidence. Again, this can prevent a child from gaining confidence in her own ability for insight. For instance, 'The real reason you spilt that water over Jamal's drawing was because you were jealous of it!' or, 'You have a problem with authority!'

- **Telling a person how they feel** Jumping to a conclusion about what a child is feeling does not allow him to be aware of his own experience and is, in effect, telling him how to feel. This can be especially difficult if offering pity or sympathy, 'You poor thing. I bet you feel so embarrassed don't you?'

When emotions are discounted (and this may be more likely if negative emotions are experienced or there is a possible conflict situation), we are not only discounting a valuable learning opportunity, we may also be escalating a situation. To discount feelings can enrage and the child may become angry, sullen or uncooperative – if the adult becomes angrier in response to this, escalation is evitable. Tempers may fray and shouting or worse may result. If emotions can be expressed appropriately solutions may be found but sometimes children, not unlike adults, can find it hard to find the words or ways of expressing their feelings. Some children will, for many reasons, have particular difficulties in appropriately expressing different emotions. Reflective listening is a process that can help children give words and expression to their emotions and have them listened to. It can overcome many of the blocks where emotions are denied.

The importance of empathy in reflective listening

Empathy is about taking the perspective of another. When we are interested in knowing more about a child's emotional experience and helping them express this, we become empathic. It is being curious rather than judgemental about how the child sees the world, their feelings, intentions, desires and motivations. We are seeing the world as they see it and how we communicate this to the child may help them see their world more clearly. When we listen and are curious about a child's feelings we communicate that feelings are important. When we accept a child's emotions we accept him and in so doing help his confidence in himself. Empathy is an attribute of emotional intelligence and in applying it to children we facilitate their own emotional development. When they have feelings listened to they become more aware of them, more able to manage them and more sensitive and empathic of the feelings of others and thus better able to communicate effectively with others. With this confidence their motivation for new experiences, including learning experiences, grows and they are able to risk failure.

When feelings are put into words, they are more open to rational cognitive processes. We can solve our own emotional problems rather than have them solved for us by people too ready to tell us how to think and feel. How often have we seen things more clearly simply by talking things through – the process of having someone listen to all that we are saying is helpful. Children are struggling to make sense of their experiences and empathy is a powerful tool in helping them do this. Children can have many different feelings at the same time, which can be confusing and overwhelming and at times leave them feeling out of control or reacting in ways that seem strange or quite cut off from their feelings, for instance, laughing when they are really feeling worried. Reflective listening is about listening to a child's experience rather than trying to persuade them differently or talk them out of it. If a child feels that he is being treated unfairly we need to know why he sees things that way, and this can open the door to a different kind of conversation about what fairness is about.

Reflective listening doesn't mean that a child can do what he wants to do; behaviour still needs limits and consequences and children gain a great deal of security from knowing this. However, reflective listening may be all that is needed to help a child change his behaviour or it can be used with other skills to encourage behaviour change. If a child's behaviour causes too much anxiety in adults, perhaps because it is unsafe this may need to be managed and made safe before it can be explored with reflective listening. If a child is saying things that are too negative about himself we may want to make sure that even if we accept that the child might have those feelings about himself, we don't believe them or that we see things differently. Reflective listening is a powerful tool that teachers can bring into their everyday interactions to appropriately discuss emotions.

So, reflecting skills are about communicating empathy. When we listen and are curious about another person's view and see it as legitimate the child experiences respect. There are times when this will be extremely difficult especially if listening to strong views about racism or hatred. It does not mean that we suppress our own beliefs but rather suspend them or withhold from advocating them too early. If we can understand before we try to be understood we increase the chances of ourselves being listened to. We can say our view when the time is right. Even if an act of violence has taken place it can be important to try and understand the anger that may have led to this act. Consideration of consequences or problem-solving can follow from this curiosity into the person's experience and will be more appropriate as a result. Reflective listening skills are the building blocks of dialogue and effective communication (Issacs, 1999).

Techniques of reflective listening

The foundation of reflective listening is one of respect for the child's emotional life and it also requires skill. The techniques described here need practice until they become part of a person's repertoire of communication that feels comfortable and natural. The skills here are most helpful when used with warmth and genuineness. They do not work if used as 'techniques' to get people to talk or to try and get people to comply. However, the learning of new skills can feel artificial at first and leave people feeling 'de-skilled'. The exercises can help with practice of the skills. The best way of learning is to try them out in small steps, rather than trying to change your interpersonal style. Many of these skills we use naturally in conversations anyway and we can develop from observing ourselves using these skills effectively.

Listen with full attention

Listening is the basis for helping a child express their emotions and to experience being understood. This is not just listening to the words but an active listening in which one's full attention is given to the speaker, to notice what clues and information we are being given. This means an awareness of body language: both the non-verbal communication of the child, and our own – do we look like we are interested in what is happening or is our attention elsewhere? We often say most just with our eyes. This is not to say that we must always be able to focus our attention on any individual at any time. Often we will have to focus our attention on the wider class.

When listening, sometimes it is not necessary to speak, as our attention sends sufficient information to the speaker that we are engaged. Silence is an important part of communication and it is not necessary to fill periods of silence with comments, rather to be comfortable with it and see what emerges. We also need to cultivate our own inner silence; we are not trying to anticipate or second-guess what the child might say. If we believe we may know what is in a person's mind we may be closing down our own curiosity. The guiding principles are to follow what the child wishes to say at the pace he feels able to say it. Start where the child is and follow her lead. By giving one's full concentration to what the child is saying, and respecting whatever she feels that she wants to share, encourages the child to say more and gives the child a sense of her own self-worth.

Acknowledge feelings

Often just one-word statements or just a sound are enough to tell the child that you are listening and accepting what he is saying. 'Uh-huh,' 'I see,' or, 'Mmm,' can give enough feedback and encouragement that you are listening and keen to hear more. Also, it is useful to pick up on a key word, particularly a feeling word, and to repeat that back in a gentle, enquiring way.

Child: I think that after that happened he (a character in a story) was sad.

Teacher: Sad?

Child: Yes, he'd lost his brother. He's bound to feel upset.

By responding to a student's talk, especially if strong feelings are evoked, with just minimal encouragements to continue talking means we do not disrupt a person's own thinking processes and provide the space for that person to possibly solve any dilemma or problem for himself.

Name the feeling

Naming the feeling that is being expressed yet not voiced helps clarify the emotional issue and convey that you have an understanding of a person's experience. It also offers a strong opportunity to develop an emotional vocabulary and offers an alternative to denying feelings or giving advice that may discourage the student.

Student: Peter won't stop talking.

Teacher: That's very irritating when you are trying to work.

or

Student: I just can't get it right no matter how hard I try.

Teacher: That's discouraging. It's not easy to work out how algebra works.

or

Teacher: You sound frustrated. Understanding the difference between metaphor and similes is not easy.

Acknowledge wishes in fantasy

Sometimes a child is going to have a strong wish or desire that something in his life is very different. It is often then that adults will launch into reasoning with the intention of explaining to the child why things are as they are. However kindly intended this can often encounter resistance and resentment. A very powerful technique is to give in fantasy what can't be given in reality. Faber and Mazlish (1995) argue that by expressing a student's wishes in fantasy, we make it much easier for her to deal with reality.

Teacher: You really wish that you didn't have to do maths. It makes you so frustrated.

or

Teacher: You really wish you didn't have to work with David on this project.

or

Teacher: You're very angry with Abdi for what he did. You really wish you could hurt him.

Allowing these expressions of what someone wishes does not condone unacceptable behaviour, but help someone express more safely what they are feeling and then reduce the need to act it out. All emotions can be accepted and in the acceptance be processed. Murderous hate can transform into anger that can become a problem that can be solved. With many of these skills it is very tempting to acknowledge the feelings and then make a directive comment. This usually takes the form of a 'but'. For example, 'You sound angry but you must do as you are told.' However, this 'but' just negates the empathy you have offered and will again create resistance and defensiveness. You can hear a 'but' coming a mile off. Practise just making reflective statements and then watch and listen to see what happens.

Talk to feelings not content

When someone is overwhelmed by strong feelings what gets said might cause considerable anxiety, for instance, a young person who swears he is going to hurt another. A teacher might feel that limits may have to be stated clearly. This may be so but it may be of more importance to acknowledge the emotional content and to name it more specifically to help the student manage it himself.

> Student: He's being horrible and mean to me. I HATE HIM. I'm gonna kill him.

> Teacher: I can hear how furious you are with him (the teacher's tone of voice echoing the strength of the emotion).

or

> Teacher: You're really angry with Richard. I take that very seriously and I want to know what happened.

Responding to the violent language or to the content may (or may not) stop the outburst but it will do little to help the student resolve the situation that has so upset him, and may just serve to make him focus his resentment on the teacher. Talking to the feelings enables the young person to explore further and models more appropriate expression. It offers the young person the opportunity to calm himself and maintain his dignity. When that happens, it is not uncommon for a young person to then start making amends, to apologise for their outbursts without having to be told to do so.

Open and closed questions

Use questions sparingly. Questions do not always facilitate conversations and too many questions can be inquisitorial. Children do not always respond to questions readily and often respond just with one-word answers. Questions need to be used judiciously and it is useful to make a distinction between open and closed questions. Open-ended questions are questions that usually don't have a right or wrong answer rather they offer a person an opportunity to talk and give their viewpoint. They can't be answered with a yes or no so are better to help a child talk more fully. Helpful questions often begin with, 'What,' or, 'How.' Questions beginning with, 'Why,' can sound blaming and may prompt silence so are best avoided. Open questions can follow from reflective statements and the tone of voice is critical.

> You look angry. What's happening here?

> What you are doing is dangerous. What's going on?

> You are late for the lesson. What's up?

Closed questions, on the other hand, can be answered with a, 'Yes,' 'No,' or a brief response. They can be useful if a child is so shy that talking at all is too anxiety provoking. Closed questions can warm the child up to speaking. It helps if they are confident that their answer will be accepted not criticised. From this, they may gain the confidence to talk more fully. If someone is not communicating, then offering a simple yes or no choice may offer a way in.

> Do you need my help?

> Shall I go through that one again?

> Are you OK?

> Have I made it clearer now?

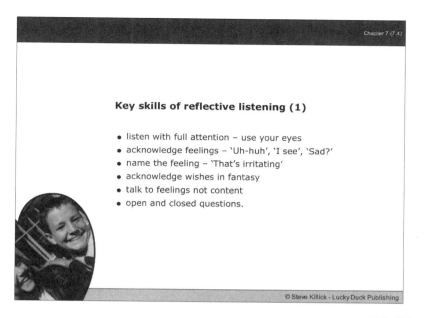

Slide 7.4

 See Exercise One (including Slide 7.5)

Checking out' statements – reflecting back feelings, meanings and wishes (paraphrasing and summaries)

We can help a child clarify her own feelings by giving her back, in our own words, what we have heard her saying. This names the emotions expressed and means we act as a mirror in which the child can see herself, her thoughts and feelings from a new perspective. She might reflect back feelings, meanings or wishes that may or may not be voiced. For instance, 'You're angry because you think you have been treated unfairly.' We do not need to distort these emotions in an attempt to influence behaviour. By reflecting back as accurately as we can we give the child the opportunity to change herself. When we reflect back the feelings without evaluating them as good or bad, we validate the person's experience, freeing the child from having to feel defensive or anxious that he will have to justify his actions or face evaluation.

Reflections can be made as statements or questions. They can be paraphrasings of what the person has communicated and made in the spirit of asking a question. This enables the person to give feedback as to whether it feels accurate to him. Statements can be made boldly with confidence but we should always be open for feedback to allow the child to further clarify if we have not got it completely right or, indeed, got it completely wrong. Depending on the age of the child, reflections might begin with the words

- It seems...

- I sense you are feeling... You wish...

- I hear... I feel...You seem to be saying...

- What you are saying is...

- You feel ... As you see it... That sounds like...

In reflecting back we are not saying that we agree or disagree with a person's perspective, rather we suspend our own view to ensure we understand the child.

Child: Mr Williams was horrible to me. He shouted at me for no reason.

Teacher: You're angry with him for shouting at you.

Child: He didn't need to and he did it in front of the whole class.

Teacher: That sounds as if it was embarrassing and you felt he didn't have good reason.

Child: Well I'd been asking Michael to help me. I wanted to get it right.

Teacher: You wanted to get your work done correctly?

Child: Yes, I suppose I was disturbing Michael. Mr Williams had asked me to stop.

Summaries reflect back the theme of the conversation as a whole. This can help either to deepen the emotional content or to conclude a conversation smoothly. Again, they communicate listening and empathy offering a new perspective on what has been said, and summaries should be offered in a way that allows the child to correct if she does not agree or is able to clarify further. Summaries can be useful both to deepen the emotional content and also to help conclude a conversation smoothly. Summaries might start with:

Am I right in thinking...? Tell me if I haven't got this right...

If I've got this right... Can I put it in my terms...

Teacher: So, if I understand you correctly, you asked Michael to help you and Mr Williams told you off in front of everybody. You're thinking maybe you should have listened to him earlier but now you're feeling a bit embarrassed and angry with him.

Summaries can also help with the learning process by helping the child clarify his thinking and communication. They can also strengthen and reinforce good work.

Let me check I have understood you. You are saying you don't understand why you have brackets at that point. Is that right?

or

So what you are telling me is that you designed that page using a piece of clip-art downloaded from the Internet which you put there with the cut-and-paste function. Then you chose that font because of the way it stands out clearly.

 See Exercise Two

Reframing

There are occasions when we can reflect back what a child is saying with 'a bit of a twist'. This is when the child needs his feelings reflected back to him in a more palatable way enabling him to think about them. A reframe changes the way something is viewed. Consider the difference between describing a child as a 'difficult child' or reframing this as a 'child with difficulties'. Reframes are particularly useful when a child might describe himself or others negatively or pejoratively. When reflecting it is important not to collude with negative statements that a child might make about himself, and reframing can accept some of the emotional content whilst challenging the negative description. Reframes can offer more helpful ways to see problems.

Child: I just can't do this. I've tried and tried. There's nothing I can do. I'm just thick I guess.

Teacher: Wow, this is something so hard it's making you lose faith in yourself.

Child: I just can't draw.

Teacher: Drawing can be hard. You feel you would like to draw better.

Child: I'm stupid.

Teacher: Well, I don't see it that way but it sounds like you are angry with yourself.

It is important to note what the response is. If you offer too different a way of seeing something it may not be accepted. It can be helpful to own it as your perspective rather than a paraphrasing of what the child has said. If it makes sense to the child they might take it on as a new way of looking at the problem.

> Child: Everybody hates me. There is nobody here who isn't mean to me. Nobody even speaks to me at break times.

> Teacher: That sounds horrible. I think it's really hard to make friends sometimes.

> Child: That's something I'm not good at.

> Teacher: Sounds like that, at the moment, you are feeling a bit stuck.

The meaning any event has for someone depends on how it is viewed or 'framed' so when something is viewed can be changed, its meaning also changes (Bandler & Grindler, 1982). A person's emotional and behavioural responses change when the perceived meaning changes. Using metaphors and simile can be really powerful in changing how things are seen.

Challenging negative talk

If a child makes a very negative statement about himself or others, it is important that some of these statements are challenged. This is similar to reframing but may more directly challenge the child's belief or, at least, make clear that you do not accept it. This can be done most effectively by the use of I-messages that accept the child's feelings whilst at the same time stating that you have a different viewpoint.

> Child: I hate this and I just can't do it. I'm stupid!

> Teacher: I can see that you're pretty frustrated at yourself but I can't say I agree with you. Maybe you can't do it yet.

Accept ambivalence

The experience of ambivalence, of having mixed feelings is common for all of us. Children, like adults, can have both negative and positive feelings in their attitudes and relationships. They can feel ambivalent about their friends, their family and their teachers. They may also be ambivalent about trying something new. Ambivalence can be difficult to tolerate – many adults find it uncomfortable and confusing and may respond with, 'Make your mind up'. Accepting ambivalence means tolerating uncertainty and complexity. Learning that this ambivalence is a natural state of mind, that we can feel conflicting emotions about things and that we can change our mind helps children feel less confused. Where there is love there is also hate, where there is fear there is often excitement.

These mixed feelings can be accepted for what they are and reflecting them back to the child helps him see them more clearly and weigh them up in balance. The adult does not need to resolve it but to state the dilemma that helps the child see it clearly.

> On one hand you really want to have a go at singing in front of the whole school. On the other you're worried that you might mess it up. That's a tough one; I wonder what you will choose.

> Sometimes you like Rachel, sometimes you don't.

> The good things about French are that you like it and you're good at it. On the other hand if you choose it for GCSE it means you can't do drama. It's a difficult choice.

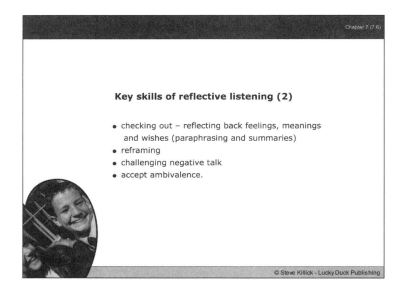

Slide 7.6

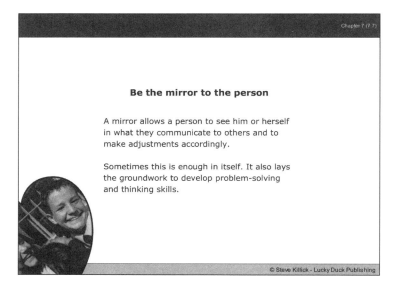

Slide 7.7

Summary of Chapter Seven

- Reflective listening helps the child feel accepted and safe, enabling them to use their own thinking and problem-solving abilities. In short, these skills facilitate a child's own emotional intelligence.

- Key skills to reflect back to a child what they are thinking and feeling are:

  Listen with full attention

  Acknowledge feelings and name the feeling

  Acknowledge wishes in fantasy

  Talk to feelings not content

  Open and closed questions

  Checking out – reflecting back feelings, meanings and wishes (paraphrasing and summaries).

  Reframing

  Challenging negative talk

  Accept ambivalence.

Exercise One – Reflective Listening Skills

Divide participants into groups of three and have them allocate themselves as A, B or C.

A is to be a speaker.

B is to be the listener and enquirer.

C is to be the observer and recorder.

A is to talk on a subject for five minutes. This can be a subject of that person's own choosing and should be something they are happy to talk about. Possible subjects include:

- Why I became a teacher (or whatever profession)

- A hobby or interest – something the person is passionate about.

- A conflict or dilemma in the classroom.

B's task is to listen and, when appropriate, use some of the reflective listening skills described I so far. C's task is to time-keep, to observe and record what skills B used in the conversation.

Reflection

At the end of the five minutes, C stops the conversation and the small group has a discussion about the experience of talking and listening. C gives her view of what skills helped and hindered the conversation. Slide Five can displayed to help give questions for reflection.

This exercise can be used in many ways to develop skills. The format can be used to experiment with learning skills discussed in future chapters. If the group are confident enough they can try role-play different situations, for instance, talking to a child about a problem or meeting with a parent to discuss an issue. Extending the time can deepen the content of the discussion.

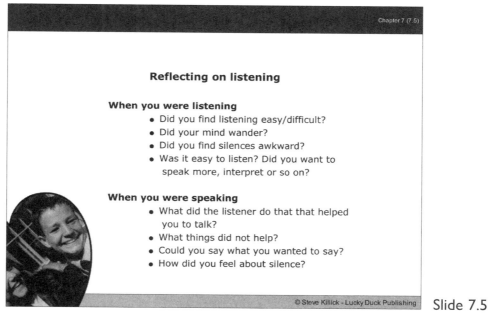

Slide 7.5

Exercise Two – 'Checking Out'

This exercise can be presented as a game that can be played in pairs. A topic for discussion can be decided on such as 'what makes a good holiday/novel/film' or so on. The pair can decide on any topic they choose as long as they think they can have a discussion about it. It maybe something they could debate such as a current affairs topic or an issue in education.

One person starts by making some statements about what they think about the topic. When they have finished, the second person responds by summarizing what the first person has said and checking for clarification then adding their own opinion. The first person then responds by summarizing the second person's viewpoints and checking out whether her summary was correct and then adds something else in response. It can continue in this fashion for some minutes.

As a variation, it can be played in a small group of about six where one person starts by making some statements. The person next to them summarises this and adds their own statements. The third person summarises both speakers statements and adds some more and so on.

Chapter Eight

Encouraging Cooperation – Motivation and Feedback

More on motivation

Motivation benefits learning, behaviour and personal development.

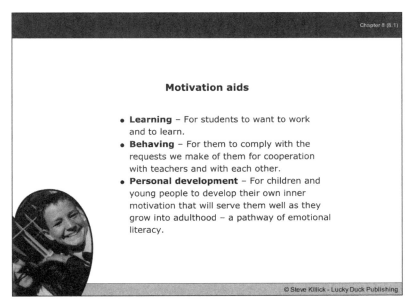

Slide 8.1

Enhancing motivation is one of the greatest challenges in the classroom. Many children, particularly in secondary school, are so poorly motivated that trying to engage them in learning can be a disheartening experience. There are many factors that teachers have to compete with: a history of negative learning experiences, poor support and encouragement from home or the lure of more immediate pleasures amongst others. Many young people are disaffected with education and have to meet their needs for self-esteem and excitement outside the school. There is mistrust and suspicion towards adults and resentment towards having to comply with activities in which they experience no success or accomplishment. Some learn that by being good at being bad is one way at least to gain some self-esteem. Some do not experience self-esteem at all or feel motivated in any areas of their life, they may have learnt, at great cost to themselves, that if you don't try, then you don't fail. Yet self-esteem is built on action, effort and a sense of achievement.

There are many young people who feel that no one knows them in their school or who cares about their experiences and with whom they can talk about their feelings. Initiatives such as Connexions aim to provide mentors for disaffected children by providing a relationship with someone who is concerned about their progress yet trying to engage such children will remain a challenge. Providing such relationships is not always easy in the secondary school setting. That so many teachers are able to do this is an achievement that needs greater recognition. Just one such relationship can make a considerable difference to a child.

Teachers are often in the position of having to correct behaviour and encourage more effort. What the child often experiences is constant criticism. There are no easy answers when motivation to learn has failed. Yet there are also many ways teachers can communicate in ways that encourage motivation in learning, cooperation and social behaviour. Using feedback as an alternative to praise and criticism can help build more positive relationships by placing a focus on what the child is getting right. An understanding of the skills in using feedback can help to make teachers more effective, build better relationships and increase motivation.

The problem with praise and criticism

Many teacher comments to children are often about approval and disapproval whether about learning or behaviour. These comments are meant to either reinforce or encourage what is seen as appropriate and desired or to correct and discourage undesired behaviour. But praise is not always motivating and criticism can be ignored. The difference between effective and ineffective praise is that effective praise gives real information about how that person is doing. Ineffective praise gives a judgemental evaluation of good or bad. Often children are very aware that in being given praise they are being manipulated. Older children may not welcome praise from adults and experience it as patronising, particularly in public situations. Perhaps more useful than the concept of praise and criticism is the idea of feedback. Feedback gives the child information about what they are doing, that what they are doing has been noticed. It does not evaluate or judge. It uses I-messages rather than You-messages to give children the opportunity to decide whether to carry on or choose to change. Descriptive praise is for more effective than evaluative praise.

Features of effective feedback

- The emphasis should be on the positive. There should be more positive than negative feedback. Positive feedback builds confidence and relationships. Negative feedback will be more likely to be listened to if it comes from a source that provides positive feedback. It is less likely to be listened to if most messages from that source are negative. Good feedback acknowledges and celebrates effort and achievement.

- It is based on giving information about behaviour and does not attack or judge character as ineffective criticism might. It is behaviour-specific.

- It gives the young person information from which they can make choices about what to do to change as opposed to telling a person what to do.

- It can be given immediately. When children are learning new skills they gain from knowing quickly whether they are getting it right or not. Immediate knowledge of results aids motivation. This is not to say that delayed feedback is unhelpful, rather that its effects are different.

- It can be given to the child directly or to others such as parents or colleagues.

- It can be verbal or written such as marking work, letters, postcards, certificates or emails.

- It enhances emotional literacy through acknowledging feelings and linking behaviours with consequences. It also informs children about adult feelings and that actions, both positive and negative, impact on others. This can increase their sense of personal effectiveness and confidence.

- It can be spontaneous and unpredictable. An unexpected compliment can create considerable wellbeing and teh benefits can last for days.

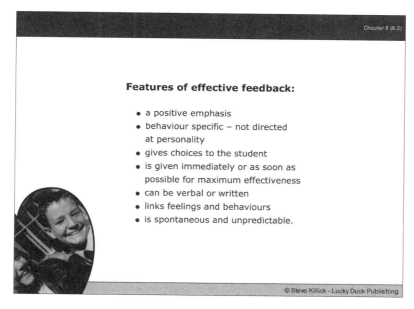

Features of effective feedback:

- a positive emphasis
- behaviour specific – not directed at personality
- gives choices to the student
- is given immediately or as soon as possible for maximum effectiveness
- can be verbal or written
- links feelings and behaviours
- is spontaneous and unpredictable.

© Steve Killick - Lucky Duck Publishing

Slide 8.2

 127 See Exercise One

Getting more of what you want – positive feedback

We all need positive feedback. It can make us feel wonderful whoever we are. To understand the effect of such feedback on children we need to know how important it is for adults. To know our actions are appreciated, that we can make a difference to others and even that people are thinking about us, is very important. A common experience for many people in their working lives is that they only discover how valued their work was by their colleagues when they leave their jobs. It was only then that they were told what they and their work meant to people. Positive feedback keeps us going and it makes us happier. With that we are encouraged to keep going, even to do more. In many organisations there is little emphasis on the fact that most people are working effectively most of the time. It is as if when people do what is expected, there is no need for recognition. Yet recognition reinforces and motivates and can thereby improve performance.

With children, as with adults, if there is a culture when positive feedback is given frequently it makes it easier when we have to make or receive criticism. Complaints are not easy to make; they may not be made directly but turn into disgruntled gossip or criticisms that are personal in nature and leave people feeling defensive and undervalued. Using feedback is a vital part of teamwork that builds collaboration and motivation. It creates a supportive organisational climate rather a critical one. The skills in giving feedback to children also apply to working with colleagues. The considerable stresses that are continually faced are made easier with specific recognition of the things that are done effectively. These skills are also useful in communicating with parents. Giving and sharing news about specific positives makes the task of communicating about negatives easier.

Feedback not only has benefits for learning and motivation but assists the development of other areas of emotional literacy by enabling useful communication about feelings. Feedback lets children know how their actions are affecting you and that helps children understand the connection between their actions and their effects on others. Positive feedback gives children confidence in themselves and in their relationship with the teacher. This, of course, may seem very fundamental, but many children will expect to receive criticism. That they get clear information about what they are getting right is very important information. Positive feedback puts the emphasis on catching people doing things right, the basis of helping people reach their full potential (Blanchard & Johnson, 2004). Recent research by

115

Swanson & Harrop (2005) found that even brief training for teachers (in both primary and secondary school) in making instructions clear, focusing on posture and feeding back success had significant improvements on learning and behaviour.

Giving positive feedback

Many actions deserve recognition, particularly those associated with achieving goals related to learning. What also is important is how children relate to others, when they listen to each other, work together or act in consideration towards others. Not all such behaviours can be recognised all the time, what is important is that such acts are noticed frequently and the feedback isn't bland or evaluative (that's good, you're good, etc.) but specific and meaningful. Appreciation should come from the heart and can be given frequently and freely.

Having high expectations of behaviour and academic performance is important but when these are achieved they shouldn't be taken for granted. Feedback offers a chance to restate those expectations and to reinforce the behaviour.

Instant feedback

- Have eye contact.

- Describe the behaviour that you want to acknowledge This might be a bit of work or appropriate or excellent behaviour. Be specific about exactly what you are noticing. We often speak to children about what they are getting wrong rather than what they getting right. Recognition and feedback about what the student is getting right reinforces the learning and makes it easier to tackle what is not understood.

- Describe how it makes you feel Tell the person how this makes you feel or how you positively evaluate the action. Whatever observations are made they should be genuine and honest. Such techniques also serve to introduce and develop a child's emotional vocabulary.

    'I notice you have drawn that to the exact proportions in the face. You took a lot of care to get that right.'

    'Will, I noticed you checked the work area to make sure it was safe before you picked the drill up. I feel I can trust you with the tools.'

    'I like it when you look at me because I know that you are listening.'

    'What really impressed me about how you handled that piece of work was…'

- Label the behaviour as a positive characteristic It can be appropriate to link a behaviour with a positive personal attribute. Such feedback is powerful as the child can see herself in a positive light.

    'Daryl, I saw you lend your pencil to Ciara when she couldn't find one. That is what I call considerate.'

    'Simon, I saw you stick up for Larry when the others were having a go at him. I was really impressed by that. That takes courage and shows loyalty. You're a good friend.'

By connecting actions and feelings we are helping build, in a child's mind, the connection between actions and consequences, particularly between effort and results.

    'You worked hard on that piece of work. I think you should feel proud of yourself.'

    'Now you have worked that out you can relax. How can you reward yourself for your effort?'

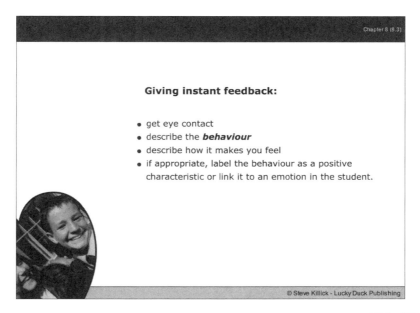

Giving instant feedback:

- get eye contact
- describe the *behaviour*
- describe how it makes you feel
- if appropriate, label the behaviour as a positive characteristic or link it to an emotion in the student.

© Steve Killick - Lucky Duck Publishing

Slide 8.3

This feedback should not be given to help motivate others who may be watching. The child should not be set up as a 'model' for how other children should behave. This is counter-productive. The purpose is to let the child know that you have experienced him acting positively. By describing the action it reinforces and strengthens behaviour. By describing your feelings you are letting the child know about the positive consequences of his actions. By labelling him positively he is given a way of seeing himself as others see him. The effect of this can be dramatic. Feedback like this can be written on cards, even given by emails if readily accessible. It can help if someone is struggling with a difficult task to encourage further effort and it can be linked with more tangible rewards if appropriate. Most of all, it is important to be genuine. If it is done as a way of manipulating behaviour this is often conveyed non-verbally and will not achieve this aim.

Feedback systems

Feedback systems can be introduced for whole classes that can give recognition of positive behaviour. These can be tied in with points and rewards or be used towards house competitions. These are most effective, not when everybody gets a point every time for the predictable behaviours, but when they are more spontaneous and allow for individual differences. Points are received when you improve on your own behaviour regardless of how others are doing. One school developed what was called a blob-cheque system (this was a name devised by students and staff together). A blob was awarded for acts of achievement, effort or consideration. A blob was simply a mark on a chart. When five blobs were collected the young person was awarded a cheque. These were handed out at assembly that was turned into a weekly ritual. Cheques were not easily gained and the young people recognised the effort of those that achieved it through their applause. Cheques could be 'cashed in' towards small privileges or collected and then used to select rewards from a reward menu. The system worked so well that the school was able to increase the resources to create very meaningful rewards. The rewards can also be used to encourage cooperation. If a group of young people could collect a required number of cheques each then a privilege or reward can be organised for all of them. This system worked well because it rewarded success particular to the child. A blob was given not if a child performed better than others but better in relation to their own performance and standards. Everyone had an equal chance of receiving one. It was not always the rewards that were motivating, rather that positive feedback and recognition could be given at so many points: when the blobs were given, at assemblies when progress was described and when the cheques were cashed in. It was most effective because of the elements of fun and spontaneity it provided as well as placing an emphasis on the positive.

Getting less of what you don't want

Positive feedback aims to build motivation and positive relationships and diminish negative behaviour through increasing positives. However, this will not eliminate all negative behaviour. Attention must be given to interventions that might lessen and prevent such behaviours occurring, and also what to do after such behaviours occur. Children will need guidance on being kept on task. Orders, threats, warnings and lectures may serve to create an atmosphere where compliance is gained through fear and create an underlying feeling of resentment. Positive discipline is aided by skills that respectfully allow children to change, firstly by aiming to prevent such behaviours happening in the first place.

Gaining cooperation – preventative skills

- **State your expectations clearly** The value of positive and widely known rules has been discussed and teachers can develop this further through the clear statements about expectations. Such statements inform the child of what behaviour is expected of them.

  'I expect you to be on time.'

  'I expect you to turn up with your PE kit.'

  'I expect you to share the equipment with Mike.'

  'I expect you to talk respectfully to each other. Could you tell me what that means?'

When behaviour is according to expectations there should, of course, be a high likelihood that it is reinforced through positive feedback.

Faber & Mazlish (1995) outline several skills, adapted here, that can help children become aware of their actions and correct them without feeling criticised.

- **Describe the problem** Often all that needs to be done is to point out the difficulty without any further comment. Bill Rogers (2002) has called this technique 'Describe Obvious Reality'. In so doing, it gives the student a chance to act responsibly and take the initiative in correcting the problem. If we tell the student what to do, we may immediately get the problem of reactance or a denial ('It wasn't me, sir').

  'Running in the corridor causes accidents.'

  'When you sit next to Simon, you always talk to each other.'

  'When you all shout at once, I can't hear anybody.'

  'The noise you are making can be heard by the people next door.'

- **Give information** Similarly, it can be sufficient to just give information without any accusation or criticism to motivate a change in behaviour. It is often so that the less said, the better. Lectures are not appreciated. It may be to remind people of specific rules in the classroom.

  'Your class has started.'

  'Chairs are for sitting on, not jumping off.'

  'A ruler helps for drawing a straight line.'

- **Offer a choice** Directives can lead to defiance but by offering a choice, from usually two acceptable alternatives, the student can feel more involved.

  'I can see it's hard to get started. Would you like to work on the computer or on the other table?'

'To get through this bit of work you need to work with someone. Do you want to work with Michael or Dave?'

- **Say it with a word or gesture** A simple cue or gesture may be much more effective than a long sentence in reminding someone what they should be doing. Often just the use of our physical presence, moving closer or watching, is sufficient. At other times, just saying the word and then walking away with the expectation that this will lead to change avoids the confrontation. This is about making body language work. A prompt allows the child to take the initiative.

- **Describe what you feel** As with positive feedback we can simply state how this action is making us feel. This can be far more effective than attempting to correct through shaming and attacking character. Talking about our feelings helps the child know that their behaviours impact upon other people and helps the child know that we notice and we care. It also helps the student know what the teacher is thinking. Yet, the child needs to know they can affect us positively as well as negatively. If they have no sense of being able to make someone think positively about them, why should they care if they only hear negatives?

    'Tony, I'm really frustrated to hear talking when I'm trying to explain this to the class.'

    'I'm angry that you have used such unacceptable language to express your feelings towards Martin.'

- **Put it in writing** What adults say can easily be blocked out, forgotten or not even heard by children. Messages in writing, either as notes or posters, can act as cues or reminders in a stronger way than speaking can.

    Dear Radha, I was disappointed not to get your homework this week. Could you let me know when it will come?

- **Use humour** Humour is one of the most effective ways of diffusing situations or making a point, from talking in a funny accent or seeing the funny side (although, obviously, belittling, sarcastic or offensive humour would not achieve this objective). Being able to use humour is a gift for many teachers and can do much to create a fun environment for learning but it is worth noting this is increasingly being seen as a learnable skill in training.

Don't say, 'Don't'

These skills can all contribute to a climate of cooperation. Giving positive direction and choice about what to do suggests better ways of getting along. Talking about your own feelings as opposed to comments that may negatively evaluate a child also may contribute to a calmer atmosphere. It can also be useful to avoid giving negative suggestions. When we give instructions that begin with the word 'Don't', we are giving a linguistically complex instruction. When the brain hears an instruction such as this it has to picture, or think about, the behaviour that is not wanted and then cancel it out. For a child who is impulsive (and this might include someone who is emotionally aroused), they are more likely to respond to the suggestion rather than cancel it out. When we give 'Don't' instructions we are suggesting the very behaviours we don't want to see. It is also gives no indication of the behaviours we do want to see. Describing the behaviour we want is more likely to gain cooperation.

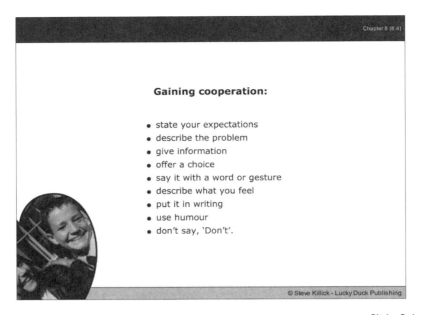

Slide 8.4

Negative feedback

The techniques for encouraging motivation and cooperation should impact upon keeping students clearer about the tasks they need to achieve, but may not be sufficient to eliminate all difficult behaviour. Non-compliance of children is always a challenge facing staff. Although feelings can be accepted, limits may need to be placed on behaviours. However, nagging, shouting and threatening consequences of non-compliance can have a negative effect. Negative feedback techniques aim to give information to students about what the problem is and to help correct this quickly. It takes account of emotions, both the young person's and the teacher's, and aims to build cooperation by working collaboratively. Here, a range of options is offered depending on the behaviour that is presented and these skills can be used in combination.

- **Have eye contact.**

- **Describe the problem** Be specific, refer to the problem behaviour and stick to that issue. Do not comment about character or personality. State exactly why it is a problem, perhaps because it contravenes a rule or the effect it has on others.

  'You have missed the beginning of class. You have missed what I have asked everybody to do and it is disruptive to others when you come in late.'

- **Express your feelings** Link the behaviour with your feelings about the issue.

  'This has happened several times and I am very irritated by this.'

- **Invite the child to problem-solve with you** You can offer or ask the child to solve the problem either immediately or to prevent it recurring again. Similarly, the conversation may turn to how the situation may be rectified or amends made. Techniques for problem-solving are discussed in more detail in the next chapter.

  'It appears it is difficult to get to class on time, what can you do to make sure that you get here on time?'

These techniques can be put together in many ways. One such way, described by Goleman (1995), is known as XYZ. In XYZ, the format of the feedback is simple and follows the formula of, 'When you did X, it made me feel Y. I'd rather you did Z.'

'When you threw that ball at Didy, I was shocked that you wanted to hurt him. If he has upset you, you need to tell him in words why you are angry with him.'

'When you ran down the corridor, I was very worried that you would hurt yourself or somebody else. Please walk.'

Try to avoid threatening consequences of misbehaviour. It can sound like a threat and therefore get an adverse reaction. Also, if someone is highly aroused, perhaps in a state of being emotionally hijacked, they will not be able to reason clearly enough to be able to link behaviours and consequences. This is a time to de-escalate the situation.

Return to positive feedback as soon as possible

Such communications can deal with many problem situations quickly and help the child learn more appropriate ways of behaving. When teachers express their feelings clearly and appropriately in front of young people, this can be useful in helping motivate the child to better behaviour; they can think better of their actions. There is also a danger that the feelings of shame and humiliation are so great that the child cannot tolerate them. For that reason, it can be helpful to remind that child of his or her strengths. If the child feels humiliated he may end up only resenting the person who has made him feel thus. By talking about the child's strengths and ability to do better immediately after highlighting the fault, the child can focus on the feedback about the problem behaviour rather than feeling criticised. Finishing with genuine positives means the child is less likely to leave the conversation feeling blamed and resentful.

'I know you are much better than this. I've seen you stick up for yourself without having to hit anybody. Now deal with this properly.'

So, essentially, follow negatives with positives. However, this principle does not work when reversed. To give positives first then give a negative (usually a 'but' comment) is not a helpful message. It is usually obvious that a 'but' is coming. The 'but' is what is listened for and the positives are ignored and certainly not trusted.

Follow up on your intervention

If your intervention has contributed to the child changing their behaviour it is important to notice and feed back that appreciation. This reinforces progress. If it hasn't there is now a problem that can be returned to and a new attempt to solve it can be made. If things haven't changed then more action or problem-solving needs to be made.

'I've noticed you have made it on time to the last few classes. I appreciate that. How have you managed it?'

'Things are definitely getting better since we last talked about this and I appreciate that. But it's not quite there yet. We need to have another think together about ensuring you make it to class on time.'

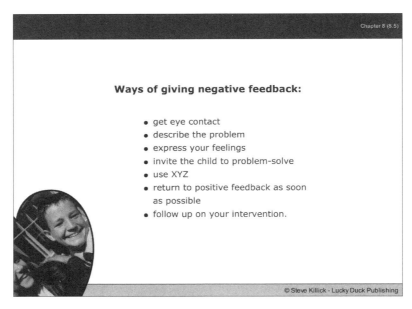

Slide 8.5

Consequences for inappropriate behaviour

Using negative feedback strategies may prevent or lessen the need for using sanctions and punishments. There will, of course, remain instances when children will not always behave as we would wish and their behaviour will be such that we have to take some kind of action. As discussed in Chapter Five, that children experience the consequences of their actions, both positive and negative, helps in the development of responsibility. However, traditional methods of dealing with behaviour that over-rely on reprimands and punishment are not always effective. Verbal reprimands may be met with indifference and punishments can breed resentment and ill feeling.

However, there are effective actions that increase the possibility of positive learning taking place and that help link behaviour to consequences. Again, they work best in the context of a positive relationship. Faber and Mazlish (1999) list several alternatives to the use of sanctions and punishments.

- Express your feelings strongly – without attacking character.

    'I am FURIOUS that you did not return at the time we agreed.'

- Restate your expectations clearly.

    'We agreed that would return by 2 o'clock. I expect you to stick to your word.'

- Show the person how to make amends.

    'I would like an apology to all those you inconvenienced through keeping them waiting.'

- Give the young person a choice.

    'This project work is important. You can either do it now or over the weekend. You choose.'

- Say it once then take action. Don't lecture or repeat yourself trying to find further reasons after you had made a request. If you say it once then take action, this helps a young person learn to listen, rather than switch off from the adult's voice. For example, a child was playing football in an inappropriate place and ignored an instruction to move. The teacher then walked over, picked up the ball and took it to where it could be kicked appropriately. This was done without producing any bad feeling in either teacher or child.

    Young person: 'Why have you locked all the art materials away?'

Teacher: 'Perhaps you can tell me why you think I might have done that?'

'Will, I said if you continued to talk in a way that was racist we would have to discuss it. Come and see me after the lesson, please.'

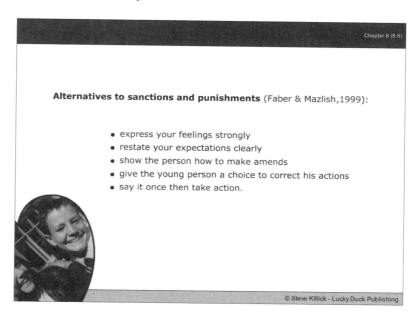

Alternatives to sanctions and punishments (Faber & Mazlish, 1999):

- express your feelings strongly
- restate your expectations clearly
- show the person how to make amends
- give the young person a choice to correct his actions
- say it once then take action.

© Steve Killick - Lucky Duck Publishing

Slide 8.6

Such interactions can be the beginning to a conversation between the teacher and child that can lead to a better understanding and a reduction of problem behaviours in the future.

A young person can learn much through experiencing the natural consequences of her action. However, for many, it may not be enough and then the use of problem-solving conversations, discussed in the next chapter, can be helpful. Consequences work best if they are immediate, proportionate to the offence and time-limited. Sometimes, informing parents is necessary, not as a punishment but simply because the behaviour is such that it is appropriate to inform them and possibly discuss with them how to respond. Consistency also helps yet this is difficult to apply. Some teachers will tend to use sanctions more than others. General guidelines for teachers developed by the school can be helpful.

However, if experiencing the consequences of our actions was enough to help us learn, we would have all learnt much more than we already know! It's not just consequences, it's how we think and feel about them that count. Also, different children have different learning styles. Some need clear direction and positive authority (rather than authoritarian responses), while others respond to sensitivity and encouragement.

The therapeutic reprimand

Reprimands, when necessary, are best when the focus is on learning. An adult can forcefully express her displeasure at a particular behaviour. This technique, adapted from Blanchard & Johnson (2004), is only effective if you are sure the child knows better and has control over her actions. It also must be used sparingly. If it is overused, the young person will soon learn to ignore it and to resent the individual whose only tool in managing behaviour is to elicit shame. A reprimand becomes therapeutic when it focuses on the problem behaviour and helps the child understand that she can act better. As always it is more effective if an 'audience effect' is reduced as much as possible.

- Describe the problem behaviour or the transgression of a 'rule'.

  'I saw you really try to stick your pencil in Richard's eye.'

- Describe any consequences, especially how it affects you. This may also include a strong expression of your feelings but not so forcefully expressed that it is threatening to the child. 'That behaviour is extremely dangerous. I do not know what made you do such a thing but I will not tolerate such dangerous behaviour in my class. I am FURIOUS that you did such a thing.'

- Having pointed out the problem, it is not useful to have the child wallow in negative feelings. This is a time to state your higher expectations of the child, or to explore how he might make amends. Your case is strengthened if you have examples of how the child has met your expectations previously and it can be useful to point this out. If you do not have examples then you do not know that the child is capable of better, which may indicate that a reprimand may not be effective.

   'I know that you are able to concentrate on your work and disregard distraction. You have worked well this morning already.'

- At this point it may be appropriate to listen to the child's point of view although it may not be forthcoming. If not then, explore ways that the child might make amends and/or ways of resolving the problem should it happen again (this might identify skills that the child needs to work on).

   'It is frustrating when someone winds you up but next time perhaps you could tell the person clearly that what he is doing is bothering you. If that doesn't work then let me know. Right now I would like you to apologise to Richard and return to your work.'

Results may take time – the importance of following up

To see changes in frequent and well established difficult behaviours may take time. Instant responses may often not be sufficient. The child may need to learn new skills such as a basic emotional vocabulary, emotional regulation or understanding and communicating with others. In such cases, following up is essential. For many children, knowing that certain behaviours will be followed up may be sufficient to help motivate them. For example, a child might want to avoid 'a boring talk' with a teacher. For those whose behaviour is not a question of lack of motivation but a skill deficit, such a follow-up is the opportunity to learn skills.

The act of following up on such behaviours is possibly more important and effective than the reliance on ever-increasing sanctions. Effective follow-up can be based on key skills already discussed such as reflective listening, and developed through the use of problem-solving and other skills (discussed later). The Follow-up Review, discussed in Chapter Five, can also be a useful tool.

Features of effective follow-up

- Find the right time and place to discuss an issue. If you or the young person is in a state of high emotional arousal, this makes a productive discussion less likely than when you are both calmer.

- Help the child be very clear what the problem is. It can be useful to either help the child clarify this or for you to explain the problem and what makes it a problem. 'Can you remember why I wanted to meet with you? I wanted to meet to discuss exactly what happened when you tried to attack Richard with a pencil.'

- Listen and explore the child's point of view. Reflective listening can help the child express what his side of the story is. It can help to understand this without condoning any problematic behaviour and increase your understanding of what the child may need. 'Can you tell me exactly what happened that led you to attack Richard?'

- When you have gained an understanding of the child's point of view, he may be more likely to listen to yours. Exploring his and your feelings may be important in this conversation. 'So, if I understand you right, Richard was winding you up and actually called you some pretty hurtful names. That could not have been at all easy to deal with and I guess you were angry. However, whatever he said does not justify an attack that may have caused a serious injury. You also said you were calling him names which may have contributed to the situation.'

- Explore how a repeat of this situation can be prevented in the discussion. It is helpful if the child can produce or agree to possible strategies, especially if they are realistic. Natural consequences may come into play here. If the child is unable to find a realistic strategy then techniques in the next chapter may be helpful. Remember, the key point is to explore future situations rather than get into argument over what has already happened. If there are disagreements about what happened then agree to disagree. 'What do you think you can do if Richard starts winding you up again? I like your idea of not listening to him. It's pointless fighting fire with fire and I've found it can help just to go and talk to someone else to really show it doesn't bother you. However, until I'm sure you can really manage not to get worked up I want you to sit on a different table.'

- Agree to meet again to review how it is going. 'We will talk again next week to see how it's going. If it's working well you can feel pleased with yourself for mastering a new skill. Maybe we can see about going back to that table. If not we can think about it together some more.'

Ensuring you do follow up is, of course, critical. If a child thinks the matter is forgotten he may lose some motivation. It is also important that the child is not left feeling excessively shamed, hurt, blamed or humiliated. If he can feel hopeful and helped then he can progress. If, when you follow up again, there has been success or, at least, no repetition of the problem, this becomes a time to give strong positive feedback. If it hasn't, it is not the place to reprimand but to further problem-solve. Some problems may take several conversations to work out.

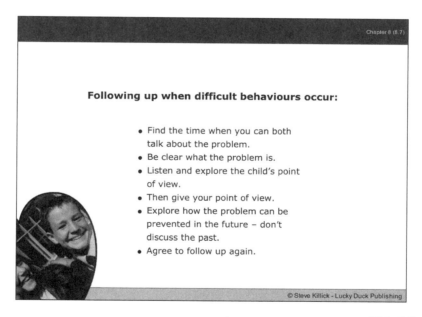

Slide 8.7

 See Exercise Two (Including Slide 8.8)

Building internal motivation

The feedback we give to young people can assist in building inner motivation. When young people (or adults as the principle applies equally to all) receive information about their competence and capabilities their confidence grows. They also become more receptive to learning about how they could do things better. This confidence fuels the internal motivation to achieve and succeed. The confidence to dream of what can be achieved and to feel one has the confidence to pursue this, to be able to persist through setbacks and overcome obstacles, is fundamental to the achievement of one's potential.

Too often criticism is rooted in making the child experience shame or anxiety in the hope that this will lead him to correct his actions ('If you don't learn your maths you won't get a good job, you will never amount to anything') yet this approach is often counter-productive and further de-motivates the child. He might think, 'If I can't succeed why should I try'. If positive feedback is given often and negative feedback is delivered in a way that respects the child's integrity and does not leave him feeling shamed, the internal motivation and confidence that is inherent in every child is enhanced. Ultimately, strong inner motivation will be more powerful than external feedback received yet the confidence to believe in one's own goals is built through interactions with others.

Painting pictures

Helping children focus on positive achievable futures is more useful than dwelling on past problems. Children vary in their capacity for thinking about the future, be that five minutes, five months or even five or more years hence. The skill in building inner mental pictures for the child of what is going to happen can help her learn planning skills, manage transitions (both in the short-term such as moving from one activity or class to another or major transitions such as moving from primary to secondary school) and lessen the anxiety created by the unknown. Helping children imagine what things can be like helps them paint internal pictures in their minds of what the future holds, and helps in developing the capacity to dream about achieving those goals. It is about being clear about where you want to get to, having a clear goal. Internal motivation comes from having internal goals in which one can believe what can be achieved.

Summary of Chapter Eight

- Motivation plays a key role in learning, behaviour and development. How we give feedback to children over their performance can increase or decrease their motivation.

- Effective feedback is more positive than negative and is behaviour specific. It can be given in many ways, encourages choice and cooperation.

- Instant feedback reinforces motivation and learning and helps build confidence in developing inner motivation.

- A focus on positives makes it easier to address negative behaviours and poor motivation. When this is done clear communication, reflective listening and problem-solving can all play a part.

Exercise One – Reflecting on Feedback

This exercise aims to increase participants' awareness of the power of receiving positive feedback in the shape of compliments and appreciations.

In pairs, ask participants to share when somebody last gave you some positive feedback or descriptive praise either at work, at home or elsewhere.

Reflective discussion with the whole group.

Ask them, in pairs, to discuss how this made them feel and what effects it had on subsequent behaviour.

How far back did they have to go for the last bit of positive feedback – a day, a week, a month? Longer?

What makes good feedback?

Does it affect mood and motivation?

Do we get enough positive feedback? Are there dangers in too much?

Was Mark Twain overstating the case when he said, 'I can live for two months on a good compliment'?

From this, the discussion could move into considering how and when participants give positive feedback to others and to explore the relationship between giving and receiving positive feedback.

Exercise Two – How to Respond?

This exercise aims to help participants think about how they may respond to a number of undesirable behaviours.

Divide the large group into groups of about four or five and ask them to consider what, out of the range of ways described for dealing difficult behaviours, they might think would be the most appropriate for each of the behaviours listed in Slide 8.8.

It may be useful to remind the groups of the main possibilities for intervention from which to draw on and who would be best placed to give this intervention: ancillary staff, teacher, form tutor, year tutor, or head or deputy head.

> Giving negative feedback.
>
> Alternatives to sanctions and punishments.
>
> The therapeutic reprimand.
>
> Following up when difficult behaviours occur.

Each group works through the behaviours and decides which would be the most appropriate way of responding. After 15-20 minutes, return to the large group and go through the behaviours, one at a time, exploring what each group decided and why.

What would be the most appropriate response to the following behaviours?

- Verbal abuse directed towards an adult.
- Running off the school premises and being found just outside the gates.
- Hitting another child hard on the arm.
- Trying to repeatedly distract another child from working by mouthing to them.
- Making a threat to beat up another child later.
- Stealing a personal item.
- Not attending a lesson.
- Racial abuse towards another child.
- Spitting at another child as they enter class.
- Throwing a ball hard at another child in playground.

Slide 8.8

Chapter Nine

Problem-solving Conversations

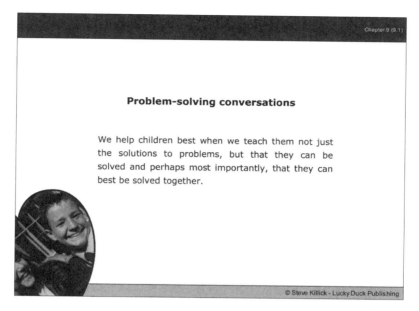

Slide 9.1

Not many people would want to be part of a society (or for that matter, a family, a workplace or even a school) where everybody did exactly as they were told. Such a culture could only be described as authoritarian. Nor would many want a society where everybody could do as they liked without thought for others. We have evolved to be best able to meet our individual needs through working together to solve problems and working towards shared goals that advance us. Yet this is a complex process and one in which we do not always succeed. A key skill in developing emotional literacy is being able to solve problems with others, to know how to negotiate, compromise and invent novel solutions together. Education develops problem-solving skills and there is much to be gained through the solving of academic problems, be that a maths formulation or learning to plan and organise how work is tackled. These skills can assist in learning how to solve emotional and social problems. However, learning how to solve these problems directly can give children invaluable skills. Indeed, it helps them with the problems that most directly concern them and how they get on with others. It is this aspect of problem-solving that this chapter is directly concerned with. Problem-solving is a thinking skill, and the use of such skills is further explored in Chapter Ten.

Much of growing up is concerned with learning how to deal with feelings and get along with others. Children have plenty of opportunities in their lives to develop skills in this area and work out their differences with others, with their siblings, their friends and their parents. Arguments with parents, rivalries with siblings and peers and the making and breaking of friendships are offering children the chance to learn these skills. Some learn these skills readily but others may struggle. No one learns without making many mistakes. However, how adults interact with children can assist greatly in this learning process.

The skills of reflective listening can help a child think more clearly and facilitate his own problem-solving skills. Feedback can give the child clear information about how his actions affect others and reinforce and strengthen what he is getting right and help him think of new things to do. These are the foundation of problem-solving skills upon which further ways of thinking about and solving problems can be built. There are plenty of formal and informal ways of developing problem-solving skills, from formal problem-solving as a class to finding ways of sorting out disputes, both when children are in dispute with other children and when in dispute with adults.

This chapter presents a number of different problem-solving strategies related to emotional development and literacy. These strategies contain many common features and can be used interchangeably. In describing them, the purpose is to make explicit how problems can be solved, for we help children best, not when we give them answers or solutions for problems, but when we let them know that problems can be solved. The different strategies are illustrated in Slide 9.2.

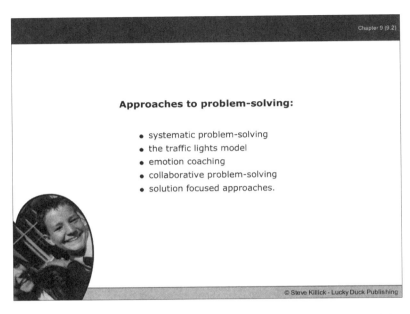

Slide 9.2

These approaches can be used formally in the class and during activities such as Circle Time. The strategies can be used when working with a whole class moving systematically through the steps, or they can be used flexibly and informally in brief conversations with individual pupils. These skills are also useful in communicating with parents over difficulties their children may be having.

Life is a series of challenges, demands and problems, both big and small. Being able to master them helps to give a sense of confidence and competence. The human brain is a wonderful piece of apparatus for solving problems and it continually generates ideas about what to do. However, we can lack confidence in our ability or ideas, or possibly rush to carry out solutions without thinking through what the consequences of our actions may be. Some children won't get the opportunity to develop confidence in using these skills. Children's lives are full of problems and they need to have a way of learning how to solve these problems. Children will do much better if they know they can solve problems rather than have problems solved for them. This does not mean leaving them to sort these problems out alone, as they benefit from adult support and confidence in learning ways of solving problems. Social problems especially give children the opportunity to develop problem-solving skills for themselves by using other people as sources of help. Often when children have problems adults will offer advice and solutions too readily; the child is told what to do. It does not help a child to be told their problem is easy and all they need to do is whatever the adult thinks is a good idea at the time. This often frustrates the child rather than helps. The adult may also be frustrated that their advice, offered with good intent, is not followed (they may often think to themselves that the child just never listens or is just not motivated). It is better for both teacher and child that problems are explored, clarified and possibly redefined together before solutions are suggested. The adult and child can work together to generate lots of creative solutions. The person with the problem then has the responsibility of choosing a solution that might work for him and can use any advice appropriately. The child can try out something new and evaluate how effective it is and if it doesn't work, try to find another possibility.

When children solve their problems too easily

We are all natural problem-solvers and many of a child's behaviours result from his attempts to solve the problems that they have at any particular moment. The child who hits another child in response to name-calling is often attempting to solve the problem that they have when they feel insulted. When a child says, 'I want,' something, it maybe an indicator that she has a problem and the object she wants is now seen as the solution to that problem or need. What is not so often seen is how her solutions may breed new problems and she can best meet her needs through working with others. However, it is in the nature of problem-solving that even good solutions can create unforeseen and new problems that will need to be solved.

Teachers can have conversations with children that might facilitate the child's own solution or to come up with a collaborative answer. Problem-solving generates both creative and critical thinking involving thinking about what is desired and what is possible. Problem-solving also develops linguistic and reasoning skills. Teachers will be familiar with problem-solving strategies and will commonly use the strategy of systematic problem-solving. This technique has been practised for many years in many different situations, including schools. It has been described by Brandes and Phillips (1979) in the excellent source book of ideas for working with groups, *The Gamesters' Handbook* and is often described as 'brainstorming'. However, it is rarely used as effectively as it could as a problem-solving technique and is more commonly used for the much more mundane activity of making a list. It is with familiarity of the steps that the teacher can find many ways to use this technique creatively.

Systematic problem-solving

The following stages represent a step-by-step approach to tackling a problem. This approach is particularly useful for dealing with social and learning based problems. It can be helpful to become familiar with the distinct steps involved in the process and to use this in dealing with complex problems. Familiarity with the steps makes it much easier to use the skills informally.

The six steps are:

1. **Define the problem** The aim is to get a shared agreement and clear picture of what exactly the problem is. Often there are different perspectives to a problem. A teacher might have a problem because a student has not done her homework. The student might have the problem that she doesn't have somewhere to do her homework. This is the problem that the child needs help with rather than to be burdened with the teacher's problem as well. If there is shared definition that the difficulty is, say, how the child can find somewhere to do the work then the process of finding a solution can begin.

2. **Generate ideas about what to do** This is the creative process of thinking about all the things that might possibly be done that might solve the problem. It is important to accept all the ideas that are suggested. Often children may be reluctant to offer ideas for fear that they will be criticised as impractical or dismissed altogether. We are all capable of dismissing our ideas as not worth trying as we think to ourselves, 'That will never work'. When we do this we close down our own creativity as ideas that at first seem impractical may have the germ of a very practical solution. To help facilitate children to produce ideas it can be useful to write all ideas down without any critical evaluation, to offer some suggestions yourself or ask what the person thinks somebody else, a friend or someone they admire, might do in that situation. Writing down all the ideas sends a very strong message that they are being taken seriously. If the child who can't find a place to do her homework suggests that she doesn't do the homework at all, write this suggestion down but invite her to keep thinking of other strategies.

Often children will need practice before they begin to have the confidence that their ideas are valid. Our emotions can also block our creativity. A child who feels very angry may want to hit someone and until that idea is acknowledged it can't be moved past. Accepting it makes it then possible to think of other ideas, for example, writing a letter. Unusual ideas (thinking 'outside of the box') are very acceptable at this point and should be encouraged. It doesn't mean they will be acted upon.

Younger children will often find it hard to keep more than one option in mind and will often want to leap into action right away. For children in the early years of schooling it may be enough just to have two options to consider. Older children will, of course, be able to deal with far more alternatives.

3. **Critically evaluate ideas** Once a list has been generated that might contain some feasible ideas it is time to think through some of them. Sometimes ideas can be grouped together; some ideas might be dismissed easily at this point. To help evaluate ideas it can be useful to ask questions that help children think things through: that link actions with consequences. For instance, 'If you do that what would happen next?' or, 'How would others respond?' The teacher might add their perspective, for example, 'I guess from your point of view it would be great not to do your homework, but that would be difficult for me to accept. I can't evaluate how you are learning and it would not be fair on the others.'

From all these ideas select the ones which are worth trying and discard those not worth pursuing or that no one wants to discuss.

4. **Select a solution** From the possibilities generated that are the most feasible select one to try out. If necessary develop an action plan. The child needs to have commitment to try it out so the more he is involved in the selection process and the final choice the better. It is important that any solution fits with the school's values and beliefs about what is acceptable behaviour.

5. **Try it out.**

6. **Evaluation** Arrange a follow-up where you can hear about what has happened and whether the problem has been resolved. If it has worked positive feedback is clearly in order. Remember that sometimes solutions breed new problems so there might be new problems to be solved. If it hasn't worked, it does not mean the process has been unsuccessful and should be abandoned. It is better to see what has been learned. It is a process that needs determination and persistence. With repeated use may come new understanding or definitions of problems or more creative and thoughtful solutions.

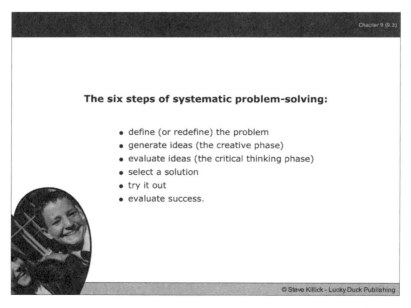

Slide 9.3

Systematic problem-solving may be used with a class to help teach problem-solving skills and working together, for instance, how to solve a problem as a group. It may be used to solve problems that the class are facing as a whole and can be used to tackle particular social situations such as:

- Resisting peer pressure (What could you do if someone wanted you to take drugs/skip school?)

- Friendship skills (A friend tells you that they are really unhappy, what do you do to help?)

- Conflict resolution (Two old friends have argued over a hurtful comment one of them made to the other. They both want you as their friend and for you not to like the other one. What can you do?)

When familiar with the problem-solving steps, the class could work in small groups to discuss these problems. Discussion of various social approaches to tricky social problems can help build new social skills. Teenagers, particularly, enjoy trying to solve these problems as they face them regularly and if they feel their ideas will not be ridiculed. They will also be able to add new situations to try out and think about what they might do. The focus is on thinking things through and it is important not to start evaluating their solutions as good or bad. It is better to think through the costs and benefits of each solution or if a particular action was used then what would happen next. It is the process of thinking about the complexities of the issues, how others might think or feel, to be able to see alternatives and possibilities that is important, not the end result. Activity sheets can be used to help prompt children and some examples are given in the exercise section. The approach can also be used with individual children to help them solve problems they are facing, particularly those related to school.

Formal problem-solving with the whole class

Faber & Mazlish (1995) describe how this technique can be used with a class as a whole. A class was struggling with the issue of talking over each other and putting each other down, and it was leading to increased conflict and unhappiness. Nobody liked the situation but it was hard for anybody to stop behaving in this way. The teacher invited the class to think of things they could do to stop talking across each other and to be more considerate of each other. The teacher then wrote down all the ideas on the board without evaluating any of them, sometimes just helping to clarify them. These included such things as:

1. Have a 'no interruptions' rule.

2. If you are afraid you will forget your idea, write it down.

3. Anyone who interrupts gets a zero.

4. Have a 'No Put Down' rule.

5. If you say, 'That's stupid,' you can't talk for the rest of the week.

6. Class makes up a list of things they can say instead of put downs.

After a list was generated, the class debated it. Some members felt that some of the ideas were too punitive but the last idea of having more respectful ways of speaking instead of put downs was seen as a very good idea and the following list was generated from their ideas. It was stuck up on the wall to help remind the class what they might say instead. The list was often referred to by a class eager to learn new ways of communicating.

Instead of Put-Downs	⟶	Use Respectful Talk
That's stupid	⟶	I don't see it that way.
That's not true	⟶	Where did you get your information?
You forgot to say	⟶	I'd like to add.
What a stupid idea	⟶	Could you explain how that would work?
You're wrong	⟶	Here's another way to look at it.

Informal problem-solving one-to-one

A boy in Year 6 frequently was made angry and upset by another member of the class who had many ways of 'winding him up'. This boy's response was to retaliate and often hit out. His teacher found a time, not long after an incident where he had to intervene to make the situation safe, to open a problem-solving conversation.

Teacher: It looks to me that Mark annoys you a lot.

Student: Yeah, he's always making fun of me or my brother.

Teacher: I can understand why that would make you pretty angry but I can't let you hit him. Could we think about other things you might do when he's annoying you?

Student: OK.

Teacher: Great, let's think of as many things as possible. Got any ideas?

Student: No.

Teacher: It's not easy. I remember someone a bit like you who just pretended to go deaf whenever someone tried to wind him up. He found it had a pretty good effect. (Jots that idea down.)

Student: (Laughs) Sometimes I just think about something else and he doesn't bother me at all.

Teacher: Hey, so ignoring him can work sometimes. Let's write that one down. Hey, how about if you got my attention when he starts doing it?

Student: Maybe, would you move him to another table?

Teacher: That's an idea too. (Teacher writes both ideas down).

The conversation continued like this for a few more minutes. The teacher then summarised some of the ideas and asked what the student thought of them. Together they discussed all the strategies and the student decided to try one where he would just repeat back what was said to him. If he felt himself getting annoyed he would walk away. The teacher encouraged the child to try it out and said he would be interested to know what happened.

 See Exercise One

The traffic lights model

The steps of the problem-solving model are broken down into three clear steps in the traffic lights model that is particularly useful for children with impulse control difficulties. However, as described by Rae (1998) and Stallard (2002), it can be useful for a much wider group, especially those who get frustrated and angry. It can be used as an anger management model. Steps can be rehearsed using activity sheets. There are three concrete steps so the visual image of traffic lights provides a strong visual prompt to stop and think. Some classes display a colourful picture of the traffic lights to act as a constant cue to remember to think before acting.

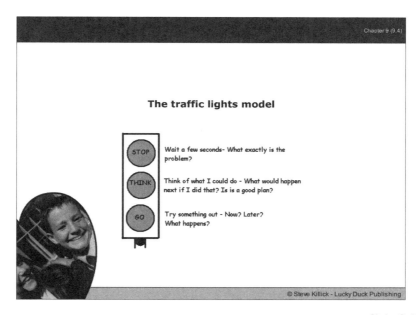

The traffic lights model

STOP — Wait a few seconds- What exactly is the problem?

THINK — Think of what I could do - What would happen next if I did that? Is is a good plan?

GO — Try something out - Now? Later? What happens?

Slide 9.4

Keeping conversations focused on solving problems

In using the traffic lights model, or indeed any of the approaches to problem-solving, the following strategies can assist young people in using their own problem-solving skills.

Don't rush to answer questions (including your own)

Teachers will know the importance of not hurrying to answer questions that children ask but reflecting the question back in a way that enables the child or others to answer it. It's also important when asking questions to give time for the child to compose an answer. It can often take five to ten seconds for a child to process a question and think of how to answer it. In practice, however, teachers do not often give this length of time and expect a response within two to three seconds. Children need time to work things out.

Help thinking through

When evaluating ideas it can be good to think through both the positive and negative consequences. Asking about what would happen next helps a child build predictive skills. Questions can help elicit both positive and negative effects of actions, and by looking at both outcomes one may be more likely to reach a more balanced decision. For instance, it may make a person feel better if she avoided tackling something difficult with a friend but the negative consequence may be that the friend gets upset. It would be very common to feel ambivalent over any particular course of action. To explore that ambivalence can help a person be clearer about the issues, more aware of possible pitfalls as well as advantages and thus make a positive choice. Useful questions that help think through and link actions to consequences are:

'If you did that, what would happen next?'

'How do you think that would affect ...?'

'What would be the good things in doing that?'

'What would be some of the less good things if you did that?'

It can be useful to use summaries to reflect back what a person is thinking:

'So, on one hand doing that has the advantages of... but on the other hand it might also mean... What do you think you will do?'

In the questions above, the term 'less good things' is used in preference to 'bad things' as this might be heard as a critical or evaluative comment that might create resistance. Exploring ambivalence about decisions is useful in facilitating motivation and a key feature of motivational interviewing (Miller & Rollnick, 2002). The use of words and language is important. Persuasion, or giving solutions, is avoided unless the person is clearly seeking advice. The focus is on exploring ambivalence and then letting the person make her own choice. Many young people will make a decision on what they say to themselves as opposed to what others may say to them.

Depersonalise the problem

When a child has to think about new ideas or strategies they can find it hard to think in ways that they haven't done before. To help generate new ways the child can be asked to think as if they were someone else. This might be someone they know, or admire, or of a certain profession – an engineer, a politician or a musician. People have been found to be more creative simply by being asked to imagine that they were creative people. To then ask them questions as if they were someone else can open up new possibilities.

Use resources that might be available

You can assist children in solving problems by using resources that are available. Obvious examples are the Internet or the library. Also, they should be encouraged to talk to other people, such as friends or parents, to hear different views.

Keep optimistic about the child's ability to solve problems

Some problems are very difficult and answers may not come straight away. To find the solution that works for that child may take time. Encourage persistence to stick with the problem and keep optimistic that the child will find a solution that works for him. Frustration with difficulties or dismissing the difficulty may send the message that the child is not competent to work it out.

Keep motivation high

It doesn't help a child to hear that a problem she is dealing with is easy. It's useful to acknowledge the struggle involved rather than saying that the solution is easy. If children anticipate failure, their anxiety can only increase if they hear that they are going to fail at something most people find easy. At the same time, paint a picture of what things will be like when the problem is solved, 'What do you think you will feel when you have managed it?'

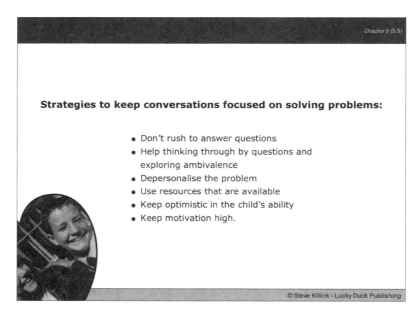

Slide 9.5

Emotion coaching

John Gottman (1998) devised a way of helping parents manage strong, negative emotions in their children with the aim to help children regulate and master these emotional states for themselves. Very similar to systematic problem-solving, this method can be adapted for use in the school setting by teachers. This method, called 'emotion coaching', helped children trust their own feelings, regulate their own emotions and solve problems. Gottman, a pioneer in emotional intelligence research in adults and children, found that this technique could help self-esteem, social confidence and positive learning attitudes. He identified four different types of approach to emotions in their children that parents have. There may be similarities with teachers' attitudes to dealing with emotional problems in the school. We can all show features of these different attitudes towards different problems at different times or situations.

1. **Dismissing** These parents would see their children's feelings as unimportant or trivial and pay little attention to them. They may see negative emotions as harmful or a sign of poor adjustment. They would want to try and fix things quickly. An effect of this is that the child may come to learn that his feelings are somehow wrong or invalid and that there is something wrong with him. Such a child may be poor at regulating his own emotions.

2. **Disapproving** Similar to dismissing parents but more likely to judge and criticise the child's emotional expression. These parents are likely to assume the child is manipulating them through negative emotions. It is easy for them to get caught up in power struggles that can place an overemphasis on compliance and authority. The effects on children are very similar to the above.

3. **Laissez-faire** The laissez-faire parent freely accepts all of a child's emotions and will offer comfort but they will not help the child problem-solve or set limits for the child. They might believe that the only way to get rid of negative problems is to let them out until they dissipate. Children of these parents have trouble concentrating, regulating feelings and forming friendships with other children.

4. **Emotion coaches** Parents who help children manage emotions see negative emotions as an opportunity to get close to the child. They can tolerate being with an angry, fearful or sad child and will not be impatient with the emotion. They respect the child's emotion but see moments of emotional expression as opportunities to comfort, help problem-solve and label feelings, also to set limits and offer guidance on regulating emotions. Children who experience this kind of parenting are more likely to develop emotional literacy.

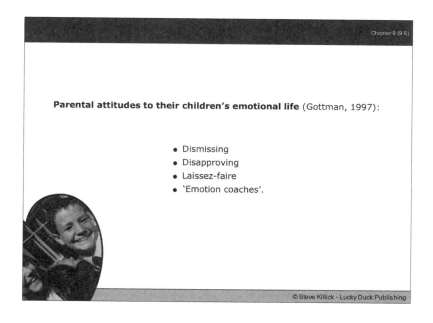

Slide 9.6

137

Gottman identifies five steps in emotion coaching that call upon skills of reflective listening, building motivation and problem-solving:

1. Become aware of a young person's emotion whilst also being aware of your own feelings. Recognise that the expression of emotion may be an opportunity for communication and learning.

2. Use reflective and empathic listening to help the young person verbally label their emotions. Look for opportunities to validate the feelings expressed.

3. Help the young person to problem-solve through defining the problem, generating ideas and evaluating them. Yet, at the same time, set limits for behaviour – this is particularly important for children who are learning what the limits are. As previously discussed the teacher can help the child accept the emotion but limit any problem behaviours. This helps the child learn that the feeling is not the problem but their behaviour might be. For instance, a teacher might say, 'You're angry that Richard took your game from you. I would be too. But it is not OK to call him horrible names. What could you do instead?'

4. Goals and solutions can then be considered. Ideas can be generated through writing down lists or discussion. Encourage the child to select an option to try out. Try to prevent yourself from imposing your ideas too readily. If you do have particular concerns these can be raised, for example, 'The problem is if you get up to leave the classroom a lot, other children will want to know why and I will have to do something about it.' If the child makes the final choice within the limits defined she will be more motivated to follow it through as well as gaining confidence in her decision making abilities.

5. Follow up to see what happened. If it wasn't successful the process can be repeated. If it was, the successful outcome is reinforced and the person complimented on their problem-solving skills.

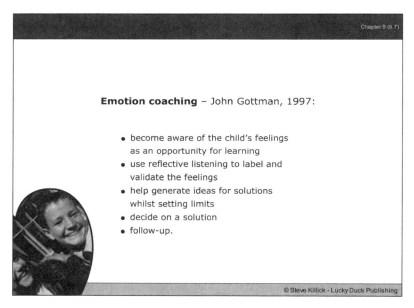

Slide 9.7

Collaborative problem-solving

Collaborative Problem-solving is a method developed by Greene (2005) to help children who have problems in dealing with frustration that can make them explosive in temperament. There may be deficits in thinking, social and emotional regulation or language skills (including the lack of an emotional vocabulary) that lead them to be over-irritable and unable to deal well with change.

Collaborative problem-solving is where the adult and child work together to solve the problem. There are three distinct steps to the approach that can help children develop problem-solving skills to deal with the situations that frustrate them. Again, as with other approaches, these conversations may not sort the problems out in one go and it may take many conversations until the child is able to use these skills by himself. The stages use the skills of reflective listening, defining the problem and inviting the child to problem-solve with you. They can be used when the child is in a state of distress or frustration over something or when he is calmer to look at how he might solve the problem.

- Stage One – Empathy and reassurance. If a child is frustrated and attempting to solve the problem inappropriately, empathy and reflective listening can be used to communicate to and reassure the child that you understand his difficulty. In the case of the child who snatches another child's pencil, the teacher might first respond by feeding back to the child that she understands what the child's problem is, 'I can see you need a pencil to do your work,' or perhaps, 'I see you just grabbed Bill's pencil. What's up?' The purpose is to help the child define what the problem is.

- Stage Two – Re-define the problem. This stage helps the adult to define exactly what the problem is and that the child's solution to it may have created new problems. Redefining the problem can help the child become more aware of the needs of others and increase his skills in empathy.

'OK, you need a pencil and the first one you saw was Bill's. The problem is that Bill needed it too and when you grab it like that, it's going to annoy him.'

- Stage Three – Invite the child to problem-solve. Here the teacher invites the child to think of new ways to solve the problem using the stages of systematic problem-solving. 'Having a pencil is important for work. Can we just think of ways you can get one for yourself without annoying someone?' The child is asked if he has any ideas first before the teacher makes any suggestions. If the child can't think of any then the teacher can give some alternatives and ask what the child thinks of those. This process helps the child see that alternatives exist and can learn how to think these ideas through. The child can choose a new option and if it works, the situation is changed. If it doesn't, it gives the opportunity to try again.

Greene's model succinctly combines many of the communication skills that help facilitate emotional intelligence and build new thinking skills. With expertise it is particularly useful for children who may be experiencing emotional and behavioural difficulties.

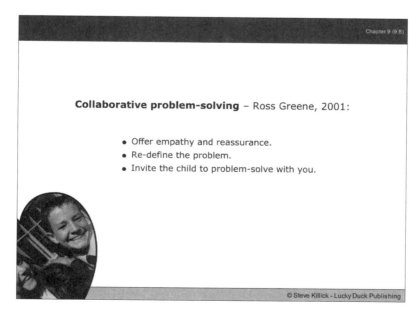

Slide 9.8

Solution focused approaches

'My interest is in the future because I'm going to spend the rest of my life there.'

Charles Kettering

Understanding or re-defining a problem is not always a necessary prerequisite for solving it. Finding a solution, rather than focusing on fault finding, blame or what has gone wrong in the past, is one of the most important principles in emotional competence. There are many useful strategies that are based on solution orientated psychology and therapies and many of these ideas have been applied in school settings (Rhodes and Ajmal, 1995, Ajmal & Rees, 2001). They are also particularly useful in working with parents. The focus is on ensuring the child or parent concentrates on what works rather than what doesn't work and builds on strengths and competencies in finding solutions. Often, when we try and deal with a problem we repeatedly deal with it in a way that doesn't work, we just do more of the same. If shouting doesn't work, a person's solution may be just to shout louder, meaning she's become stuck with just one approach. An emphasis on the past and on details of the problem is not necessary for the development of a solution (Rhodes & Ajmal, 1995). Solution focused approaches aim to help people find other ways of thinking. There are many skills and types of questioning involved in the solution focused approach, some of which are summarised here.

Look for exceptions to the problem

When problems exist, there are always exceptions, that is, times when the problem behaviour does not occur. For instance, the habitually late child will have times when he does arrive on time. It can be informative to be curious about when problems don't happen just as much as when they do happen. These exceptions, or unique outcomes, can tell us about what might help when they do occur. Often problems are related to power struggles over somebody not doing what somebody else wants. When this happens people often get into more polarised positions and they find it harder to understand each other and be flexible in their thinking. Also, problems can dominate and distort our thinking. A parent may say to herself, 'He never does his homework,' or, 'He is always watching the television.'

This kind of thinking can blind us to seeing when there are exceptions and if we can't see this then we are unlikely to reinforce and build on such situations. Yet we might learn much that might help if we ask ourselves why this person is managing well at this time or what might be done to make this more likely to happen.

Teacher: You say that Mark is finding maths homework difficult and not spending much time on it. Are there times when he is able to manage it even if it only for a little while?

or

When was the last time he was doing it without any difficulty?

Be future focused

This is about focusing on the future, on where the child or parent wants to get to and on working out the quickest way there. An important intervention is to help families or an individual realise achievable goals to aim for. The emphasis is on the future rather than the past or even the present. Small changes are significant. Small changes can introduce further changes to a system as they ripple through the system. Minimal intervention is sometimes all that is necessary to facilitate the client's own problem-solving skill.

The task is to collaborate with the child to help him focus on resources and solutions not problems and on success rather than failure.

Problem free talk

A problem can lead to a conversation. A problem in learning, behaviour or in how people feel will often initiate a discussion about what to do. Sometimes the child, parent or teacher may enter the conversation feeling they are going to be blamed, such a fear might lead to defensiveness. Problem free talk might lessen such fears. It also has another very important function – it can locate strengths and resources in the person that they might be able to use to help sort out the difficulty. A teacher decided to have a conversation with a child in a maths class who was becoming increasingly disruptive. The child was expecting to be told off but the teacher wanted to find out how he could regain the child's motivation for working. He began by saying that, as he didn't know the boy well, he wanted to know what things he liked doing. The young person spoke about his interest in football. The teacher was interested in what the boy thought was needed for someone to be a good footballer. Among the ideas that emerged was the idea of achieving goals and working as a team. The boy became more excited as his ideas were listened to and the teacher could see ways of talking about the lesson as a place that needed teamwork and cooperation and the importance of being clear of what the goals of the lesson were. When problems in class were discussed it was in the nature of what could happen in future classes, not what the boy had done in the past. The teacher used the football metaphor and could genuinely compliment the boy on his skills. The child left the conversation clearer about what things would help him learn and more motivated to cooperate.

Conversations with children, and equally with parents, can help identify skills and competences that can transform areas of difficulty or potential conflict. Having curiosity about areas of a person's life where things are going well, such as interests and hobbies, work, things they like doing, aspirations or things they are looking forward to such as holidays, can not only bring forth a change in how that person communicates but also give valuable information about how problems may be solved. Recognising these strengths makes it much easier to explore change.

Coping talk

If people are experiencing difficulties, coping talk reframes a perspective from looking at people as having difficulties in coping to looking at how people are coping with difficulties. The child who thinks he can't do something after repeated effort may feel there is no point in making further effort and may eventually give up. The child may respond to an acknowledgement of his persistence in the face of difficulties rather than just be encouraged to further effort. Coping talk focuses on what the child has done already to deal with problems. Recognition of this can make it easier to acknowledge frustrations and can help reinforce and strengthen appropriate problem-solving strategies. A teacher met with a child and his mother after the child had been falling behind with his work. The child's father had died two years ago and conversation with the mother soon became filled with some of the financial and housing difficulties that had dominated their life since the loss. The teacher was able to empathise with the difficulties and both compliment and comment on how well the child had done in the face of these difficulties and how schoolwork had played a part. She asked, 'What did you do to stop things from getting worse?' It became possible to think about what things had helped in the past and then ideas and solutions emerged about how both the school and the parent could support each other and the child.

Using rating scales

Solution focused approaches place great importance on the value of giving genuine compliments and noticing where things are going well. The use of rating scales is also important. By asking a child to rate herself on a continuum of one to ten enables the child to give a fine discrimination of how they are doing and to consider small steps that might lead to change. One teacher asked a class to rate themselves at how good they felt that day with one being very low and unhappy and ten being really high spirited and feeling great about themselves. In pairs the children shared with a partner about why they were at that number, what stopped them being just one number below and what they might do to get one number higher up the scale.

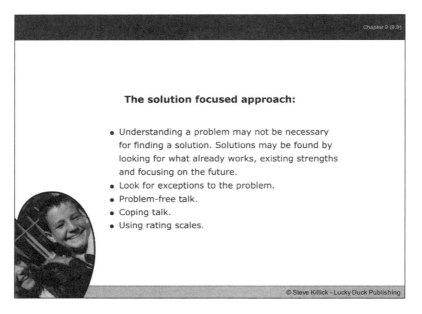

Slide 9.9

144   See Exercise Two

Solution focused approaches, like the other problem-solving strategies, rely on the judicious use of reflective and empathic listening and giving feedback, especially with the focus on the future. The techniques briefly described here can be integrated into all sorts of conversations where problems or difficulties can be addressed in a way that is positive, non-blaming and sees that problems can be solved. They put an emphasis on helping a child value and utilise her own problem-solving skills and to develop those skills to apply in many situations. They are also specialist skills in their own right that can take time and practice to be applied with high levels of expertise. Such approaches may become part of a school's ethos and approach to dealing with the many problems that emerge in the school setting.

Summary of Chapter Nine

- There are always problems to be solved in life and children face multiple problems that impact on their learning every day – not only in their work but also in their social and emotional lives.

- Reflective listening and feedback can help a child clarify their thinking to be become more effective problem-solvers. Beyond these skills there are a number of strategies to help such as:

- Systematic problem-solving – A six-stage model to help generate ideas, select from alternatives and develop a plan.

- The traffic lights model – A three-stage model of 'stop, think and go' to help children develop self-control.

- Emotion coaching – This model uses the systematic problem-solving model to help children develop emotional regulation.

- Collaborative problem-solving – A model developed for children with explosive temperaments and used with children with emotional and behavioural difficulties and helpful in developing social skills and other aspects of emotional intelligence.

- Solution focused approaches – These put the emphasis on what the person is already doing right and build on strengths and competencies to solve problems.

Exercise One –
Applying Problem-solving Strategies

This exercise aims to develop skills and provide practice in using the systematic problem-solving model.

Generate a list of problems that might be solved using the systematic problem-solving method. Encourage the group to think widely including not just situations where it might be used in the classroom but also in discussions with parents or with colleagues. It could be used to tackle whole school issues like bullying. The purpose is to help participants see some of the issues that they deal with in their working life as problems that can be solved. It is useful to get a range of problems from quite straightforward everyday ones to more complex challenges that people may have been struggling with for some years.

Part One

Allocate the participants into small groups of about five. Ask them to think of a problem that they would like to solve as a group. This is not a role-play so it should be a problem they can work on together as a group. This may range from a problem an individual has, such as 'How could I help X to concentrate on his work more effectively' or a whole school issue such as 'how could we make the transitions between classes easier?'

It can be useful to emphasise that it is easier to solve a problem if it is 'positively framed' rather than 'negatively framed'. A positive frame puts an emphasis on what could we done (i.e. 'how could we do something rather than how can we stop or not do something).

An ideal problem for this exercise would be one that would have real benefits if solved. Each group should be given 5-10 minutes to find a satisfactory problem to work on together. It is important to ensure each group has a realistic and well-defined problem before beginning Part Two.

Part Two

Having defined the problem, the task for the group is to find ways of solving the problem by working systematically through the stages to the point where they have an action plan of things they may do to solve the problem.

The group should appoint a facilitator who guides the group through the process. The facilitator writes ideas down, preferably on a piece of flipchart paper and might point out if the group is diverting from the task, for instance, evaluating ideas when they should be generating ideas.

The groups should be given about half an hour for this task.

Part Three

Each group presents to the others the problem they were working with, some of the ideas they generated but did not develop and the ideas they developed into an action plan.

Reflection questions may include:

Do you think you have developed a plan that might be worth trying?

How could you evaluate its effectiveness?

How did you find the process of working through the steps?

Note

Groups may vary considerably in their ability to work through the steps; some will find it easy and have people who are familiar with the technique. Some will find it does not come easily and is quite alien to their own problem-solving strategies.

If you anticipate it may be difficult and you are sufficiently comfortable with the process, you can work through the stages with the large group before they attempt to do it themselves. Alternatively, if there are people familiar with the model, ensure they are distributed around the groups and possibly act as an facilitator.

Exercise Two –
Contrasting Problem-solving Approaches

This exercise aims to help thinking about some of these approaches that may be applied in the classroom and to help evaluate and compare and contrast some of the approaches.

Divide the participants into small groups and ask each group to generate a list of problems that commonly occur where children may have difficulties in learning or behaviour that have an emotional basis.

After generating a list of between five and ten problems consider which approach may be most helpful for these particular issues and what any obstacles might be to using them. The group can also reflect on what strategies are frequently used (individuals will, after all, be using problem-solving strategies all the time).

A whole-group discussion may follow reflecting on some of the issues that emerged in small groups.

Chapter Ten

The Kindling of Curiosity – Thinking Skills and Emotional Intelligence

> I cannot teach anybody anything, I can only make them think.

Socrates

> Life does not consist mainly, or even largely, of facts and happenings. It consists mainly of the storm of thought that is forever flowing through one's head.

Mark Twain

Intelligence is about our cognitive abilities, that is, our ability to think, to analyse, to recall, to predict and to calculate. Emotional intelligence is about our capacity to think in these ways about emotions; to be able to recognise and consider our own emotions and that of others and use our insights with wisdom and compassion. Developing emotional intelligence means learning thinking skills specific to feelings.

Helping children learn thinking skills is increasingly seen as vital to the education process. Education is not about learning knowledge and facts but about learning how to be able to think about the information we receive, to be able to analyse, discriminate and evaluate. This transformation from learning knowledge to learning thinking skills perhaps reflects the changing context of schools and society. Our model of education and schooling was developed in a time when society was information poor and relationship rich. That culture has changed, we now live in a time that is information rich but is now, perhaps, relationship poor (Parks et al 2003).

Thinking skills are often seen as a way that more able students can be developed in the classroom. However, thinking skills are useful for all children and can be applied across a range of subjects. This chapter considers some of the key thinking skills that can be developed and then discusses thinking skills particularly useful to thinking about feelings. Many of these techniques are used in cognitive therapy, a therapeutic approach that develops thinking skills to overcome emotional difficulties. How some of this key thinking can be used to help children who are having difficulties with anxiety, anger and depression are given. How these skills can be developed rests not on what we tell children but the questions we ask them.

Thinking in social situations

Our ability to think is critical in all situations. It is key in our social skills and relationships with others. Some children may find it hard to 'read' or interpret social cues expressed through body language. A child may not realise he is upsetting another until that child expresses his anger forcibly. Another child may not realise that their inability to listen to others is making other children avoid her. Children will have thoughts about themselves that will influence their feelings and behaviours. A child who believes that 'no one likes me' or 'everyone is picking on me' may feel distressed and upset. However, although these thoughts may not be entirely accurate they may be based on experience that becomes exaggerated in the child's mind beyond what is real and out of perspective. These are errors in thinking. Being able to evaluate one's thoughts accurately makes one less likely to be emotionally overwhelmed and more able to think clearly in learning and social situations. To be able to examine the evidence for one's own thoughts and beliefs helps to develop key skills in emotional literacy.

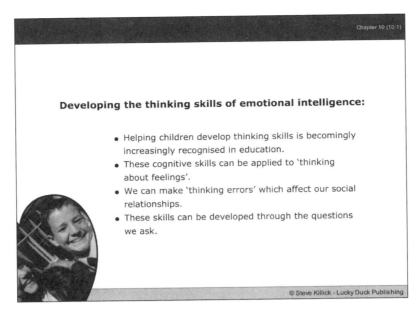

Developing the thinking skills of emotional intelligence:

- Helping children develop thinking skills is becomingly increasingly recognised in education.
- These cognitive skills can be applied to 'thinking about feelings'.
- We can make 'thinking errors' which affect our social relationships.
- These skills can be developed through the questions we ask.

© Steve Killick - Lucky Duck Publishing

Slide 10.1

The application of thinking skills

Thinking is critical to learning. Cowley (2004) links thinking skills to concentration, motivation, behaviour and learning. Being able to think develops curiosity, which is not only one of the key character strengths identified by Seligman as central to wellbeing but also a central motivation to learn. There are many strategies for developing thinking that are linked to and build upon problem-solving skills. Cowley described some key strategies such as:

- Being able to define the key question.

- To be able to think 'laterally'. This is about 'what if' and hypothetical thinking (De Bono, 1992). Hypothetical thinking can be developed by encouraging thought experiments. In a thought experiment, the student is asked to consider an imaginary situation and to consider how they would deal with it and what would happen.

- To be able to take different perspectives or viewpoints, to consider how different people might respond to the same situation. Such mental exercises can encourage empathic and perspective taking skills. For instance, how would a rock concert or a crowded town festival look to a teenager, a policeman, a shop owner and an elderly person? Debates on such issues as fox-hunting, or building a supermarket on a site where birds live, can be explored by looking at the issues from different sides: the animal lover, developer, shopper, scientist and so on. Personal and ethical issues might be explored by asking people to take on roles using formats based on TV chat-shows (Cowley, 2004).

These skills are not about helping provide answers to solutions that are 'right' or 'wrong' but helping generate creativity and being able to see things differently. This can lead to a greater understanding of complexity. Key principles are about listening to others' viewpoints, respecting difference and being open to influence. However, once such creativity has been generated, then more critical thinking can be applied. Students are helped to develop evidence-gathering skills through the skilful use of questioning which uses language to emphasise the importance of observation and thinking.

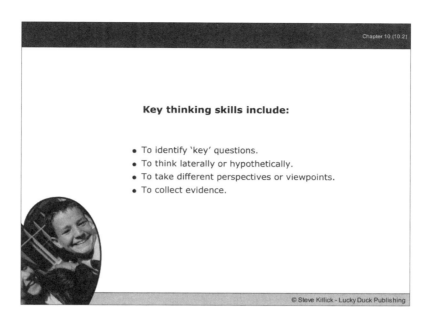

Key thinking skills include:

- To identify 'key' questions.
- To think laterally or hypothetically.
- To take different perspectives or viewpoints.
- To collect evidence.

© Steve Killick - Lucky Duck Publishing

Slide 10.2

Fisher (1996) describes the creation of a 'community of enquiry' in which children of a very young age are helped to learn key philosophical thinking skills. A key tool for doing this is 'Socratic Questioning', based on the philosopher, Socrates', renowned method of questioning that probes for reasons and evidence. Rather than the traditional role of imparting knowledge and informing people what to think or believe, questions are the stimulus for discovery and thought. The Socratic questioner acts as a guide who understands how to question, enquire and explore issues in such a way that helps others do the same (Fisher, 1996). Such questions, also known as 'guided discovery', bring information into the student's awareness making it available for reflection (Neehan & Dryden, 2004). They come from taking a position of 'not knowing' and curiosity to find out more. Such questions can help children to develop their own ideas, views and theories that they can test out. It encourages them to ask questions, contribute to discussions and give reasons for what they think. It helps debating skills both in arguing their own point of view and listening to other people's viewpoints. This lays the foundation for what is one of the most important principles in becoming a good scientist: to be able to change your ideas in the light of new information and evidence. This is what Fisher describes as 'flexible thinking'. It should be very obvious that these skills relate to the fundamental pathways of emotional intelligence.

Three key types of Socratic questioning, identified by Paul (1993), are:

1. Questions of clarification, for example, 'What do you mean by ...?' 'If that were true, what would it mean?' 'Could you put that another way?'

2. Questions that probe assumptions, for example, 'You seem to be assuming...', 'Do you think that is always the case?'

3. Questions that probe reasons and evidence, for example, 'Why do you think that is true?', 'Do you have any evidence for that?' 'What are your reasons for saying that?'

For instance, such questions might be used in exploring a GCSE text or a story.

- That's an interesting point. How do you know that?

- What makes you think that?

- Who could you speak to who would be able to tell you more about that?

- When you say 'weird', what do you mean by that? (Picking on key word)

- What did you see that makes you think that?

- Are there other possible reasons for what that person did?

- What if that person's mother had been killed by a terrorist, would that make a difference to how you viewed him?

- What was he/she feeling at that time?

- What else could she have done to deal with that problem?

- How did that change how that person behaved?

- What if everybody thought the same way?

- What do you think that character's attitude would be towards fox-hunting, pollution or abortion and so on?

- How angry is he feeling? What could he do to calm down?

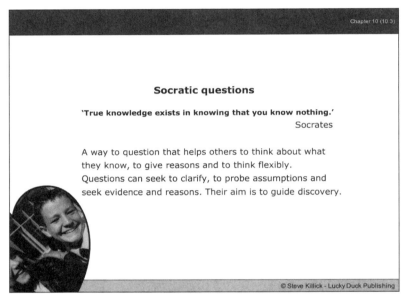

Slide 10.3

Fisher (1996) describes how such questioning can be used effectively with even very young children, preparing the ground for 'higher-order thinking'. Using these questions to explore poems, pictures and stories helps in the development of key thinking, particularly thinking about feeling skills. Fisher developed Philosophy for Children (P4C) to help develop key skills of thinking, questioning and dialogue (Parks et al, 2003). P4C is now a well established strategy for helping children develop thinking skills. Such skills aid not only cognitive but also social and emotional development. P4C is demonstrated in action in a primary school in the video *Thinking Together* (Antidote, 2004).

Higher-order thinking could also be thought about as 'thinking about thinking', that we can think about what we are thinking about. This is also known as 'meta-cognition' or 'reflectivity' and plays a critical part in the learning process. Thinking skills help the child 'learn how to learn', and encourage an engagement with the learning process. They also encourage reflection about what is being learnt. These skills can be applied in all curriculum areas and can help develop the key skills of evaluating and classifying information and evidence. Benjamin Bloom's (1956) well-known taxonomy of learning styles can be used to identify key areas in which children can develop thinking skills:

- to be able to compare and contrast and identify similarities and differences between objects

- to distinguish between what is fact and what is opinion

- to be able to sequence and order information

- to generate and extend ideas
- to know how to test for and identify cause and effect relationships
- to be able to sort, group and classify
- to analyse and identify relationships.

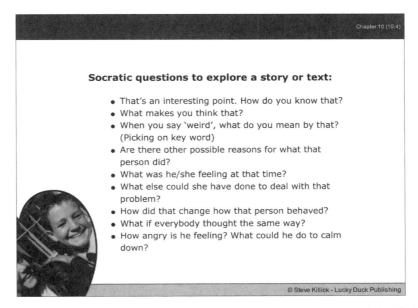

Slide 10.4

Relaxation

To be relaxed is important for thinking in a more creative way. If people are feeling as if they are being evaluated this is likely to lead to increased arousal. Ideas need to be generated and explored even if those ideas are not right, they can still be used to gather evidence and predict consequences. It can be useful to develop relaxation skills in classes although this is often easier to do in smaller groups. Visualisation exercises or tasks that ask people to be aware of attending to other sensory stimuli, smells and sounds can be useful in introducing ways of relaxing and thinking differently.

Think good – feel good, feel good – learn good

So, thinking skills help in the development of learning and also facilitate and aid emotional and social development. Thinking skills also have a specific application when working with both children and adults with difficulties in managing emotions. Cognitive therapy is based on the principle that we are rational beings who are able to make conscious decisions about how to act based on our thoughts and beliefs. Emotional problems may results from unhelpful beliefs or faulty reasoning based on our feelings. Socratic questioning is one of the key techniques that is used in cognitive therapy. Paul Stallard's book on cognitive therapy for children and young people, *Think Good – Feel Good* (2002) contains many examples of activities and activity sheets to help develop strategies for managing emotions that can be adapted to the classroom situation. Its title emphasises that if we can develop good thinking strategies it influences our mood and feelings. There is a clear link with this statement to that of Peter Sharp's statement of emotional literacy, 'feel good – learn good'.

So, cognitive strategies can help develop learning skills and, particularly, help children who may be having difficulties in managing emotions. Sometimes these difficulties will be to the extent that they can be described as mental health problems and children may benefit from additional specialised help. However, there are many ways that teachers can help children learn useful thinking skills without having to intrude or delve into personal areas. Knowledge of some of these skills may also help teachers when working with mental health workers who are increasingly working with schools as a whole rather than just individual children. These skills, which can be developed through Socratic questioning (or guided discovery) with the aim of developing insight and emotional regulation, are illustrated in Slide 10.5.

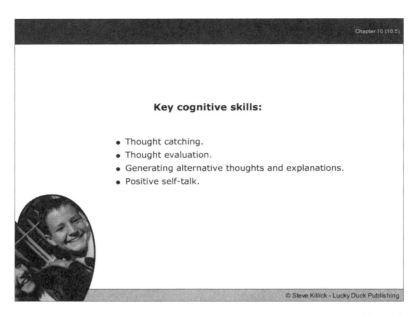

Slide 10.5

Thought catching

Constantly, thoughts flit through the mind that influence our mood and behaviour. Many of these thoughts are involuntary and irrational. Richard Carlson (1997) suggests we average about 20,000 of these thoughts a day. For many people, a significant proportion of these thoughts are negative in nature. They may relate to what may happen (I am going to mess it up or everyone will laugh at me) or to bad things about ourselves (I'm stupid, I'm a bad person). Often we are not aware of these thoughts and how they influence our mood, particularly the effect they may have on our feelings of anxiety, anger or sadness. Becoming aware of these thoughts and feelings is the first stage of being able to stop such thoughts having a negative influence. Self-awareness is one of the key pathways to emotional intelligence. This involves awareness of thoughts and feelings for which an emotional vocabulary is necessary and recognition that it is our thoughts that can influence those feelings.

Becoming more aware of these thoughts can be developed in a number of ways. Socratic questioning and exploration ('When I asked you to read that passage to the class, what thoughts went through your head?') is a useful way of helping children identify the thoughts they are having. Another way is to encourage writing thoughts and feelings down, for instance, through the use of a 'thoughts and feelings diary' in which a child might record what he was doing at a particular time, what he was thinking and what he was feeling. Thoughts and feelings diaries can be difficult for many children to keep and although they may work well for some young people, they work less well for others. Activity sheets, such as those used by Stallard, can be more effective in helping children identifying the links between thoughts and feelings.

Thought evaluation

Once we are aware of the thoughts that come into our minds we can begin to evaluate them. The process of talking is often helpful as it brings our thoughts and beliefs into the rational linguistic realm. It may become clear to someone who is thinking that everybody hates him, that as soon as he utters this belief, it is an exaggeration of reality. Sometimes, we need help to identify some of the thinking errors that we all frequently make. There are a number of thinking errors that commonly occur (Stallard, 2002, Seligman, 1995):

- Seeing only negatives and discounting positives – negative events tend to get magnified, positive events are ignored.

- All-or-nothing thinking – this is often thinking in absolute ways such as, 'You are either my friend or my enemy,' or, 'If I am not a total success then I am a failure.'

- Predicting failure (fortune telling) or catastrophising – when we make predictions about what may happen to us they may tend to be negative or predict total disaster. For instance, 'If I don't do well on my maths test, I will fail my exams, this means I won't get a job, I will be unemployed for ever, what's the point?' Catastrophising is about ruminating on and imagining the worst possible outcome if any event goes wrong.

- Mind reading – when someone thinks they know what other people will think of them, 'She thinks I am an idiot'.

- Emotional reasoning – this is where we think something is true because we feel it to be true as in, 'I feel stupid therefore I must be stupid.'

- Self-blaming is when we feel responsible for bad things that happen, for instance, if a friend does not speak to you then it is because of something you must have done rather than for some other reason.

What's your evidence?

Some students can learn about these thinking errors best by thinking about them in hypothetical situations, such as stories, rather than identifying them in themselves. Once these errors have been identified it becomes easier to recognise them in one's own thinking. One way of evaluating thoughts is to search out the evidence that either supports or refutes the belief. For instance, what evidence would you need to support the belief that, 'Everybody hates me', 'I will never succeed at anything' or 'Richard is mean'. Ideas such as the 'Thought Detective', a character who searches out the evidence both for and against an argument as a detective might do in an investigation, work well here.

The evaluation of thoughts helps recognition that not everything we think, especially about ourselves, is necessarily true – a thought is not a fact. Once we recognise that our explanations for things are not always accurate we can then look to find more helpful and realistic explanations.

 See Exercise One

Generating alternative thoughts and explanations

By being able to think of other explanations and reasons and not necessarily jumping to conclusions or accepting the thoughts that come into our heads, we are able to think more flexibly and more positively about ourselves. One student who saw himself at being poor at maths was becoming increasingly frustrated in class. After exploring some of the areas that he was competent in and some of the areas that he hadn't grasped his explanation of, 'I'm bad at maths,' changed to, 'There are some parts I haven't understood yet', he felt more able to try out some of the exercises and eventually mastered the skill. Generating alternative ideas relates to problem-solving skills that develop the idea of looking at things in different ways and being able to generate and evaluate possible solutions.

There are also ways of using stories and hypothetical ideas, illustrated in cartoons and scenarios, to help understand how thinking processes can lead to emotional reactions.

> Luke was with a group of his classmates. Everyone was having a good time and messing around. Then Luke made a joke that nobody understood. Then somebody said he was weird because his jokes never made sense. Everybody started laughing at him.
>
> Luke ended up feeling rejected by his friends and very sad. Why do you think he felt like that? What thoughts went through his head to make him feel so unhappy?
>
> Several days later, exactly the same thing happened but this time it didn't seem to worry Luke. When others laughed at him he was able to laugh at himself. How was he able to feel like this? How was he thinking now that he was able to feel OK?

The difference between these two outcomes is how Luke evaluated the situation. In the first outcome he may have interpreted his friends' reactions catastrophically, in the second he was able to dismiss their reactions as having no serious implications for himself as a person; not being able to tell a joke well is simply not that important. There will clearly be differences in the degree that children are able to identify and alter their inner explanatory systems, and this may relate to the degree of anxiety they feel. The higher the anxiety, the harder it is to think flexibly.

Decatastrophising

Seligman (1995) identified decatastrophising as a key skill for young people who may be vulnerable to depression. Many people will tend to catastrophise about the future. Human intelligence enables us to predict the future, to calculate and assess what the consequences of our actions may be. On one hand it may be useful to foresee what might go wrong which enables us to act wisely. However, if we think too pessimistically about the future the anxiety of expecting many unrealistic horrors may be overwhelming. Catatrophising can be counter-productive when the worst case scenario is actually very unlikely. Learning to evaluate realistically the outcome of actions is a useful skill to develop.

Positive self-talk

Sometimes the constant stream of thoughts that flow through our minds may be predominantly negative. This can lessen confidence and increase anxiety. Positive self-talk is a way of disputing and overcoming this internal critical voice. Helping children focus on positives – past achievements rather than failures and anticipating success rather than disappointment – builds confidence. In positive self-talk the child is encouraged to find and praise his own successes and achievements and to encourage himself (Stallard, 2002).

An internal negative thought such as, 'I'm going to get all the answers wrong, I'm rubbish at science,' might be replaced with, 'I've always managed to get some answers right. If I read the questions properly and think about what I know then I will do better'. Instead of, 'Everyone is looking me. They'll laugh at me if I make a mistake,' a more positive view is, 'I can manage to do this. I've done it before and it went OK.'

It can take time to develop the skills of positive self-talk, creating an inner monologue that is optimistic and realistic. One powerful way of developing this is to model such a monologue for children. A teacher told his class about how he had to give a talk at a conference. He described the feelings of anxiety he was having, his worries about drying up and his audience being bored in response to what he was going to say. He then also described how he started answering and overcoming those thoughts. He told himself that it was perfectly normal to feel anxious and that there was no need to worry – after all he had plenty of experience of talking to groups. He knew what he was going to say was interesting and most of the audience probably would find it so too. Anyway, even if some of them didn't, what would it matter? One student said to him later, 'I've never heard a grown-up talk like that.' It is very powerful for children to hear adults talk about their own feelings and how they can master their feelings of anxiety.

Another way of helping children who continually criticise themselves is to help them gain a more external view. This overcomes the natural tendency to be more critical of ourselves than we are of others. Encouraging the child to act towards himself as though he was a kind friend can do this. This technique, being your own best friend, can be encouraged by asking questions such as, 'What do you think a good friend might say to you about this?' or, 'If a friend of yours, who you really liked, was in this situation, what would you say to her?'

Helping children learn about dealing with feelings

Problems with emotions lie at the root of mental health problems and can severely affect not only children's education but also their whole development. There may be difficulties, perhaps in the children's early experience or in their family life, that may mean they need more than a school can provide. A teacher may be the first to notice such difficulties and begin the process of ensuring a child receives the appropriate help. Increasingly, mental health services are now working with schools, often as part of teams, which means it can be easier to discuss possibilities rather than take no action or refer to a mental health service. Sometimes, teachers will work in contexts where it will be possible to help children work directly on managing difficult feelings. The following are some ideas based on using thinking skills for helping children learn about expressing and competently managing their feelings.

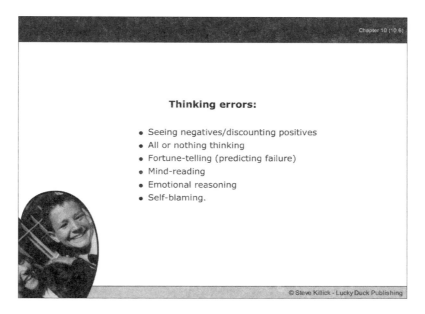

Slide 10.6

Ways of working with anger

Anger, as discussed in Chapter Two, often results in how we appraise a situation. If we feel unfairly treated or threatened it may stir up the impulse to react to the event. However, it may be that our appraisal is incorrect – if we are suspicious or untrusting we may jump to the wrong conclusion. If our appraisal is correct we then have to make a decision how to respond – aggressively, assertively or, perhaps, timidly.

Stories and scenarios can be used to illustrate situations where a character might become angry, and then reflective listening and Socratic questions can be used to explore the internal worlds of the characters. Problem-solving dialogues can act to identify strategies that may be used. Role-plays, if appropriate, may even be used to experiment with and evaluate different strategies. An example of such a scenario is given below.

A 14-year-old boy is walking home when two older boys come up to him and start a conversation. At first they appear to be friendly but then one of them asks to see the boy's mobile phone. Reluctantly he hands it over and is getting more suspicious of their intentions. He starts to ask for it back but as the older boys see the effect they are having they begin goading the boy and eventually they say that they are going to keep the phone. The boy is getting angrier and angrier.

Questions may explore the following areas:

- What are some of the thoughts going through the boy's head? Why is he angry? What else is he feeling? The aim is to identify or 'catch' thoughts and to see how they can be evaluated. Are they realistic and accurate and do they need challenging?

- How is the situation developing, how might it end? Are there situations where you have got into an argument where people got angrier? The process of escalation can be explored, both how a person's internal thought processes can lead to anger and in a situation where two people are interacting with each other The earlier one steps off the 'escalator' the better. Timing is important. Are people's assumptions about each other always correct or are there other ways of looking at the situation?

- As the boy gets angrier, what might be happening in his body? Explore the physical sensations of anger and how students experience sensations of anger. This can be used to increase their awareness of how anger affects them, and might suggest a cue to help people identify early what they are feeling and start to think next about what to do rather than just acting or speaking out in anger.

- What things could the boy do? What strategies might he use? Should he attempt to deal with the situation alone or seek help? At this point some teaching about types of strategies can be given which students have to adapt to this particular problem. Strategies might be classified under three approaches: Aggressive – physical or verbal, Assertive – respectful and confident communication and Timid – to do nothing whilst experiencing strong feelings.

Some general anger management strategies can be discussed to see if they would be appropriate or not for this situation:

- Have a cooling down period to gain a sense of relaxation. This might counter any emotional hijacking and switches off the physiological reaction. If possible go and do something that is particularly calming or relaxing.

- Do something different like folding your arms or putting your hands in your pockets. This can act as a strong cue to think and calm down. Teachers can help children learn these skills by modelling in situations when emotions get raised, 'I'm feeling very frustrated by this, I am going to take a minutes time out while I think what to do.'

- Question things that others do that you see as hostile and see if they could be seen differently. For instance, if there is someone you are not getting on with who is staring at you, don't jump to the conclusion that they are being challenging and respond by saying, 'What you staring at?' This might begin an escalation. The look might even be friendly, expressing interest or might not mean anything at all. Don't jump to conclusions about social cues.

- Counting to ten inhibits the physiological response and gives time to think about doing something differently. The impulse to act aggressively may pass.

- Find something else to think about to break the chain of thoughts.

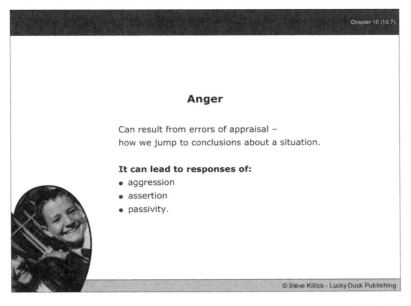

Anger

Can result from errors of appraisal –
how we jump to conclusions about a situation.

It can lead to responses of:
- aggression
- assertion
- passivity.

Slide 10.7

 160   See Exercise Two

Anxiety

The same structure of using a scenario, questioning and skill teaching can be used when dealing with anxieties. Scenarios to explore the physiological and psychological reactions of anxiety might include situations such as finding a spider or a snake in your desk, or hearing a loud noise in the middle of the night. Other scenarios might include looking at sources of social or academic anxiety. These areas lay the foundations of learning how to manage stress.

Some important skills in dealing with anxiety are:

- An essential element for dealing with anxiety is to firstly feel as safe as you possibly can. Anxiety can freeze the brain making it very hard to think. Trauma and events like bullying can increase the anxiety that someone is experiencing and it is very hard to be able to work out what to do if one doesn't feel safe. Seeking out help can be essential in creating a sense of safety. If you can soothe yourself do so, if not find someone who can help.

- Try and recognise worry thoughts as soon as possible (thought catching). When these thoughts are recognised then they can be evaluated: How likely is it that this will happen? If it does what can you do? How do you know the consequences will be as bad as you think? Are you catastrophising? What other things could you do? Does it help to go over these thoughts over and over again? Sometimes, anxiety can lead to rumination so when you catch yourself doing this, make yourself stop and think of something else.

- Monitor yourself for physical cues of worry, such as a fast heart rate, pacing and sweating. Relaxation can be very helpful. Often children and young people will have methods that they use to relax or switch off without knowing what they are doing. Hobbies and interests or activities like watching a favourite film can be helpful. It can be useful for young children to share what works for them with each other as this can stimulate ideas as well as giving the chance to discuss the values of relaxation.

- Using positive self-talk. Make positive statements about yourself and what is happening, for instance, 'I can do this, my legs feel a bit wobbly because I'm nervous and this feeling will soon pass.' Anxiety can be like throwing a ball up in the air, however high it goes it must come down.

Often, facing the fears is the best way to achieve mastery over them rather than avoiding situations that cause anxiety. Facing situations helps people learn that what they were most worried about is actually not likely to happen and also helps people learn the skills that they need to be accomplished. In this way it is like riding a bike. If you fear falling off you do not want to learn, but if you learn how to ride well you reduce the likelihood of hurting yourself if you fall.

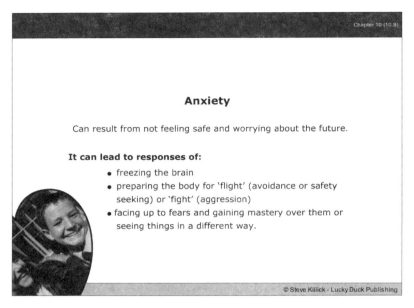

Slide 10.8

 See Activity One

Sadness, loss and depression

Children continually have to deal with loss, change and setbacks and to explore ways of dealing with such events can help build resilience. Scenarios about loss and setbacks and how to think about them can lay the foundation for developing coping skills. It can be useful to think of helpful ways of thinking about dealing with loss, change or setbacks in a number of scenarios appropriate to the age and development of the class. Here are some examples of scenarios:

- failing an exam
- a good friend who is moving away
- the loss of a pet
- the break-up of a relationship
- someone who thinks they have no friends and rarely goes out.

Children and young people who are depressed or vulnerable to depression will often have symptoms of irritability and anger, especially towards parents and care givers. They often cannot recognise or talk about feelings. Therefore, developing an emotional vocabulary can help. The thinking style is significant as small defeats can become huge setbacks and trigger depressive thinking for some. Those with a pessimistic style of thinking, of expecting the worst and feeling powerless to do anything, are more vulnerable to depression than someone with optimism. Optimism is a characteristic that can be developed. When emotions swamp concentration, it is working memory that is emotionally hijacked and paralysed. This stops the person from functioning well and remembering positives. This maintains the depression.

In social settings, children will often perceive another child's actions as rejecting. They then withdraw or may respond aggressively which other children experience as rejection. A pattern of social withdrawal is established and the child is isolated.

Ways of helping to overcome depressive or pessimistic thinking

The emotionally sensitive helper can help in a number of ways with someone who is vulnerable to depression. Firstly, noticing the degree of isolation and withdrawal that may be a sign of depression. There may be rumination, continual negative thoughts going around in one head, is significant. The greater the degree of rumination, the worse the depression is likely to be. Depressive thinking can, in extreme cases, be a factor in self-harm. Self-harm can be an act that both gives release from and, simultaneously reinforces, very strong uncomfortable feelings of self-hatred. Techniques described in the section on anxiety are applicable here too. Referral for counselling or therapy for depression should always be considered

Thinking styles

Cognitive behavioural therapy, which believes that how people think affects what they feel and do, has been shown to be useful for many cases of depression. Cognitive approaches help people to be aware of their thoughts. Techniques described in the section on anxiety are applicable here too. In a relationship that is empathic and accepts feelings it is also possible to gently challenge the negative thoughts that maintain a depressive mood. The idea is to 'reframe' how a person sees things.

Activity scheduling

This involves ensuring there are plenty of enjoyable things to do that are pleasant and stimulating. For the young person who may not be 'in the mood' for this, they may need encouragement for some activities such as socialising, going to the cinema, doing things with peers or adult friends and carers. Small but achievable tasks can be encouraged and achieved so that the person experiences a sense of achievement, however small. It can also be useful in thinking how to increase happiness by doing things for others. Compassion and kindness in helping others can have the additional benefit of helping a person feel much better about him or herself. Most of all it is about being kind to yourself.

Helping recognise emotions can be useful in helping children to learn how to deal with them. Exercises around emotion recognition and their effects on physical feelings, thoughts and in relating to others can help children be aware of how feelings and mood influence behaviour.

Increasing optimism

The Penn Prevention Programme, a preventative programme for depression in schools, is described in the book *The Optimistic Child* by Martin Seligman (1995). Here, key cognitive skills of thought catching, evaluating, considering alternatives and decatastrophising are taught to young people. The programme lasts eight weeks and helps children to learn that it is not an event (such as being criticised) that leads to an emotional reaction, rather it is how they think about the event. Young people learn to recognise thinking styles that are unhelpful and learn how to generate alternative explanations. There is good evidence that training in these techniques helps provide a 'psychological inoculation' that reduces the risk of depression developing.

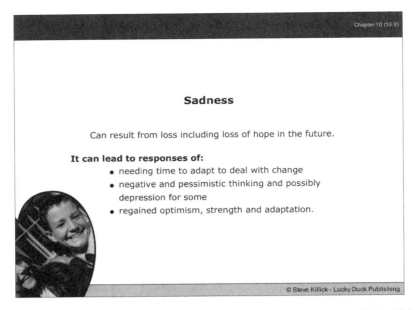

Sadness

Can result from loss including loss of hope in the future.

It can lead to responses of:
- needing time to adapt to deal with change
- negative and pessimistic thinking and possibly depression for some
- regained optimism, strength and adaptation.

© Steve Killick - Lucky Duck Publishing

Slide 10.9

To be able to think about feelings, which includes awareness on how these influence us physically, psychologically and socially, is the key to learning the skills of managing emotions. Programmes that develop such skills are providing evidence that helping children learn these skills has a positive effect upon how children feel about themselves and how they get on with others. This can also have benefits for their academic achievements. Although there will always be children who will need additional help to be offered to them and their families, the use of thinking skills can contribute to their overall wellbeing as well as to the emotional literacy of all.

Summary of Chapter Ten

- The teaching of thinking skills to young people puts an emphasis on how children learn and think rather than what is taught to them. Thinking skills help children to analyse, evaluate, examine evidence and predict. These skills are critically important in their own right but they have specific benefits in encouraging emotional literacy.

- 'Socratic questioning' is a particular style of questioning that helps develop thinking skills in young people. Projects such as Philosophy for Children (P4C) have demonstrated that children from very young ages can use these skills effectively.

- Techniques developed in the field of cognitive therapy such as thought catching, thought evaluation, generating alternative ideas and positive self-talk can help children develop both personal and social emotional skills and competencies.

- The skills listed above can be used in class situations and in helping individual students learn about dealing with strong feelings. Although there will always be children who need additional help, either through the school or through other services, helping children learn about managing feelings can contribute to their health education.

Exercise One – Thinking Errors

This exercise aims to help participants identify common thinking errors that children and young people can make and to consider how they might use Socratic questioning to help the child think differently.

In small groups of three to four, ask the participants to think of examples they can call to mind where children have exhibited some of the thinking errors described in Slide 10.6.

After they have listed some examples of thinking errors, then they should pick one or two specific examples and think of questions that would explore the child's thinking. This could be developed into a short role-play where some of the subjects of these questions can be practised.

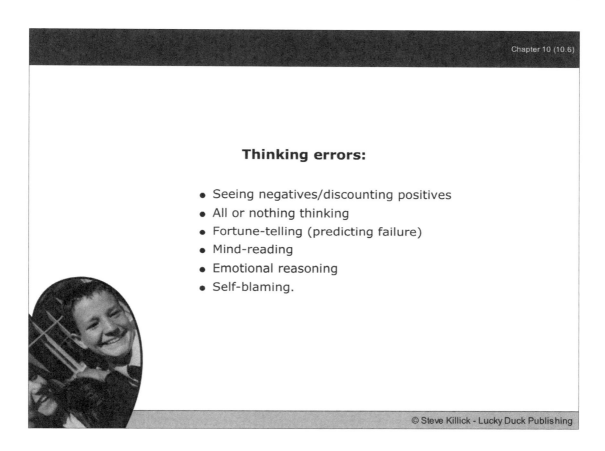

Slide 10.6

Exercise Two –
Managing Feelings

This exercise aims to help participants think about how to help a student manage feelings of anger by talking to them about how they are thinking and developing strategies. The same exercise structure can be used to think about anxiety and sadness.

In small groups of four, one participant selects a young person (who should not be identified in any way to protect confidentiality) who often exhibits angry or excessive behaviour.

The group then generates questions and strategies that the young person might learn to manage that emotion at school and use this to develop an action plan. Each group then presents their action plans to the whole group giving the opportunity to discuss specific strategies for managing anger and how they might help the young person learn new skills.

Activity Sheet One –
What Happens When I Get Anxious?

Think about a time when you or someone you know has been really worried or anxious about something.

How did that feeling show in the face? What facial expressions do people make when they are worried? Can you draw it?

How does it show in people's bodies? What signs show that someone may be worried?

What sort of things do people do when they are worried or anxious? How do they behave?

How much of the time do you get anxious or uptight?

Never   All the time

1	2	3	4	5	6	7	8	9	10

(Adapted from Stallard, 2002)

Chapter Eleven

Working Together – Developing Interpersonal Skills

It is through working together that many of the interpersonal skills of emotional literacy are developed. There are also many areas of interpersonal conflict between children. It is through the making and breaking of friendships, the rivalries and disagreements that children learn many of the skills of getting on with each other. The arena of children's play is a natural learning environment for developing skills in resolving conflict and learning how to get along with others. If children develop these skills their confidence grows and they become better learners. If there are problems, children's anxieties may grow to the point of giving them problems in learning and may lead to social isolation, unhappiness or even school refusal. If the culture of the school takes these experiences of children seriously, they can do much to help them learn new social and communication skills which can make them more effective in helping, and learning from, each other.

Many interpersonal disputes may not come to the attention of teachers, so helping Learning Support Assistants and ancillary staff such as Playground Supervisors practise communication skills can be helpful. Children can also be taught these skills directly through Circle Time, Peer Support and Peer Counselling initiatives. Children can also, through developing these techniques, be encouraged to participate in the democracy of the school through School Councils. Such programmes can help foster emotional literacy in the everyday workings of the school. It is possible for children of young ages, even in Key Stage One, to start learning these skills. Indeed, many at this age are emotional intelligence experts already. Not only do these skills extend and develop key listening and speaking skills, but also the skills of collaboration and cooperation lay the foundations for citizenship (Rowe, 2001).

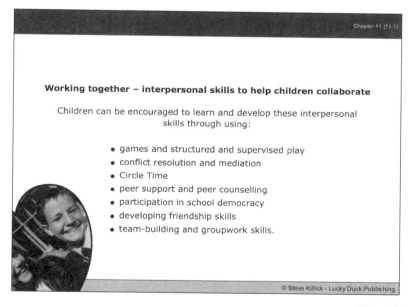

Slide 11.1

There are many areas of school life that can be tackled by taking an emotional literacy perspective. Many of these areas will fall under the PSHE curriculum and include bullying, resolving conflict and mediation skills, child protection, making and keeping friends, working with parents, social isolation, sexual health and education and drug and alcohol education (see Slide 11.2).

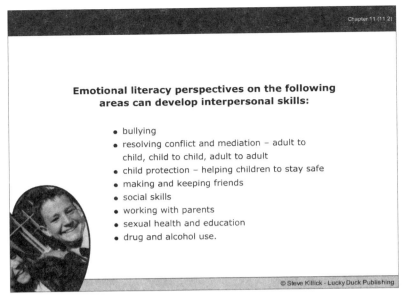

Slide 11.2

The characteristics of an emotionally intelligent approach to these issues are an emphasis on accepting and respecting feelings, rather than just evaluating behaviour as good or bad. Bullying and conflict in relationships is tackled and resolved through listening and being able to respond with a large repertoire of skills and actions as opposed to jumping to conclusions, blaming individuals or imposing sanctions.

There is an emphasis on looking at the thoughts and underlying feelings of what people say and do. Feelings of hurt, jealousy or mistrust on both sides can underlie conflict. It is important to address conflict rather than let the relationship deteriorate. When students know relationships can be repaired after conflict and that assumptions can be questioned they learn valuable interpersonal skills that can overcome prejudice.

Mediation and conflict resolution

Mediation and conflict resolution techniques have been taught successfully in schools. Both staff and students can be taught these conflict resolution and problem-solving skills (see Stacy and Robinson, 1997). As well as listening and problem-solving skills, children are taught how to deal with conflicts and problems that a rise between their peers. Among the skills to help them act differently when there are fights or arguments are:

Learning about the process of escalation (as described in Chapter Five). If somebody does something that raises the emotional temperature, try to ensure that others don't react in a way that further inflames the situation. Rather, recognise that there is a problem that needs to be addressed.

Help people to be calm rather than become emotionally engulfed. Distress, upset and anger can be acknowledged but children may need to be helped to calm down or given space for them to be able to calm themselves down. Without this, 'emotional hijacking' may result. Either party should be able to claim 'time out' to calm down and find something that will help individuals relax before the issues are addressed.

The point of view of all parties needs to be listened to and in such a way that the parties can listen to each other. The principle is 'try to understand before you try to be understood'. If you listen to someone else's point of view, they are much more likely to listen to yours. Help people to listen to each other non-defensively and talk about feelings and actions, not attack character. Possibly establish boundaries about how people talk to each other such as 'no name-calling' or 'no hurting –

164

and that includes feelings'. Look out for statements that suggest someone is jumping to conclusions about the other party's actions and explore with them their evidence for thinking that.

It can be easy to see a solution for others in conflict and to advocate that solution but just supports the point of view of one party. However, this might only contribute to further negative and resistant responses. It can be useful to take a position that there is not one correct point of view and that acknowledges that varying perspectives can exist.

Look to the future, to find how the problem can be avoided, rather than analysing the past. The focus is on what might happen next time if the situation occurs rather than who did what last time. At this point, participants can be invited to problem-solve together to offer suggestions that might move things forward.

As with all the problem-solving approaches, don't offer practical solutions too quickly. Consider alternatives, and then evaluate them. If it can be found, select the one that suits all parties. The principle is to find a 'win-win' solution for all parties as opposed to one person winning, the other losing.

If necessary, agree to meet again and review the outcome or maybe try new solutions. Finish with positives and strengthen positive feelings.

The above skills are complex and take time and practice to learn, and training must be pitched at a level that young people can comprehend. But there is great value in such training. Young people are often in conflict with their parents and carers so training both young people and staff in conflict resolution can be useful. With practice these skills can be used quickly in resolving conflicts that arise and help model good communication and interpersonal skills in children. They become better able to work out difficulties amongst themselves. To collaborate and cooperate both mean the same thing: to work together towards common goals.

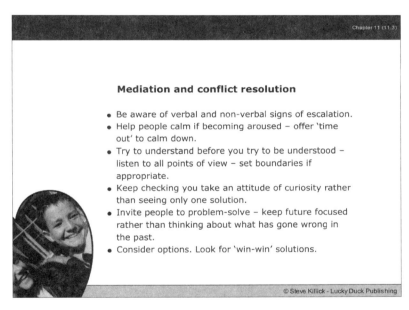

Slide 11.3

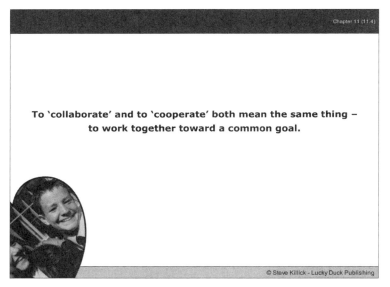

To 'collaborate' and to 'cooperate' both mean the same thing –
to work together toward a common goal.

© Steve Killick - Lucky Duck Publishing

Slide 11.4

Developing friendships skills

A friend is someone who is walking in the door when everyone else is walking out.

Chuck Spezzano, Psychologist and Teacher

Emotional intelligence is not contained solely within the child but exists within the context of relationships. For children, their ability to form friendships develops their sense of confidence. Friends are able to provide comfort and help or can distract from worries. Friendships are a considerable source of happiness and joy. For some, forming friendships comes easily, for others the skills have to be encouraged. This makes learning friendship skills a vital component to emotional literacy programmes, when children are helped to identify the qualities and skills involved in friendship.

Goleman (1995) describes a friendship coaching programme, devised by psychologist Steven Asher, that is used in schools. Friendship skills were facilitated by asking groups of children (in this case those identified as having difficulties with social skills) to help the teacher learn what they thought it meant for them to be a good friend and what they would like their friends to be like. This enabled children to apply thinking skills to defining what are the qualities of friendship. Different types of friendship were explored: qualities in friendships of the same or opposite sex, friendships with younger or older children or from different ethnic backgrounds. Areas such as the sort of things that make friendships break up, or what happens when there are problems and disagreements and the best ways of sorting these difficulties out were explored. Often, the three most important friendship skills that emerged most often were to be friendly, fun and nice. Activity sheets can also be used to help develop these skills

 See Activity Sheet One

Having identified skills that children thought were important, the skills could then be modelled and demonstrated through the use of games. Games were used to help children build confidence and raise their social skills through the following ways:

- finding ways of compromising if they disagreed over rules

- encouraging listening, observation and turn-taking skills

- helping children give praise when someone does well or to help someone if they became stuck.

- encouraging children to ask questions of each other while they play

- strengthening skills such as eye contact or appropriate touch.

Games are natural facilitators of social and friendship skills and the regular practice of doing this had a significant effect in reducing isolation and building confidence. Some examples of the kinds of games to develop social skills that can be used in Circle Time are given, and can be found at the end of this chapter.

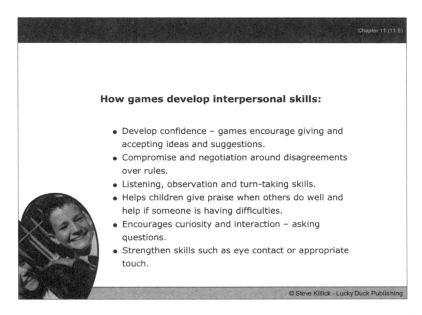

Slide 11.5

Friendship skills lay the basis being of able to initiate intimate and sexual relationships, that are caring, mutually pleasurable and healthy. A vital component of sex education includes exploring relationships especially between the genders. McConnon (1989) gives lesson plans and activity sheets designed to help promote successful relationships and explore some of the issues of gender and stereotyped attitudes.

Children are learning about sex and sexual attitudes and behaviours from an early age whether they are taught formally or not. Sex education involves learning about sexual health, to reduce the frequency of sexually transmitted diseases and unwanted pregnancies. It is also important to place this education in the context of appropriate, reciprocal and mutually satisfying relationships. This can impact upon inappropriate sexual behaviour and aggression. However, those that need this education most may be the least likely to receive it. For example, children in care may miss such information, perhaps through interruptions in learning due to family disruption, and they are less likely to receive such education at home (Patel-Kanwal & Frances, 1998). Another vulnerable group are those exposed to domestic violence. Talking about sex and relationships is difficult, despite the myth of living in a liberated society, yet the learning of appropriate sexual knowledge and attitudes lies at the heart of young people being able to manage their emotional lives and participate in meaningful relationships with adults. It plays as critical a part to wellbeing as literacy and numeracy. Formal sex education can be reinforced by using information provided in other parts of the curriculum. Brevity and repetition are important here and the issues of appropriate relationships should be referred to frequently as opportunities to model and illustrate appropriate skills. Real life dilemmas can be explored to raise awareness of issues, for example, issues about how men and women are portrayed in the media and the arts can be referred to in class. This includes how male and female bodies are depicted, how they relate to each other and raising issues of power, trust and conflict. It is not about providing answers to the complex issues that exist but helping young people to think about these issues and to be able to question their own and others' assumptions.

 See Exercise One

Developing problem-solving skills in groupwork

There are no problems we cannot solve together, and very few that we can solve by ourselves.

Lyndon Johnson

None of us is as smart as all of us.

Ken Blanchard

Games are suitable for children of all ages to develop social skills. The goal of such group activities is to develop the participants' concept of self by developing trust and competent behaviour in the group. The skills needed in communication can aid confidence and also do much to eliminate challenging and destructive behaviours (Ruberti & Holden, 2005). However, in secondary schools it can be useful to introduce more formal group problem-solving exercises to encourage shared problem-solving skills and teamwork.

The exercises, which can also be used to develop team working skills in adults, help participants realise that some problems can only be worked out together through cooperation. Such exercises also help people realise that when a group works together it can equal more than the sum of its individual parts, that the solutions that are reached can be given by people who don't always get heard or that in thinking together more creativity is unleashed. The exercises used in this chapter are examples of group problem-solving activities suitable for adolescents and adults. These exercises can be used to develop a sense of teamwork in teachers working together. Setting a tone of trust, fun and enthusiasm rather than of criticism and judgments of behaviour best facilitates leading such exercises.

As well as learning through action and participation, students can reflect on their participation. This can be stimulated by giving feedback of what people did well to facilitate the group working together, for instance, giving examples of group members thinking about each other's needs or listening to and constructively evaluating each other's ideas. They may also be balanced by examples of when group members did not work so well together, for example, poor listening or awareness of some members' needs.

The exercises in this chapter are examples of the kind of activities that can be used to develop teamwork and group problem-solving skills. The exercise should be given a set time in which to be completed. Appointing some members of the groups to act as observers while the group complete the task can enhance feedback. They then give feedback to the group members at various points throughout the exercise.

Both facilitators and observers watch the group during this process to see how they are attempting the task that has been set for them. The exercise may be stopped for short periods for the observers to share their comments with the group members. Specific observations about the interactions that observers may like to make might focus on the following areas:

- How able are group members to listen to each other?

- Who is generating ideas about how problems might be solved, is it just a few or many members?

- Are ideas being thought about and debated or just discarded without thinking through, are any strategies emerging?

- Are leaders emerging? Are they dominating the group or helping facilitate the group to involve others? How are tasks allocated?

- Are the ideas of less dominant or vocal members listened to?

- How are decisions made and agreed on? Is there evidence of methods such as consensus or majority decision making efforts? What are the most appropriate methods for the task?

- Is the group taking time to plan and think through their actions or are they just rushing into action?

- What emotions and feelings are emerging from the group? Is there a sense of enthusiasm and persistence or 'stuckness' and boredom?

- What roles are emerging in the group? As well as leadership, who clowns, disrupts, considers the feelings of others and so on?

- What issues about gender and role emerge? Can both sexes work together or do they work better separately?

- Is there evidence of the group learning or are they repeating similar mistakes in their approaches to problems?

- How do they talk to each other? Do they give each other positive feedback and encouragement? How is negative feedback given to each other? How did people respond to criticism?

- If negative feedback was destructive as opposed to constructive how might it have been given in a way that was more useful? For instance, not attacking character but talking about how the behaviour makes them feel, giving an idea of what would be more appropriate. The principle is to turn negatives into opportunities for learning.

Activity Sheet Two following the exercises may be used to encourage self-reflection in some groups. The activity sheet gives a large range of questions and for some groups it may be better to focus on just a few key issues at a time. Discussion from such exercises might focus on issues related to work or other areas of the national curriculum. These exercises can also be used to facilitate team development for staff.

 See Exercise Two

Teachers can use these or similar exercises and the feedback processes to think about their own group problem-solving skills. The exercises presented can be adapted easily to meet the interests and skills of different groups. Any task might be given to a group to think about, from planning a 'fete' for the school, a new approach to parent evenings to briefing the architects in building a school for the 21st century. It is not the problem itself that it is significant but the group's approach to solving that problem.

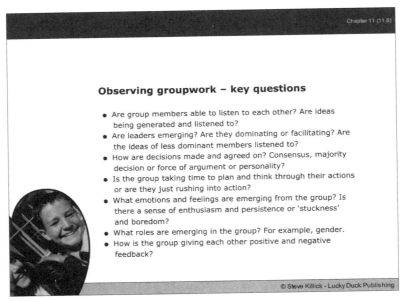

Observing groupwork – key questions

- Are group members able to listen to each other? Are ideas being generated and listened to?
- Are leaders emerging? Are they dominating or facilitating? Are the ideas of less dominant members listened to?
- How are decisions made and agreed on? Consensus, majority decision or force of argument or personality?
- Is the group taking time to plan and think through their actions or are they just rushing into action?
- What emotions and feelings are emerging from the group? Is there a sense of enthusiasm and persistence or 'stuckness' and boredom?
- What roles are emerging in the group? For example, gender.
- How is the group giving each other positive and negative feedback?

© Steve Killick - Lucky Duck Publishing

Slide 11.6

Summary of Chapter Eleven

- How children get along with each other both in friendships and conflicts can influence their emotional development. There are many ways that schools can help facilitate development in this area and thus build key emotional literacy skills.

- Peer support, peer counselling and involvement and encouragement in school democracy offers young people, even from young ages, to learn effective communication skills in resolving disputes. Young people can become active in mediation and conflict resolution in the school.

- Children, especially those with difficulties in the area of social skills and competence can benefit from learning friendship skills. Activities and games can be particularly useful in the learning of such skills.

- Exercises to encourage teamwork and problem-solving in groups can help develop high levels of interpersonal functioning in young people. These exercises can also help and assist adults in learning good teamwork and communication skills.

Activity Sheet One –
Friendship

Someone asks you what you think are the three most important qualities of a good friend. What do you think they are?

1.

2.

3.

Rate your own friendship skills	Most of the time	Sometimes	Not very often
Am I friendly to new people I meet?			
Do I tease or make fun of people?			
A friend can talk to me about anything.			
I can be fun to be with.			
I don't hurt people's feelings intentionally.			
I gossip and talk about people behind their back.			
I know my friends interests and what they do and don't like.			
I am good at listening			
It matters to me that my friends are happy.			
I have friends I can trust and talk about my feelings with.			
I think to be friends you need to agree on most things.			
I'm good at saying nice things and giving compliments.			

Example Games

Games to build interpersonal skills

These games can be played in class-sized groups but to use most effectively to help develop social confidence and competence, smaller groups of about 10 may be desirable.

All Those

1. Everyone is sitting on a chair in a circle. The Facilitator stands in the centre of the circle and there are no empty chairs. The purpose of the game is for the person standing in the centre of the circle to try and get a chair.

2. The facilitator completes the sentence, 'All those...' This can be any description of characteristics, qualities or features of the participants. For instance, 'All those with brown eyes... who watch East-Enders... who are boys...wearing a blue top...etc.' can be given. Any of the players to whom the description applies must get out of their seat and find another seat. When this happens, the facilitator then gets a seat for herself that will leave a new player in the middle.

3. The new player must then make a statement of, 'All those...' Imaginative descriptions can be encouraged and even if it only applies to one person, they must get up and move.

Human Noughts And Crosses

1. The group is divided into two teams. A grid for playing noughts and crosses is marked on a large scale on the floor. This can be done using chalk or masking tape. The individual boxes in the grid need to be large enough for a person to stand in.

2. One team is designated 'noughts', the other 'crosses'. Each team must work out a way of distinguishing itself from the other either by gesture or facial expression (for example, 'noughts' might have arms folded).

3. One team begins by one player placing herself in one box in the grid. Then a player from the other team places herself elsewhere and so on as in the paper and pencil version. The purpose is to form a line of three players of the same team or block the opponents from doing likewise.

VARIATIONS – the game may be played in silence with individuals making their own decisions or it can be discussed in teams. Acting quickly is the key and time penalties can be introduced.

Clapping Hot And Cold

1. All players sit in a circle except for one volunteer who is briefly sent outside the room. Whilst out of the room, the remaining players must think of a task for the person outside to do on his return. This might be to stand on a particular chair and take a book off a shelf or to shake someone's hand.

2. When the task has been decided on, the person outside returns to the room. He must now move around the room and try and find out what he has been asked to do. The person

is guided by clapping from the group that gets louder as the person approximates what to do, for instance, gets into the right part of the room or touches the object that is used. Clapping gets softer and quieter if the person moves away from the task.

Guessing what are appropriate tasks at which people can succeed requires considerable empathy and this games helps to practice that skill. This game can capture the imagination of the group and they can give increasingly complex tasks as members increase in skill. With time just one person can give the audio information that 'trains' the responses of the person seeking out the task. Pryor (1999) describes the use of a variant of this game, the Training Game, and its application in learning.

Zoom-Screech

1. Group members stand in a circle, shoulder to shoulder. The group leader sends a 'ZOOM' around the circle. She does this by turning her head quickly to the left to make eye contact with the person on the left and saying 'ZOOM' loudly. Then the person on the left repeats the action and sound, turning their head to make eye contact with the person on their left.

2. When the group members have mastered sending a 'ZOOM' around the circle quickly, introduce the next rule that anyone at any time can reverse the direction of the 'ZOOM' by looking directly back at the person who has given them the 'ZOOM' and saying 'SCREECH'. The person must then send the 'ZOOM' back in the other direction (or alternatively, say 'SCREECH' and again reverse 'the direction).

3. If anyone makes any errors, the game can just continue or forfeits can be given. For instance, going down on one leg after a mistake or two legs after two mistakes. Alternatively, after a mistake, a person can sit on the floor and when there are enough people sitting on the floor, a second game can start on this lower level. If anyone on the floor makes any mistakes, they stand up and join the original game.

Killer (Also known as Wink-murder)

1. Players stand in a circle, with their eyes closed, whilst the leader walks around the circle and taps one player once on the shoulder and another player twice on the shoulder.

2. The player tapped once is the 'killer'. His job is to kill other members of the group by winking at them discreetly. The player tapped twice is the 'detective'. She declares herself at the beginning of the game and her job is to identify the killer before he kills off all the other members of the group. She may have one, two or three guesses depending on the size and skill of the group.

3. When play begins the killer can wink at individual players. He should wait up to three seconds before doing a 'dramatic' death. The detective, when ready, can then make her accusation. Once the murderer is identified, the detective may then go around and select a new murderer and the old murderer may become the new detective.

VARIATIONS: there are many variations on this game, many of which can come from the participants' suggestions. Popular variants include dying in a particular fashion, for instance, in the manner of an emotion: angrily, happily, anxiously, or sadly. Another variation is to not have a nominated detective but when people believe they know who the killer is, they put their hand in the air. At this point they become immune from dying. When three people have their hands in the air, they, on the count of three, point to who they think the killer is. If they all point to the same person and they are correct, the killer identifies himself. If they are pointing to different people, the three accusers all die and the game continues.

Exercise One – Playing Games

Some of the games described here, or others that facilitators are familiar with, can be played to illustrate the value of playing games. However, there is also the risk that to be too analytical about the nature of games may destroy their spontaneity.

Some of these games can be used throughout any training sessions on emotional literacy to energise, provide light relief from more serious exercises and help the participants relax with each other.

Participants can also be encouraged to introduce and lead games that they may be familiar with.

It can also be useful to reflect on thoughts and feelings that participants may experience during games such as fears of, 'I'm going to mess it up,' or, 'I'll look stupid,' and also feelings of getting involved in the game, of enjoyment and success, concentration and engagement.

Variation

Generate ideas and skills about how to introduce games into the classroom or lead a games session. Creating a list of Do's and Don'ts can lead into a discussion about using games creatively.

Group Problem-solving Exercises

Map-makers

Equipment required: flipchart, paper, string (optional).

Time: 1-3 hours

1. In groups of between five and ten, students are asked to make a detailed map to scale of a specified area without using any formal measuring instruments like a ruler or tape measure. The area might be the class, the department building, an outdoor area, even the whole school. What is the most appropriate area will depend on the conditions in the school and the level of the group.

2. The group is given planning time to decide how it will attempt to get the measurements and information they need to construct the map. The task is to think of other ways they might measure distances and angles such as pacing, elbow length, or string and so on (but do not give the group too much guidance or they will just use the ideas you have given them).

3. After a given period of time where they can collect measurements, they have to produce their scale map on a piece of flipchart paper. Each group has to do a presentation to the others about how they solved the problem, then take time to discuss the process of how they tackled the exercise.

VARIATIONS – This exercise can be given as above with a specific time for planning, action and completion. To use the time well takes considerable planning by the group so this way is better when the group has reached a certain level of proficiency.

The Electric Fence

Equipment: a long piece of rope

Time: 20-45 minutes

1. Groups of about ten are presented with a rope tied securely between two points at height about 30 cm above waist level (or it can be held by two people at chest height). They are asked to imagine that this rope represents an electric fence. If anybody touches it, they will be electrocuted. It is not possible to pass below it.

2. The group has to work out how they can get everybody over the rope safely and without anybody touching it. They may not use any other equipment such as chairs.

VARIATIONS – The group can work together as above or one person can be appointed as leader. They can use the ideas of the group but they must make the final decision about who does what.

Knots

Equipment: none

Time: 5-10 minutes

1. In groups of seven to ten, students are asked to stand in a circle, shoulders almost touching, and to close their eyes. They then reach out their arms and find someone's hands to hold.

2. They can then open their eyes and check that they are holding the hands of two different people neither of whom is standing directly next to them. If anybody is doing this then there needs to be some minor adjustments which they can do with their eyes open.

3. The group can now try to disentangle themselves without breaking hand contact. Hopefully, the human knot should untangle to form a circle of people holding hands.

Sometimes, it will form two interlocking circles.

4. This exercise requires the group to work closely together and involves close physical contact as they weave amongst themselves. Therefore, it can be useful in groups to develop trust however, it also requires supervision to keep this activity safe for participants.

The K'NEX Challenge

Equipment: A large amount of K'NEX or another construction toy such as Lego. If this is unavailable, then variations on this exercise do not require such specialist equipment (see below).

Time: 30-60 minutes

1. Ask the group or groups to work together to construct something marvellous as a group using the materials such as K'NEX that they have been given. The group should be told what time they have and that their priorities, alongside making something marvellous, is to ensure that they have some fun, are creative and utilize the resources in the group.

2. The group is given time to complete the task, with various time to stop for feedback on the way if appropriate. At the end of the construction time they have to decide what they want to do with it.

3. Afterwards, the group discuss, reflect and feed back on how they solved the problem that was given to them. Some of the unfinished sentences on the activity sheet can be used.

VARIATIONS

Other tasks can be:

To complete a jigsaw (these could actually be made out of large sheets of patterned paper).

To paint a picture that covered every inch of a very large sheet of paper.

To decide as a group an activity that they could all engage in within a limited budget.

For an extra variation, all of the above tasks could be completed non-verbally. This puts an extra demand on the group's non-verbal skills to solve the problem.

Warp-speed

Equipment: A ball for throwing

Time: 15-20 minutes

1. This exercise, adapted from Ruberti & Holden (2005), begins with a group that can be up to the size of a class, standing in a circle. The group is informed that the ball is to be thrown from one person to another until every person has thrown and caught the ball only once. Students will have to remember who they caught it from and who they threw it to.

2. When the ball has gone halfway around the circle, stop and ask people who have not yet received the ball to put their hands up so they can be identified.

3. When everyone is sure of the order, try throwing the ball around again and time, preferably with a stopwatch, how long it takes the ball to travel from beginning to end.

4. After the initial time is established, challenge the group to see if they can reduce the time by working together. Throw the ball around again and the time for the ball to travel around should be considerably shorter.

5. After these initial attempts suggest that you think they could get the time even quicker. Encourage brainstorming and trying out of ideas to see if they work. Allow some flexibility for creativity and the time should decrease dramatically.

Activity Sheet Two – Reflecting On Group Work

Following your participation in a groupwork exercise reflect on how you contributed to the group by completing the following sentences.

1. I believed I communicated well when I...
....

2. I felt my best contribution was..
....

3. In working in the group the thing I did least well was...
....

4. I could improve how I worked in the group by..
....

5. I noticed a really good example of effective communication between group members was
....

6. The role I took in the group was...
....

7. The skills that I bring to working in teams are..
....

8. The point when we seemed to be having most difficulty was...
....

9. At that point, it might have been helpful if we had done...
....

10. The group was working at its best when ....
....

11. I think this was because...
....

12. Something I have learnt today is...
....

Exercise Two –
Teamwork

This exercise aims to help participants reflect on how they work in groups.

In small groups of about six, with one person allocated as an observer, complete either:

a) One of the group problem-solving exercises (or a variation that seems suitable for your group).

or

b) Consider a problem confronting the staff team or an area for school development such as 'building better links with parents', 'reviewing parent-teacher evenings' 'deciding on priorities for school development' or any issue that is relevant to the group. A brief presentation of conclusions should be given at the end.

Give the group about 20-30 minutes to complete the task.

After the exercise, individuals complete the activity sheet on reflecting on group work. When they have completed this, participants form into pairs and share their responses to the activity sheet. After this each person gives feedback to their partner based on completing the sentences presented in Slide 11.7

Feedback

- The impression I have of your strengths in working with groups is...

- It sounds like the thing you have learned today about how you work in groups is...

© Steve Killick - Lucky Duck Publishing

Slide 11.7

Chapter Twelve

Reflective Practice – Reflection Before Reaction

Who dares to teach must never cease to learn.

John Cotton Dana

The importance of reflecting on our own and others' beliefs, feelings and actions has been central throughout this book. Many of the exercises aim to facilitate reflective thought to inform understanding and action. To be able to reflect on our thoughts, feelings and actions is an essential component in being able to learn. This includes awareness of our desires and fears, intentions and motivations. If we can do this for ourselves we are more able to facilitate this in others. The purpose of reflection, either thinking together or alone, is to gain deeper and more complex understanding of ourselves and others.

The development of emotional intelligence in young people is, in essence, communicated through our own ability to process our emotions and those of others. So, to develop emotional intelligence in children and young people, it is important to develop it in ourselves. Reflective practice offers a way of helping develop awareness of our own thoughts and feelings upon our actions, our impact on others and their impact on us. To be able to reflect upon ourselves is at the heart of reflective practice and of emotional literacy. It is a way of increasing our awareness of the complexity and subtlety of our emotional lives. Self-reflection is an essential key in this process; it is about 'thinking about thinking', which can be described technically as a 'meta-cognitive process'.

The ability is also important for affect regulation in ourselves. Our own ability to remain regulated helps us respond more hopefully to young people when they experience strong emotions and to help transform these feelings as opposed to acting out these feelings ourselves. For instance, to consider helpful courses of action before deciding on punishment or making comments that might belittle or shame.

In education, as in many professions today, there is increasing emphasis being placed on evidence-based practice. This is a welcome development but there are limitations to a purely quantitative based approach as it is sometimes unable to provide answers to the complex problems faced in the workplace. Reflective practice is necessary to balance this approach that we can learn from our experiences and are able to gather practice-based evidence. The two approaches of evidence based and reflective practices balance and complement each other to form a holistic approach to professional and organisational development.

What is reflective practice?

Reflective practice developed in the field of adult education literature over the last twenty years and has emphasised the importance of reflection as one of the principal modes by which human beings learn and understand (Bennet-Levy, 2003). Donald Schön (1983) is one of the most prolific writers in this field who also draws upon the ideas of Kolb, Lewin and Piaget. Reflection refers to the ability of the mind to be conscious of its thinking and reflective practice is the ability to develop this skill to improve our work performance. It is a process by which we can think about what we do, why we do it, to be able to link this with theory and to develop new ideas. It is both critical and constructive self-examination based on observation to aid learning from experience. The development of reflective practice is increasingly seen as important in enhancing professional practice and is now seen as a cornerstone of learning about teamwork, leadership and development both personal and professional. It is a method to connect thought and action with the goal of improving performance.

Self-reflection is certainly not a new idea. Confucius saw reflection as an important ideal in the development of wisdom; the Buddha saw it as the key to self-understanding. It is also essential to emotional intelligence, for emotional intelligence is about the ability of the rational mind to think about the emotional mind. Emotional intelligence is not something that can be done automatically, without thought. Therefore, the practice of emotional literacy needs to incorporate reflection where action is balanced by understanding and learning. This process can make one less likely to react to a situation, to be less vulnerable to emotional hijacking, and more able to give a considered response. Reflective practice is about looking at what our thoughts and feelings are telling us.

Schools constantly have to deal with events that interfere with the learning process and this may include the continual demands of change in the education system. Many schools will have to deal with high rates of challenging behaviour that will lead to frequent crises in the classroom. Teachers will often be called upon to react to situations. Working with children, especially when they 'misbehave', triggers our own thoughts and beliefs about what children need in order to progress. Sometimes our actions will be appropriate, others maybe, on reflection, not the wisest course of action and may even escalate the problem. If we feel we have to defend our actions, we are less likely to consider alternatives, and more likely to repeat the action next time. We need to be able to look at ourselves critically yet constructively and without blame. Action without reflection can be another form of 'acting out' and an emotionally intelligent environment allows time for reflection in a variety of settings. When we reflect, we learn from the one who has the best knowledge of knowing what we need to learn and how best we can learn it – ourselves.

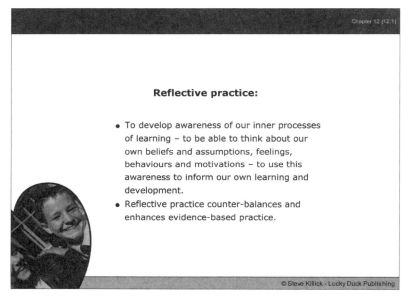

Slide 12.1

The processes of reflective practice

Lavender (2003), based on Schön's works, describes four areas of reflection:

1. Reflection in action – To be aware of what we are doing whilst we doing it.

2. Reflection on action – To consider retrospectively what happened and how we acted after an event.

3. Reflection about our impact on others – The effects both positive and negative our actions have on others – to consider relationships.

4. Reflection about self – On our own wellbeing and view about our 'self' influenced by ideas and theory.

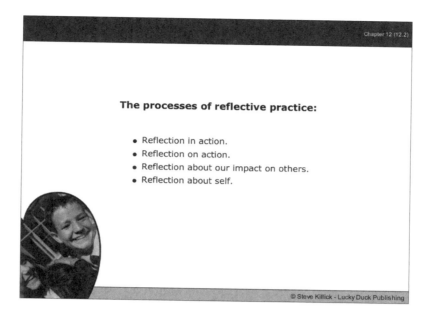

Slide 12.2

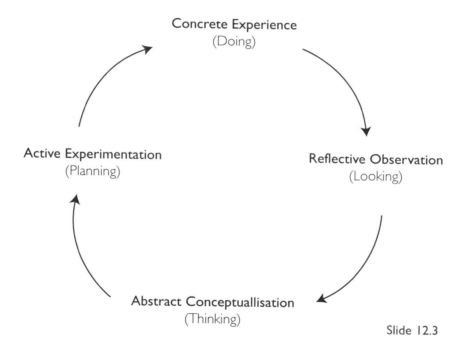

Slide 12.3

These areas, can be enhanced by knowledge of our own learning style and how to enhance this through using the learning cycle. Kolb's Learning Cycle (1984), shows a sequence that incorporates four styles of learning: concrete experience (doing), reflective observation (describing the experience clearly without judgement or assumption), abstract conceptualisation (thinking about theories or ideas relevant to what have been experienced and observed) and active experimentation (this might involve planning new strategies to think about or tackle a problem).

We often have preferences for one particular style of learning. Some people prefer action and doing, others are more observational and descriptive; another group will be more theoretical and abstract, who like thinking about ideas. Finally, some will have a preference for planning, innovativeness and creativity. Whatever our preferences, we expand our awareness through going through the stages of the learning cycle. When we rely on familiar strategies we are more vulnerable to our assumptions and prejudices blocking the taking of new perspectives. We cannot help having prior assumptions but it's what we do with these assumptions that matters. An attitude that fosters an open mind encourages curiosity. If our attitude is one of 'already knowing' we may block that curiosity. If a child behaves in a certain way, we may jump to the conclusion that he is doing it on purpose and with such an attribution our response may be governed by anger. On reflection, different reasons may become apparent and empathy may be increased. This knowledge can inform future practice. This open-mindedness can be applied to Schön's four areas of reflection.

Reflection in action

This is to be able to reflect, both cognitively and emotionally, about what one is thinking and feeling at any particular moment and to plan what to do next. For example, a teacher became aware of her own increasing feelings of irritation towards a child who was disrupting others by throwing items at other children at increasingly frequent intervals. She was planning to punish these actions by giving a detention. She became aware of how this child frequently made her feel frustrated and routine punishments had had no impact previously. She observed that other children seemed equally dismissive of the student and became aware that this child was actually struggling to make friends. She moderated her own response as she realised that his behaviour was not having any apparent aversive effect on others. From that point on she became more able to engage with him positively and help him settle in the class.

Reflection on action

This is to think back to an event, either by oneself or with a colleague, about what happened. Are there models of theory or practice that can be applied to understand the situation or does it go beyond theory or experience? How can similar situations in the future be planned and prepared for? A parent asked to speak to a teacher about her child whom she thought had been treated unfairly by the teacher and the discussion had become difficult and had not finished well. The teacher reflected that the conversation had been difficult and that he had become defensive due to the implied criticism that he had not done enough. On reflection, he recognised that he had not fully understood the parent's point of view and that maybe her criticism came from her own anxiety about the child's welfare, and that his defensiveness came from his own anxiety about not having done all that he could. He arranged a meeting where he could be more open to her concerns and explain how he saw areas that could be improved. This meeting was more constructive and led to several useful actions being decided on that improved the situation.

Reflection about our impact on others

It is valuable to the development of our own self-awareness to think about the impact we have on others and how students and colleagues see us. Understanding our contribution to the interpersonal contexts such as staff or classroom climate can help us recognise both our strengths and areas that may need development. Lavender (2003) lists several ways to reflect on our impact on others.

- Seeking out feedback from others. This might be through a variety of means: written, oral or even questionnaire. Some systems use 360° feedback which might include consideration of how colleagues, both those who manage and those that are managed, see us. Much useful information might be gained from also seeking out the views of parents and children.

- Group tasks. Use of problem-solving tasks (such as those described in Chapter Eleven) can help give information about how we interact with others. Team building exercises or even participation in training events also present learning opportunities.

- Self-monitoring. Reflecting on practice can be done by using questionnaires or self-monitoring exercises. For instance, to observe oneself over a short period of time in the classroom to see how many of our verbal interactions are questions, directions and instructions, statements of understanding and so on.

Reflections about self

Everyday we ask children to learn so it seems only equitable, as well as beneficial, that we might keep placing ourselves in the learning situation. Reflective practice, particularly with an emphasis on developing emotional intelligence, will lead us to reflect on our beliefs, feelings and what we do. Each day we experience continual feedback that over time moulds our actions and sense of how we see ourselves. Reflection on 'self' can make us more open to learning from experience and enable us to learn from our mistakes instead of continually repeating them. It is often asked of professionals with many years' practice that have they had, say, ten years' worth of experience or one year's worth of experience ten times? Are there particular issues that we seem to be stuck with that reflection may increase our awareness of?

Reflection can happen in many forms and guises, we can reflect on ourselves, others, our world, on the past, present and future – and through so doing access thoughts, memories and feelings beyond our everyday automatic responses.

Reflective practice can become a habit through finding frequent ways to apply it. It can be practised on one's own and both formally and informally with colleagues. Formal methods may include the use of supervision, consultation and mentoring.

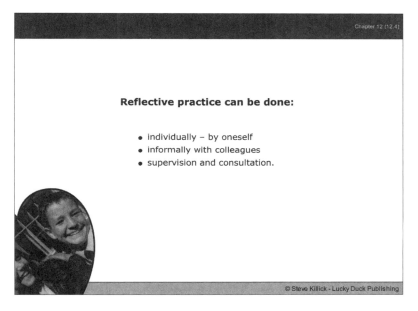

Slide 12.4

Individually – by oneself

We all need time to think about what we are doing but it can be hard to give oneself the time to do this. Schools are busy places and hectic lifestyles are common. Reflection can start with just taking a break from normal routines to consider questions such as, 'What am I really trying to achieve?' 'To what extent am I achieving it?' and, 'Am I being honest with myself?' These questions can be equally well approached indirectly through such actions as taking a break, relaxation or meditation. They might be addressed through creative methods using writing (poetry, prose, notes, essay, stories) or drawing (diagrams or pictures). This also raises the issue of the value of having places within the school environment where teachers can relax and feel calm.

Informally with colleagues

The process of thinking together is an important one, where one can have reflective dialogue and one can think about one's work in context. Finding time to discuss with colleagues with whom you feel comfortable to explore work issues aids awareness of how one operates and increases awareness of new ideas that might expand your repertoire. This might include examining perceived mistakes or areas where one doesn't feel suitably skilled. A common observation of teaching is that it can be an isolated profession, one where it can be difficult to learn from others. However, searching out those with particular skills, discussing ideas or observing others, and allowing others to observe you, can be very helpful. As everyone has something to teach, something can be learnt from everyone whatever their level of experience and skill. The finding of a mentor, someone who can act as a guide, inspiration and model, can make a difference in the learning path of professional development. Many schools are now formalising this role.

However, colleagues can also be a source of stress. Such colleagues can undermine and attack one's own feelings of confidence and competence. Identifying such people who can create these feelings and thinking how to interact with them is an important survival skill in the classroom environment. Roffey (2004) identifies some strategies for dealing with negative and unhelpful colleagues such as deciding that one's own sense of self will not be undermined and psychological disengaging with them. Professional relations are still kept although with space and distance. Also an empathic understanding as to why someone may only be able to relate in a negative destructive and destructive way, perhaps due to envy or fear, may help disable some of the power that negative interactions may have on you. In work settings, it is important to have allies, those with whom you can work together towards shared objectives. Without such allies, teachers can find themselves in vulnerable positions and perhaps more liable to enter into destructive patterns. This may manifest it self through gossip and cynicism.

Supervision and consultation

Supervision is a critical environment for reflective practice. An effective supervisor is not prescriptive but creates an environment for joint exploration of topics. There is a danger that supervision, if it happens at all, is entirely focused on task and performance evaluation elements only. However, purely evaluative supervision is likely to inhibit reflection but joint problem sharing and problem-solving discussion helps build trust and openness that allow new insights to be made. Supervisors can benefit from training and being supervised on their own supervision. Supervision can also take place in groups. There are many tasks in the provision of supervision including monitoring and evaluating work, offering advice and instruction, supporting a person in their work task and modelling of appropriate attitudes and skills.

Consultation differs from supervision in that the provider of consultation may not have any direct responsibility for a person's work practice but can still offer advice and reflection on work issues. Some schools have used facilitators from outside the school to facilitate reflective dialogue and discussion. Facilitators with expertise in emotional issues can have particular benefits in thinking about working with behavioural and emotional difficulties. As mental health services work more with education, initiatives such as offering direct work with teachers may become more widely used. Other sources may include educational psychologists or school counsellors.

Focusing on emotional literacy

Awareness of the relationship between thoughts, feelings and behaviour, both in ourselves and in students, extends our repertoire of relating to children. Mood influences a teacher's behaviour in the classroom especially to the extent that attention is given to positives or negatives in behaviour. A positive mood can influence a teacher to build on positive behaviours and to play down responses to negatives. This lessens the risk of reinforcing negative behaviour or of escalating the situation. A negative mood may increase the likelihood of negative responses or critical comments, that will, in turn, increase conflict and stress. Stress management skills can be helpful to teachers in the stressful environment of the school. Perhaps one of the most critical skills to employ is to choose our attitude (Lundin, Paul & Christensen, 2000) to the work we do. It is not always possible to choose the work that we may do on a day-to-day level but it is possible to choose our attitude towards the way we do our work. It is this recognition that our attitude is a choice that gives us the option of seeing how playfulness, enthusiasm and kindness can always be brought in.

It can take courage to examine the emotions that can be elicited in the classroom situation. It can be easier to dismiss, deny or place responsibility for negative feelings elsewhere. When feelings are repressed or seen as out of a person's control ('There's nothing I can do') the opportunity to change is lessened and one is placed in a position of permanent reaction. Individuals high in emotional intelligence are aware that they are choosing how to think and feel and they are capable of making different choices, they also recognise that negative feelings of anxiety or anger will exist but will also pass unless we choose to hang onto them.

 See Exercise One

Working with children with emotional and behavioural difficulties

These skills of reflection of emotional issues are essential if working in settings where there may be many children experiencing emotional and behavioural difficulties. Challenging behaviours inevitably provoke strong emotional reactions in those working with them. Good practice suggests that staff need ways that they can think about their own responses. Children with severe emotional difficulties need to be thought about and understood by adults especially as they will have particular difficulties in finding appropriate ways of expressing their own feelings. Often, this may be because their own distress is so intense they cannot find ways of being able to express it. It can be buried 'too deep for words' (Rose, 2004). Those that work with such children need to be able to think about their emotional lives, as to understand and address their needs is often the only way of making progress. Adults have to think for young people until they are ready to think for themselves. This task can be made harder by the constant behavioural challenges that need to be managed that can make finding the time to think and reflect even harder. The challenge facing staff in schools with a high degree of problems is to find ways of creating opportunities both for themselves and the young people they work with to think about feelings.

 See Exercise Two

Reflective practice is critical in both good practice and in developing emotional intelligence. By thinking about what we are thinking, feeling and doing, we are doing the very thing that increases emotional literacy. If we can take this into our relationships we give permission to others to do the same. But reflective practice is not easy, it can mean self doubt and acknowledging the complexities and ambiguities that can exist. It is about tolerating the 'jungle of uncertainty' and recognising the ambivalences we may feel, and acknowledging some aspects of ourselves with which we may not feel comfortable. In the face of challenging and often aggressive behaviour, we would not be human if we did not feel anger ourselves. If we cannot accept that as an aspect of ourselves, we are vulnerable to 'unconscious aggression', where we in turn can act out our feelings. Through reflection, our empathy can increase and with that we can see a wider choice of responses.

 See Exercise Three

Summary of Chapter Twelve

- Encouraging reflective practice is an essential part of any school keen to enhance emotional literacy skills. Reflective practice concentrates on the 'inner' process of thinking about feelings, beliefs and actions and works in partnership with evidence-based practice in school development.

- Central to reflective practice is an understanding of Kolb's learning cycle of action, reflection, abstraction and experimentation. We may have preferences for a particular learning style but use of the learning cycle extends the ability to learn from experience.

- There are four areas in which we can practise reflection: whilst in action – to be aware of what we are thinking, feeling and doing whilst we do it, to reflect retrospectively and plan for future events, to reflect about our impact on others and on our sense of self. It can be practised individually or collectively with colleagues. This can be done either through informal contact or more formal processes of supervision.

- Reflection in working with children who present severe emotional and behavioural challenges is essential in considering how to help them learn and progress.

Exercise One –
Identifying Supervision Needs

This exercise aims to help participants evaluate their own supervision needs through reflecting on their own experiences of supervision.

Ask participants to reflect individually for about ten minutes on the questions given in the activity sheet, 'Identifying Your Supervision Needs'. Then, with a partner, each person shares their reflections and identifies what changes, if any, they might like to make to their supervision arrangements. This might involve renegotiating their current supervision arrangements and, if this is not considered feasible, how they might create other forums that might meet their needs.

A whole group discussion afterwards might elicit shared interests in which people may wish to develop peer consultation arrangements. If participants identify a lack of supervision or mentoring this can be discussed to identify if this should be seen as something that should be rectified or not and what steps can be taken to do this.

Activity Sheet –
Identifying Your Supervision Needs

1. What features of supervision have been most helpful to you in your personal and professional development in the past and why?

....

....

....

2. What features of supervision have been least helpful to you and why?

....

....

....

3. What would you identify as being the areas in which you would most like to develop in your practice?

....

....

....

4. What kind of supervision would be most helpful in enabling you to develop in those areas?

....

....

....

5. What actions can you take to create an arena for supervision that might best meet those needs?

....

....

....

Exercise Two –
What is the Experience of the Child?

This exercise aims to help participants reflect on the experience of a child who might be having difficulties through encouraging participants to reflect on their own emotional reactions to the child.

Divide participants into groups of four or five. Each group identifies one person who has a particular child that he or she would be happy to discuss. This may be a child who may be having difficulties in the school setting; this might manifest itself through behavioural problems, or be a child that perhaps elicits strong negative feelings or where there is a poor relationship between teacher and child.

The group also nominates a facilitator who uses the prompt sheet 'What is the Experience of the Child?' to ask questions to help the teacher reflect on what feelings the child may elicit in the teacher and how this might deepen the understanding of what the child's experience may be and how the teacher may respond. The prompt sheet need only be used as a guide for the discussion, not all questions need to be asked. Other group members can also ask questions or share their observations during the discussion.

It is important to stress the conversation should be considered confidential and not discussed outside the room. Allow twenty minutes for the discussion and follow this with a whole group discussion where participants feed back about the themes that emerged from the small-group discussion.

Prompt Sheet

What is the Experience of the Child?

Use these questions to facilitate a reflective discussion about a teacher's experiences of a particular child.

Please describe something about the child.

What does this child make you feel?

What is it that makes you feel that way? How might that affect you and your actions and responses? Is it something that the child brings to your relationship, something that you bring, or some external influence?

What do these feelings make you do or want to do? Are they positive or negative in their effects? If there are negative effects what might change your perspective?

What are your motivations about working with this child? Do you have conflicting feelings?

To what degree do you feel a sense of empathy? Are there times when you feel empathic and times when you do not?

Do you have a sense of how the child sees the world? What is the experience of this child? Does this have child have a 'voice'? What would he/she want to say but might not be able to articulate?

What can you do to help them when they feel angry, frightened or upset, and content? What things work for this child?

There might be things that you don't know about this child and if you did know might change your understanding. What things might they be?

What things might you try to do differently next time you meet?

Exercise Three –
Concluding Exercise

This exercise aims to conclude the training and help participants evaluate what they have learnt.

Ask participants to reflect in pairs on the questions presented in Slide 12.5 for about five to ten minutes. Then in a large group each person can either feed back for themselves, or alternatively for their partner, the many learning points they have taken away and any ideas they would particularly like to take forward.

Concluding exercise:

- What have I learnt that has been most useful to me?
- What has made me think differently?
- What has been less helpful, or that I am not sure I fully understand?
- What would I like to know more about?
- The things I would like to take away and put into action are...

Slide 12.5

A Frightening Conclusion

I have come to a frightening conclusion. I am the decisive element in the classroom. It is my personal approach that creates the climate. It is my daily mood that makes the weather. As a teacher, I possess tremendous power to make a youth's life miserable or joyous. I can be a tool of torture or an instrument of inspiration. I can humiliate or humour, hurt or heal. In all situations it is my response that decides whether a crisis will be escalated or de-escalated, and the child humanised or dehumanised.

Haim Ginott, Between Teacher and Child.

Emotional literacy is about developing confidence and competence, both in staff and young people. Ginott's most famous quote refers to the power that a teacher has in being able to influence the young person. However, many teachers may not feel that they experience this power, rather that the continual battle of wills is more often the day-to-day reality of education. Awareness of feelings in oneself and others aids effective communication and this communication will come to be seen as increasingly important in education in the 21st century. It is through effective communication that a child learns about his own emotional state, receives meaningful feedback and learns to process emotions, solve problems and engage in satisfying relationships. This lays the foundation for the emergence of two key values that have traditionally been seen as important to foster in children: respect and responsibility. Respect for others develops through the receipt of respect of for one's own emotional life and to experience a community that reinforces the values of respect for the emotional life of others. Responsibility develops through a sense of setting boundaries and limits that help children link feelings with actions and actions with consequences – they become able to think through their actions, predict consequences and make choices. When this is difficult children need to be able to receive additional help in how to do this.

There are many resources available to schools to help develop emotional literacy practices; there are now a considerable number of publications available giving theory, classroom activities and policies. The Internet is full of resources and information. There are a growing number of organisations providing training and support for schools. They can act as 'mentors' to the school or 'critical friends' that can assist in school improvement and development. Education will continue to evolve and the next few years may see radical changes to traditional approaches in education. This will be especially so at secondary school level as new technologies and new understanding of learning processes enable a rethinking of how education is best delivered. If the ideas that underpin emotional literacy and education are placed at the forefront of these developments they can become part of schools' central ethos for learning. A strong ethos will guide the attitudes of teachers and in turn will influence the use of specific and effective communication skills. In the positive relationships that result the outcomes for young people will become apparent. Goleman (1996) described what he believed would be the characteristics of children who had received emotional literacy interventions:

- Confidence. The belief that they will succeed and that adults are helpers not threats.

- Curiosity. That finding out about the world gives pleasure.

- Intentionality. To believe they have an impact on the world and to be able to act upon it.

- Self-control. The ability to regulate one's emotions in age appropriate ways.

- Relatedness. The ability to engage with others, to understand and feel understood by others. The capacity to communicate with others.

- Cooperativeness. The ability to solve problems together.

Children with these skills are going to be prepared for adult life, they will be lifelong learners ready to grow from the obstacles they will inevitably face. Of course, schools can only do so much. After all, only fifteen percent of a child's life is spent at school and what schools can and do achieve in that time is remarkable. Perhaps what is most frightening is that so much potential in children exists and that we possess the tools, within our grasp, to unlock potential for all children.

References

Ajmal, Y. & Rees, I. (Eds, 2001) *Solutions in Schools – Creative applications of solution focused brief thinking with young people and adults.* BT Press.

Antidote, (2004) *Thinking Together – Using philosophy for children to promote whole school emotional literacy.* Smallwood Publishing.

Bandler, R. & Grindler, J. (1982) *ReFraming – Neuro-linguistic programming and the transformation of meaning.* Real People Press.

Baron-Cohen, S. (2003). *Mind Reading – The interactive guide to emotions.* Jessica Kingsley Publishers.

Baron-Cohen, S. (2003) Foreword in *Reading Faces and Learning about Human Emotions* by Barbara Maines. Lucky Duck Publishing.

BarOn, R. (1997) *BarOn Emotional Quotient Inventory Technical Manual.* Mental Health Systems.

BarOn, R. & Parker, J. (2000) *BarOn Emotional Quotient Inventory:Youth Version Technical Manual.* Mental Health Systems.

Bennett-Levy, James (2003) Reflection: a blind spot in psychology. *Clinical Psychology*, 27, 16-19.

Biddulph, S. (1998) *The Secret of Happy Children.* Thorsons.

Blanchard, K & Johnson, S. (2004) *The One-Minute Manager.* HarperCollins.

Bloom, B.S. (Ed.) (1956) *Taxonomy of educational objectives: The classification of educational goals: Handbook I, cognitive domain.*Longmans, Green.

Boxall, M. (2002) *Nurture Groups in School – Principles & Practice.* Paul Chapman Publishing.

Brandes, D. & and Phillips, H. (1979) *The Gamesters' Handbook – 140 games for teachers and group leaders.* Nelson Thomas.

Breakwell, G. (1997) *Coping with aggressive behaviour.* British Psychological Society.

Brehm, S.S. & Brehm, J.W. (1981) *Psychological Reacyance: A Theory of Freedom and Control.* London: Academic Press.

Butler, S. & Rohnke, K. (1995) *Quicksilver: Adventure Games, Initiative Problems, Trust Activities and a Guide to Effective Leadership.* Kendal Hunt Publishers.

Carlson, R. (1997) *Stop Thinking and Start Living.* Thorsons.

Carradice, P. (1994) *Borderlines.* Lucky Duck Publishing.

Collishaw, S., Maughan, B., Goodman, R. and Pickles, A. (2004) Time trends in adolescent mental health. *Journal of Child Psychology and Psychiatry 45,8 pp1350-1362.*

Cotton, K. (2001) *Developing Empathy in Children and Youth.* School Improvement Research Series. North West Regional Educational Laboratory. www.nwrel.org/scpd/sirs/7/cu13.html.

Covey, Stephen (1989) *The Seven Habits of Highly Effective People.* Simon & Schuster.

Cowley, S. (2004) *Getting the Buggers to Think.* Continuum.

Davies, G. (1999) *Six Years of Circle Time.* Lucky Duck.

De Bono, E. (1992) *Teach Your Child How to Think.* Penguin.

Defalco, K. (1997) *Educators Commentary on What Is Emotional Intelligence* by Peter Salovey and Jack Meyer in *Emotional Development and Emotional Intelligence – Educational Implications.* Edited by Peter Salovey and David Sluyter. Basic Books.

DfES (2005). *Excellence and Enjoyment*: social and emotional aspects of learning. Ref DfES 1378-2005 G

Elias, M. & Clabby, J. (1992) *Building Social Problem-solving Skills: Guidelines from a school based programme.* Institute for Rational Living. New York.

Elias, M., Tobias, S & Friedlander, B. (1999) *Emotionally Intelligent Parenting.* Hodder & Stoughton.

Faber, A. & Mazlish, E. (1995) *How to talk so kids can learn – at home and in school.* Rawson Associates.

Faber, A. & Mazlish, E. (1999) *How to talk so kids will listen & listen so kids will talk.* Avon Books.

Faupal, A. (Ed.,2003) *Emotional Literacy Assessment and Intervention.* Ages 7-11 and 11-16. nferNelson.

Fisher, R. (1997) *Games For Thinking.* Nash Pollock Publishing.

Fisher, R. (1996) *Stories for Thinking.* Nash Pollock Publishing.

Freshwater, D. and Robertson, C. (2002) *Emotions and Needs.* Open University Press.

Furedi, F. (2004) *Young Minds Magazine,* 72, 12-13.

Gardner, H. (1983) *Frames of Mind: the theory of multiple intelligences.* New York:Basic Books.

Gersie, A. & King, N. (1989) *Storymaking in Education and Therapy.* London: Jessica Kingsley Publishers.

Gibbs, Graham (1988) *Learning by Doing – A guide to teaching and learning methods.* The Further Education Unit.

Ginott, Hiam (2003, 1965) *Between Parent and Child.* Three Rivers Press.

Ginott, H. (1972) *Teacher and Child.* Avon Books.

Goleman, D. (1995) *Emotional Intelligence – why it can matter more than IQ.* Bloomsbury

Goleman, D. (1998) *Working with Emotional Intelligence.* Bloomsbury.

Gottman, J. (1998) *The heart of parenting – How to raise an emotionally intelligent child.* Bloomsbury Publishing.

Greene, R.W. (2001) *The Explosive Child.* HarperCollins Publishers.

Greene, R.W. & Ablon, J.S. (2005) *Treating Explosive Kids: The Collaborative Problem-solving Approach.* Guilford Press.

Holden R. (1999) *Happiness Now – Timeless wisdom for feeling good fast.* Hodder Mobius.

Howlin, P., Baron-Cohen, S. and Hadwin, J.(1999) *Teaching Children with Autism to Mind-Read – A practical guide for teachers and parents.* Wiley.

Hughes, D. (1998) *Building the Bonds of Attachment - Awakening love in deeply troubled children.* Rowman & Littlefield Publishers.

Issacs, W. (1999) *Dialogue and the Art of Thinking Together: A Pioneering Approach to Communicating in Business and in Life.* Bantom Doubleday.

Jennings, S. (1997) *Creative Drama in Groupwork.* Speechmark Publishing Ltd.

Lavender, Tony (2003) Redressing the balance: the place, history and future of reflective practice in clinical training. *Clinical Psychology,* 27, 11-15

Lundin, S., Paul, H. & Christensen, J. (2000) *Fish – a remarkable way to boost morale and improve results.* Hodder Mobius.

Killick, S. & Lindeman, S. (1999) *Giving Sorrow Words – managing bereavement in schools.* Lucky Duck Publishing.

Kolb. D. (1984) *Experiential Learning.* Prentice Hall.

Kyriacou, C.(1998) *Essential Teaching Skills.* Nelson Thornes.

Maddocks, J., Cooper, J. & Sparrow, T. (2005) Emotional intelligence is not personality. *The Psychologist*, 18, 1, 11.

Maines, B. (2003) *Reading Faces and Learning about Human Emotions.* Lucky Duck Publishing.

McConnon, S. (1989) *Boy Friends, Girl Friends* – (Your Choice Series). Macmillan.

Mental Health Foundation (1999) *The big picture: Promoting children and young people's mental health.* Mental Health Foundation.

Mehrabian, A. (1981) *Silent Messages: Implicit Communication of Emotions and Attitudes.* Wadsworth Publishing.

Miller, W. & Rollnick, S. (2002) *Motivational Interviewing – preparing people to change.* Guilford Press.

Mosley, J. & Tew, M.(1999) *Quality Circle Time In the Secondary School.* David Fulton Publishers

Neenan, M. & Dryden, W. (2004) *Cognitive Therapy – 100 key points and techniques.* Brunner-Routledge.

O'Moore, M. & Minton, S. (2004) *Dealing with Bullying in Schools – A Training Manual for Teachers, Parents and Other Professionals.* Paul Chapman Publishing.

Orbach, S. (1999) *Towards Emotional Literacy.* Virago Press.

Pantley, Elizabeth (1996) *Kid Cooperation.* New Harbinger Publications.

Patel-Kanwal, H. & Frances, G (1998) *Let's Talk about Sex and Relationships - A policy and practice framework for working with children and young people in public care.* National Children's Bureau.

Paul, R. (1993) *Critical Thinking: How to Prepare Students for a Rapidly Changing World.* Santa Rosa, Ca: Foundation for Critical Thinking.

Park, J., Haddon, A. and Goodman, H. (2003) *The Emotional Literacy Handbook.* David Fulton Publishers.

Parks, K. (2004) *Interactive Storytelling: Developing Inclusive Stories for Children & Adults.* Speechmark Publishing Ltd.

Petrides, K.V., Frederickson, N. and Furnham, A. (2004a) The role of trait emotional intelligence in academic performance and deviant behaviour at school. *Personality and Individual Differences*, 36, 277-293.

Petrides, K.V., Furnham, A. and Frederickson, N. (2004b) Emotional Intelligence. *The Psychologist*, 17, 574-577.

Pryor, K. (1999) *Don't Shoot the Dog – The New Art of Teaching and Training.* Bantam.

Rae, T. (1998) *Dealing with Feelings.* Lucky Duck Publishing/Sage.

Rendall, L. & Robinson, L. (2005) *Emotional literacy: what are the needs of pupils at Headlands School and how do we measure it?* Headlands School, NCH Cymru/Wales.

Rhodes, J. and Ajmal, Y. (1995) *Solution Focused Thinking in Schools – Behaviour, reading and organisation.* BT Press.

Robinson, G. & Maines, B. (2000) *Crying for Help – the No Blame Approach to Bullying.* Lucky Duck Publishing.

Roffey, S. (2004) *The New Teacher's Survival Guide to Behaviour.* Sage.

Rose, J. (2004) The residential care and treatment of adolescents. In: *From Toxic Institutions to Therapeutic Environments: Residential Settings in Mental Health Services*. Eds. P. Campling, S, Davies & G. Farquharson. Gaskell.

Rowe, D. (2001) *Introducing Citizenship – A practical handbook for primary schools*. A & C Black.

Rogers, B. (2002) *Classroom Behaviour: A Practical Guide to Effective Teaching, Behaviour Management and Colleague Support*. Paul Chapman Publishing.

Rogers, B. (Ed. 2004) *How to Manage Children's Challenging Behaviour*. Paul Chapman Publishing.

Rogers, C. (1983) *Freedom to Learn for the 80's*. Merril Publishing.

Rogers, C. (1987) *Client Centred Therapy*. Constable.

Ruberti, M. & Holden, J. (2005) *Reducing Challenging Behaviour using Adventure Based Experiential Learning (ABEL)*. Residential Child Care Project, Cornell University.

Salovey. P. & Mayer, J.D. (1990) Emotional Intelligence. *Imagination, Cognition and Personality*, 9, 185-211.

Schön, Donald (1987) *Educating the Reflective Practitioner*. Wiley.

Schön, Donald (1983) *The Reflective Practitioner*. Wiley.

Seligman, M. (1995) *The Optimistic Child*. HarperCollins.

Seligman, M. (2002A) *Authentic Happiness*. Nicolas Brearly Publishing.

Seligman, M. (2002B) Positive Psychology: Fundamental assumptions. *The Psychologist*, 16, 126-127.

Sharp, P. (2001) *Nurturing Emotional Literacy*. David Fulton Publishers.

Sharp, P. (2002) *Emotionally Intelligent Teams*. Presentation to Headlands School.

Stacy, H. & Robinson, P. (1997) *Lets Mediate – A teacher's guide to peer support and conflict resolution skills*. Paul Chapman Publishing.

Stallard, P. (2002) *Think Good – Feel Good – A cognitive therapy workbook for children and young people*. John Wiley & Sons

Steiner, C. (1979) *Healing Alcoholism*. Grove Press.

Swinson, J. & Harrop, A. (2005) An examination of a short course aimed at enabling teachers in infant, junior and secondary schools to alter verbal feedback given to their pupils. *Educational Studies*, 31, 115-129.

Treasure, J. (2004) Motivational Interviewing. *Advances in Psychiatric Treatment*, 10, 331-337.

Ward, B. & Associates (1996) *Good Grief 1 – Exploring feelings, loss and death with the under elevens*. Jessica Kingsley Publishing.

Ward, B. & Associates (1996) *Good Grief 2 – Exploring feelings, loss and death with the over elevens and adults*. Jessica Kingsley Publishing.

Weare, K. (1999) *Promoting Mental, Emotional and Social Health – A whole school approach*. RoutledgeFalmer.

Weare, K. & Grey, G. (2003) *What Works in Developing Children's Emotional and Social Competence and Wellbeing*. The DfES, UK.

White, M. (1999) *Magic Circles – building self-esteem through Circle Time*. Lucky Duck/Paul Chapman.

Worden, William, (1996). *Children and Grief – when a parent dies*. Guilford Press.

Zeidner, M., Roberts, R. & Matthews, G. (2002) Can emotional intelligence be schooled? A Critical Review. *Educational Psycholgist*, 37, 215-231.